Astrology of the Astro-Shaman

By Michael Erlewine

Startypes.com
315 Marion Avenue
Big Rapids, Michigan 49307
Fist published 2006
© 2006 Michael Erlewine/StarTypes.com

ISBN 978-1-4404414-4-8
All rights reserved. No part of the publication may be reproduced, stored in a retrieval system, or transmitted, in any form or by any means, electronic, mechanical, photocopying, recording, or otherwise, without the prior permission of the publisher.
Graphics designed by Michael Erlewine

This book is dedicated to

Andrew Gunn McIver

Foreword by Steven Forrest 15
Astro-Shamanism 24

What This Book is About 24
A Personal Account 24
Life Initiations through Astrology 26
Traditional Shamanism and "Core Shamanism" 27
What is Astro-Shamanism? 28
Not the Same as the Vision Quest 28
A One-Way Street 30
Shamans Are Not Priests or Ministers 31
Societies and Brotherhoods 32
The Shaman Is Not a Doctor 33
Shamanism in Astrology 33
Dead and Alive 35
Out-of-the-Body Experiences 36
The Astrologer as Shaman 38
Are Astrologers Shamans? 39
Seeking The Shaman 39
Altered States 40
Beyond Convention 41
The Inner Meaning 43

Astrology of the Heart 43
Self Secret 43
Esoteric Teachers 44
The Planets as Chakras 45
The Chakras in the World 46
Reflected In the World 46
The World is as 'We' See It 48
Living in the Chakras 48
Wandering In the Chakras 49
Successive Chakras 50
Planetary Landscapes 50
Mastering the Chakras 51
Background: Digressions 53

Expectations Can't Define 53
Backpedaling 54
Intellectual Understanding 55
Approach Is Everything 56
We Sail Our Ship Alone 57
Figure and Ground 58
Pointing Out 58
Understanding 58
Experiencing 59
Realization 59
Three-Step Process 59
The Monad: Divine Astrology 60

Monad. The Sun Is Shining 60
The Astrology of No Time 62
The Solar System as a Tree Of Life 63
A Divine Astrology 63
The Tree Of Life 63
The Flame of a Flashing Sword 64
The Four Beasts 65
The First Generation 65
The Mystery of the Seven Seals or Planets 66
Formation of the Seals 66
Opening of the Seven Seals 67
Formation of the Seven Seals through Time 67
Repeating Itself 68
Saturn Is the Timekeeper 69
Mercury 69
Venus 69
Earth 70
Mars 70
Jupiter 70
Major Planetary Aspects 71
Major Planetary Aspects 72
The Planets as Chakras 72

Inner Key to Outer 72

The Planetary Key 73
The Inner is the Key 73
Saturn: A Formal Definition 75
Saturn the Shaper 75
Saturn: Walls That Make Homes Possible 76
The Test of a Lifetime 76
The Seven Chakras 77

Saturn (Muladara Chakra) Base of Spine 77
Jupiter (Svadisthana Chakra) Genital Region 78
Mars (Manipura Chaka) Navel 78
Chakra: Earth (The End of Meaning) 79
Mercury (Ajna Chakra) Third Eye 79
Sun (Sahasrara Chakra) Crown of Head 79
What Chakra Are You In? 80

Identifying the Saturn Chakra 80
Can't Make a Living 81
Invoking Jupiter 82
Identifying the Jupiter Chakra 83
Crossing the Gap 83
Jupiter's Lightning 84
The Lawyer: Skillful Means 84
Mars: The Key to Jupiter 85
Still Unmarried 85
Career Problems 86
Identifying the Mars Chakra 88
The Most Common Form of Yoga 88
Identifying the Earth Chakra 89
The Earth of Heart Chakra 90
The Chakras Inner to Earth 90
Identifying the Venus Chakra 90
Identifying the Mercury Chakra 91
The Saturn Chakra 91

The Beautiful Soul 92
The Jupiter Chakra: Guru 93

The Key to Your Saturn Is Your Natal Jupiter 93

The Sanskrit Word is Guru 94
Success or Succession 94
The Vision of Jupiter — Baptism or Rebirth 95
Born Awake In Time..96
Faith as a Force 96
The Sword of Faith 97
Handling Saturn 99
Jupiter Is the Lawyer 99
Jupiter Phases 100
The Asteroid Belt..101
Journal: First Moments Of Jupiter Awakening: 102
Journal: Eternity's Door..105
Journal: Reading from the Outside..........................105
Journal: My Trial of Faith..106
Journal: The Beast Claims the Whole 107
Journal: The Test of Faith 108
Journal: A World That Knew Me Not 110
Journal: Do Not Do a Thing......................................110
Journal: I Was My Pain 111
Journal: Refusing To Breathe...................................112
Journal: Roaming Purgatory....................................113
Journal: Pride's Examples 114
Journal: Self-Reference..114
The Mars Chakra 116

Journal: I Am Led To the Sea of Love 116
Journal: The Sense of Life 116
Journal: Balboa and the Sea of Sense 117
Mars Is the Activity That Generates Space 118
Mars Is Meaning...119
Journal: The Vision of Mars Is Our Marriage 119
Journal: Marriage Is Quite an Affair.........................120
Journal: Dewdrop Slips into the Shining Sea 121
Journal: Why Marriage Is Like a Funeral................122
Journal: Relieved Of Duty 123
Peace Terrifies 124
Journal: The Shell of the Self 125

7

Awake In My Own Dream 126
A Life of Response 127
Journal: Awakening In Response 127
Journal: Take a Good Look 128
Journal: Out to Pasture 129
Clearing the Subconscious 131
The Sewer 131
Open Subconscious 132
Journal: The Poetry 133
Journal: Awakening of the Earth or Heart Center ... 134
The Earth Chakra 136

The Earth Is the Heart of Meaning 136
Journal: Everlasting Life 136
Journal: The Consummation of the Marriage 137
Journal: Childbirth 138
Journal: Looking Out the Window 139
Journal: Through God's Looking Glass 140
Journal: A Midwife of the Spirit 141
Journal: My Heart Went Out 141
Journal: The Heart Center 143
Journal: The Valley of the Shadow of Death 143
Journal: Hard Thoughts 144
Journal: Pain Is Fear 145
Journal: The Vision of the Heart Center 146
Journal: Could Care Less 147
Journal: The Silence 148
The Inner Chakras 150

Venus Is the Key to the Heart or Earth 150
The Bodhisattva 151
Mercury Is the Light of Love 151
The Sun Center Itself the Whole 152
The Moon 152
The Lights: Sun and Moon 153
The Moon as Our Mother 155
The Moon as Our Child 155

The Sun 158
The Outer Planets 160

Saturn and the Outer Planets 160
The Transcendental or Outer Planets 160
The Meta-Physical 161
Pointing Out: Saturn Is Form 162
Saturn is the Physical End 163
The Prime of Life 163
Straight Lines Curve 164
The Straighter the Line, the Finer the Curve 165
The Physical End of Life 166
The Bewildering Display of Time 166
When Time Stops 167
Entering the Silence 167
The Vehicle is Launched 168
One Generation 168
The Outer Planets 169
A One-Way Street 170
Sidebar: Out of the Body Experiences 171
Somewhat of a Big Deal 171
Revelation and Rendering 172
The View from Earth 173
Lineages: Outer Planets 174
Outer Planets in the Chart 175
The Outer Planets: A Step toward Interpretation 178
The Uranus Journey 178
The Neptune Journey 179
The Pluto Journey: Identification is Circulation 181
The Fixed Stars And Beyond 184

The Fixed Stars 184
The Life and Death of Stars 185
The Solar Mysteries 191

Our Self and Sun 191
The Self in the East 193
Seeing the Self 194

Sunrise	196
Beyond the Heart Center or Sun	198
THE POINT OF NO RETURN	201
Reincarnation	203
Incarnation and Re-incarnation	203
Incarnation — A Work in Progress	203
Bodies of Knowledge	204
Abandoned Bodies	205
Putting Our Self into Things	206
Bind and Last	208
Lasting the Test of Time	208
Nothing Lasts Forever	209
The Birth of Stars	210
The Sum Total of Our Involvements	211
The Body of Knowledge	212
The Point of No Return	213
Our Flood and Ebb Tides	214
Our Cycles of Up and Down	215
Extending Ourselves in Experience	216
We Ask For It	217
Moment by Moment Incarnation	218
Let Me Have It	218
Reincarnation: The Sun Is Shining	219
Honeybees and the Hive	220
The Constant Generation	220
The Life in Common	222
The Terrible Crystal	222
In My Past Life	223
Re-Incarnation: More	224
A Moment's Infatuation	225
The Word Must Be Made Flesh	225
Sowing and Reaping	226
A Child is Life	227
Saturn the Sequencer	228
Cycles Are Returns	228
Saturn or Chronos	229

Life beyond Saturn or Time 230
Our Soul Memory Stirs 232
The Prime of Life 232
Hide in Plain Sight 233
Leaving the Womb of Time 235
The Noise of Time 236
Setting the Sails 237
After the Fact, There is but the Poetry 238
Journal: Person the Product of Time 239
Journal: Personal Ties 240
Saturn the Timekeeper 241
The Circle of Repetition 242
The Womb of Time 242
Go Spell 243
The Monad or Space Ship: The Silence 244
The Quality of Time 245
The Rush of Time 245
Time Curves 246
Beyond 247
Time and Eternity 248
Saturn the Sequencer: More 249

Looking Forward to Looking Back 249
The Straighter the Line, the Finer the Curve 250
The Event Horizon 251
The Sun is Shining 252
Karma & Re-incarnation 253
The Shining Sun 254
Outgrowing Our Body 255
Beyond Time 256
Do Look Back 257
Be the Book 258
Saturn: The Body of Our Enlightenment 259
An Object is the Product of its Use 260
The Body is the Ultimate Talisman 261
Rush To Leave the Body 261
Getting Some Body Out Of Our Body 262

11

The Esoteric Concept of Bodies 263
High Times 263
Low Times 264
When Words Live 265
As Above, So Below 266
When We Say "Yes!" 266
Issue by Issue 267
Recapitulation 268
The Last Judgment 268
He Who Laughs Last 269
Making Choices 270
Credit With Interest 270
W. H. Auden, on the death of Yeats: "He Became His Admirers 271
A Crack in Time 272
Personal Choices 274
Unconventional 274
Future-Oriented Choices 275
Most Significant Subset 276
A Stellar Personality 277
That Fascinating Person 278
Saturn and Cycles 278
The Tracks of Time 279
The Astro-Shaman 280
Within or Without? 280
The Last Judgment 282
Planets As Chakras In A Natal Chart 283
What Interests the Client? 283
Looking at the Chart 284
Strong and Weak Planets 285
Planets: A Process and a State 286
Interdependent 287
Astrological Techniques 287
Astrology as an Oracle 288
Astrology Is About Our Lives 288
Can Astrology Predict Events? 289

Financial Astrologers 290
What Can Astrology Predict? 291
Electional Prediction 291
The 'Last' Of Life 292
Collecting Light 293
Realized Realization 294
Spiritual Work 295
Inner Teacher 295
Just Passing Through 296
The Degrees of Experience 296
Endless Description 297
The Straighter the Line, the Finer the Curve 298
The Hierarchy of Age 299
Gradual Exposition 299
Falling to Repetition 300
The Limits of Time 301
The Beat of the Planets 302
Time's Noise 303
The Roar of Nature Living 304
Of Purgatory and Hell 305
Have You Heard About the Lord? 307
Shamanism and the Bardo States 308
The Bardos 309
What Is Ignorance? 311
Mind Training and Meditation 311
Meditation and the Bardo States 312
The Mind's True Nature 313
Preparing the Mind 314
What Is Pure Land Buddhism? 315
Amitabha's Buddha Field 316
The Bardo Realms Are the Default 317
Summary: Astro-Shamanism and the Bardos 318
Astro-Shamanism and Meditation 318
Our Western Tradition 319
What's In It for Us? 320
The Ego or Self 321

Is The EGO Bad? 322
The Two Techniques..323
Experience It for Yourself 325
Pointing Out Instructions 326
Taking the Training...326
My Personal Story 327
Waiting 330
The Teacher..331
The Rule of Personality 332
Being Recognized 333
Giving In 333
Meeting the Karmapa 334
The Meeting 336
About Michael Erlewine..340
A Brief Bio of Michael Erlewine 341
Personal Astrology Readin.....................................342
The Heart Center House 343
Heart Center Library..343
Heart Center Meditation Room..............................346
Heart Center Symbol...350
Music Career 351

Foreword by Steven Forrest

Astro-shamanism. What could such a term possibly signify? Shamans shake rattles, wear scary masks, and go on psychedelic journeys into the Underworld. Astrologers sit safely in front of their computers under bright electric lights. The world that astrologers inhabit is essentially rational; it operates according to laws that can be studied and learned. The shaman's world is trans-rational, daemonic, magical. The shaman improvises in the face of chaos.

So what is Michael Erlewine doing here? How can he claim to build a bridge between these two worlds? Read on. You'll find out. He pulls it off. He rocks the paradigms. This book will mess with you.

Shamans heal souls. In our modern western world, we often expect the same of psychotherapists. That makes sense. "Psyche" is based on the ancient Greek word for soul, and "therapy" derives from the Greek word for healing. So it would follow that psychotherapists are soul-healers. And some of them truly are. Ditto really for some astrologers. But, to me, the crowning irony is that so many psychotherapists are steeped in the bio-chemical and mechanistic paradigms that dominate the modern world. They don't actively believe in souls at all. It is a bit like imagining podiatrists who didn't believe in feet! And even among modern astrologers, we often see something very similar: an absence of any sense of a coherent metaphysical heritage. Many are, functionally, existentialists. They describe our personalities and our "fates," and that's that. There is no framework of larger meaning or purpose.

To become a psychotherapist, one needs rigorous academic training. You have to pass a lot of tests. In astrology nowadays, it's still more of a professional free-for-all. Basically, anyone can print up some business cards and claim to be an astrologer. Many do. But the reality is that the intellectual rigor involved in becoming a psychotherapist is reflected pretty evenly in the mental effort it takes to become an astrologer—at least one who is respected by his or her peers. Among serious astrologers, there is a real affinity for complex, academic knowledge. Despite the popular image of an astrologer as a ditz or a flake, if you spend a day at an astrology conference you'll probably be intimidated by the brain-power you encounter there. The characters in the modern astrological world, in other words, seem to be drawn from the same zoological park that populates academia in general. There are some truly fine, deep, soulful people in the field, but one also encounters the same, familiar menagerie of educated fools, brains-on-legs, and psychopaths with PhDs.

It is tempting simply to say that it is ever thus—that in the modern world, every profession with the slightest pretension of academic rigor will breed these kinds of one-dimensional human beings. But why? As astrologers we purport to do something much like shamans do: to go down into the dark with our clients and help them re-assemble themselves. To heal. To recover their souls from the Underworld. This is not an abstract, intellectual process. You've got to get your body in it, and your heart too. You cannot do it "academically." Most of all, you have to have been there yourself, down in that deep dark place. You have to have done that work. And the stakes are enormously high—a human being in a vulnerable state has put his or her soul in your hands.

How can we claim to be training astrologers effectively when a typical astrology class, conference or book doesn't even mention the need for an astrologer to have inward, spiritual preparation? We are stuck in exactly the same blind spot that has crippled modern psychology: we are imagining that purely intellectual training alone will do the trick. It won't. You can't make a soul-healer that way. That's only part of the recipe. Just because we understand the physics of sound propagation, musical theory, and the evolution of the keyboard since 1492 doesn't mean we can actually play the piano!

In Astrology of the Heart, you get to know Michael Erlewine personally. His intellect, as you will discover, is fierce. He very obviously has no fear of burning the midnight oil with his nose in a book. This is rigorous work. But you also quickly comprehend that Michael has made considerable inner effort outside the narrow envelope of the academic paradigm. By the end of the book you realize that his home-base is Tibetan Buddhism, but before then he deftly demonstrates that he's ridden more soul-horses than that one: his language is sometimes mystical Christian, sometimes Rosicrucian, and of course quite often purely shamanic.

As Castaneda's don Juan would put it, he "moves fluidly between the worlds." But not just between the mental, intellectual constructs of those worlds. Michael, like a Druid's apprentice or a Buddhist monk, has submitted to the spiritual direction of men and women he was humble enough to realize were wiser than himself. He has received initiations. He has gone down into the Dark, into the Great Silence, into the

Luminous Void. He has, in other words, done something not enough astrologers do: mind-training. He has visited the worlds to which the astrological symbols refer. He speaks of them not with the authority of erudite footnotes, but with the authority of direct experience. The Zen Buddhists refer to philosophy and cognitive spiritual constructs as "a finger pointing at the moon." In the implicit joke, the student stares mesmerized by the finger, and never notices the moon at all. Michael Erlewine, however, has actually been to that moon, and he points out the way there to the rest of us.

This, to me, is the main message of Astrology of the Heart: that we must leaven the bread of dry astrological theory with the yeast of inner work. Meditation. Shamanic trance. Direct, trans-rational engagement with the planets. Experience, not just theory.

Is Michael simply saying that, along with our conventional astrological studies, we should all also practice meditation? Actually, he is saying a lot more than that. His message is integrative. It is not just about tagging meditation onto existing astrological disciplines. He demonstrates quite effectively that astrology provides a map of the inner worlds. The places we encounter directly when we enter into contemplative states are astrological, quite literally. He takes us on an ascending journey through the planets, mapping out the particular challenges, illusions and opportunities that exist at each level. It is very concrete and methodical, and he never asks you simply to "believe in it." You can verify it yourself.

One gets the impression of Michael having had quite a lot of personal experience at each of these planetary levels. In fact, with his personal cards on the table, he shares a fair amount of that biographical material. Undoubtedly sometimes his personal experience was so strong and unique that it left impressions in him that might not generalize so well to other people. No astrologer—or shaman—could ever fully avoid that pitfall. Your mileage may vary, in other words. Still, there is a feeling of something universal and objective here. Reading, I get the same feeling I get when I encounter weirdly parallel descriptions of "alternate realities" by shamans from cultures as far apart as Amazonia, Native America, Africa, Celtic Europe, and Siberia. It's clear they've all been to the same place, even though they use different metaphors to describe it. In the same tradition, Michael has linked astrology, shamanism, and Vajrayana Buddhism into a unified field, and shared the map of this same primordial territory with the rest of us. And he invites us to experience it for ourselves, to check his facts against the authority of our own experience.

Shamans are Tricksters. They have what the Native people of North America might call "coyote" energy. Cunningly, they trap us in situations where, in order to survive, we have to release some cherished illusion. Michael "got" me this way. As I read his book, I often found myself arguing with him in my head—getting caught up in my attachment to my own ideas, in other words. Technically, his astrology is very different from mine. He is, for one glaring example, inclined toward the heliocentric perspective, whereas I am purely geocentric. In this book, Michael's heliocentricity manifests primarily in his use of Earth as a planet. That really confuses me. In my cosmology, Earth has a tragic flaw as a planet: it isn't up there in the sky! It can't be in a sign or a house, or make any aspects. How can we use it? Michael does, effectively.

He messed with me in another tricky way too. The thrust of Astrology of the Heart is a kind of shamanic journey inward through the planets, culminating in our fusion with the almighty Light of the Sun. In that journey, Michael includes a magnificent enthronement of often-underestimated Mercury. With typical eloquence, he writes, "The Sanskrit word for Mercury is "Buddha," awareness . . . Mercury is the light of love, the divine light of eternal truth, the eternal corona and radiance of the Sun center itself . . . Mercury is the light of the mind, the light we see shining in each other's eyes."

    This is beautiful stuff.

Trouble is, when I am teaching my own students I take precisely the opposite road! I start with what I see as the natural egocentricity of the Sun, work outward through mere mind (Mercury), human love (Venus) . . . and eventually leap through Neptune's mystical stained-glass window out into the terrifying shamanic passage we call Pluto. I proceed from there into the wild archetypal reaches of the Kuiper Belt, and finally into true cosmic consciousness symbolized by the vastness of interstellar space.

    Just the same as Michael . . .only backwards.

I could have argued with him, or even gotten my knickers in a knot over who is right and who is wrong. That temptation lasted about a tenth of a second, then I was laughing at myself. The Trickster had struck; Michael had "coyote-ed" me, tricking me into seeing how easily I can get caught up in my own narrow mental constructs. And as I felt the rightness of what he teaches here and simultaneously the rightness of my own contradictory model, a window opened up inside me. I heard the sound of one hand clapping. I knew God could make two mountains without an intervening valley.

The spiritual richness of that immersion in paradox dwarfs any technical astrological insight. It is the inner work upon which astrology rests. What astrologer, lacking a tolerance for paradox, could conceivably honor the diversity of the clients he or she will counsel? Their reality is not the same as his or hers. This compassionate, humble spaciousness, this willingness to pass beyond the narrow straits of "rightness," is a ground teaching implicit in Michael's astro-shamanism

The modern astrological world desperately needs that openness. Over the past couple of decades something strange and unprecedented has been happening in the community of astrologers. Just as our larger social world has moved toward multi-culturalism, so has the world of astrology. Psychological astrology claimed center stage, briefly. But we now have a renaissance in Vedic astrology, which uses an entirely different Zodiac than the western traditions. And Vedic astrology has spawned a Neo-Vedic movement, with some philosophical sympathy for more western notions of free will. We have Uranian astrology, with its strange world of non-material, mathematical "planets." And Cosmobiology, Harmonic Astrology, asteroids, and an astrology based on the host of new planet-like objects out beyond Pluto. Then along came Project Hindsight and the resurrection of Hellenistic astrology. Adding to the confusion of riches, there is also a huge interest in the very distinct traditions of neo-Platonic and Renaissance astrology. I myself have become identified with Evolutionary Astrology, which essentially merges ancient reincarnation-based metaphysics with the values of modern psychology.

The frightening point is that these traditions are becoming mutually incomprehensible. I can't, for example, argue with Vedic or Hellenistic astrologers, or even speak very intelligently with them: I simply don't understand what they are saying. I don't speak their language and they don't speak mine. Modern astrology has become the Tower of Babel.

I celebrate the diversity, in principle—but I am also spooked about the future coherence of the astrological community and the loss of its beneficial interdependency and dialogue. We may simply be losing the common ground of a shared language. History teaches us that such a loss typically spells the death of a culture.

This brings me back to Michael the Trickster. He pulled me out of my narrow view, and re-connected me with that deeper ground of Being where paradox sits comfortably in the heart of the Mind.. He brought me back, like a shaman, with a renewed sense of that solid foundation upon which all astrologies rest. If the astrological community is going to have a vibrant civil future, it will be because beneath the diversity of our theoretical approaches we sense and celebrate this underlying unity of vision and experience. If we are living only up in our heads, in our cognitive intellects, we will never get there. They create divisions, not unity.

We can only experience this shared ground directly, through inner work. The nets of pure intellect are not fine enough to catch it. This is the sweet fruit of mind work—the direct experience of consciousness itself.

It is the path Michael Erlewine has walked all his life, and it is the path he invites us to consider in this fine and timely volume.

I find myself filled with gratitude toward Michael, and also with a sense of encouragement. As synchronicity would have it, he has invited me, an Evolutionary Astrologer very different from himself, to write this Foreword. And the book will be published by Robert Schmidt and Project Hindsight, known for their scholarly breakthrough work in restoring Hellenistic astrology for modern practitioners—again, a totally different philosophical vector.

Walking his talk, Michael has placed a stepping stone between two very different worlds. He stands on that middle stone, with white water roaring all around him. And his finger is pointing at the moon.

>Steven Forrest Summer Solstice, 2007 Chapel Hill, North Carolina

Astro-Shamanism

What This Book is About

Astrology is, above all, an oracle, albeit a complex one. An oracle is a direct way for the cosmos (and our own inner life) to actually speak to us, if we will listen. This book is about listening to that inner oracle and learning how to read and interpret the signs and messages that are endlessly appearing all around us each day of our lives.

The material covered here is part of what is called "inner" or "esoteric astrology." It is esoteric only because it is subtle enough that not everyone can get it, pick up on it. If they did, it would no longer be called "esoteric." I will do my very best to point this material out as clearly as I can and, if you can get it, your understanding of astrology will not only deepen, but you will begin to see these inner teachings at work in the world around you, 24x7. No longer will your astrology be just from a book or a chart form. Esoteric astrology is above all a living astrology and, if this book makes any sense to you, you will learn to see astrology is all around you in your day-to-day life, and not just out there somewhere among the stars. Esoteric astrology is the real heart of astrology and very much worth making an effort to understand and experience. And Shamanic astrology is a principle form of esoteric astrology.

A Personal Account

Shamanic astrology is a subject that is VERY hard to describe in words, but I will do my best. I have had excellent teachers and training, yet I must ask for your patience and understanding. Some of the following sections will be quite formal, like many astrological books and articles; however, still other sections will be very personal and poetic. I apologize in advance if any of this writing is too personal or too much or the wrong kind of prose for your taste. I have only my own personal account and life journey to use as an illustration. I cannot presume on anyone else's experience. And please don't read my personal account and suppose that you will experience the same thing.

We are each different, so read my account as one person's odyssey through the thicket of time. Yours will be tailored to your life and experiences. I have marked those more descriptive sections as "journal" entries, so you can take them or leave them, as you will. I suggest you read them, as I don't have all the answers. Sometimes the more poetic 'me' is all the understanding I have. I am still very much on this same journey.

I have organized all of this material into rough sections as make sense to me, but keep in mind that all of this esoteric material is interdependent and mutually reflective, so any given section may have all kinds of topics touched on other than just the main theme. There are many small sections, as well as longer ones too. Also keep in mind that many of these topics will be repeated. I will be going over the same content, again and again, from slightly different perspectives. Please have patience with this approach. Repetition is an important means to allow these concepts to sink in. It is how I learned from my teachers. Remember, this is esoteric or hidden material and by that very fact is not always obvious. Take your time.

It is best to read through each section and immerse yourself in what's there, letting it seep into your consciousness as much by osmosis as by grasping at it with your intellect. The goal is to get a feel for this approach. It is not unlike focusing a pair of binoculars until things come into focus. Read through it, but don't try to force an understanding. Let it flow. Once you begin to see what is being talked about here, you can take it from there.

And last, I dedicate this book to the benefit of all sentient beings, that each may find the right kind of energy (Mars) to propel them along their correct path (Jupiter), and help them pass through whatever challenges await them (Saturn). In the end, may each of us take full possession of Earth, our inheritance.

Life Initiations through Astrology

This book is about the shamanic tradition within modern astrology, what we could call 'Shamanic Astrology', and astro-shamanism is nothing new. Astrologers have been performing a shamanic function in society for centuries, and they continue to do so today. Astrology, and the astrologer's role as shaman or guide, is becoming increasingly more important in modern society. Shamanic astrology is not often openly discussed, and is generally considered, as already mentioned, a part of what has been called "esoteric astrology," the inner or more secret aspects of astrological knowledge. This is because it has to do with the ecstatic tradition, what is commonly called out-of-the-body experience. That ecstatic tradition is what we will be presenting here.

Before we describe the process of astrological shamanism, let's review what a shaman or shamanka (female shaman) is in the literature of the world. Here we will use the better-known term "shaman" to represent both male and female shamans, so as not to have to repeat both terms endlessly.

The word origin of Shaman (SHAY-men), from the Siberian Tungus language, means one who "knows," one who has attained some degree of spiritual realization, awareness, in particular awareness of the other worlds, the next life stage or planes.

Traditional Shamanism and "Core Shamanism"

We should distinguish here between what is called traditional shamanism and the popular-today derivative called "Core Shamanism." Traditional shamanism is a vocation that chooses you (there is no choice), while core shamanism is an avocation, a form of shamanism which anyone can choose to study and learn to use. Core Shamanism is, in a word, a sanitized form of traditional shamanism, stripped of most of the dangers and risks, something that almost anyone can sign up for, study, and eventually practice.

Both forms of shamanism exist in the world today, so it is meaningless to say that traditional shamanism is the only one to be used and the other simply an imitation, although there is some truth to that assertion. Here we are focusing on the parts of shamanism that make sense in modern astrology. Any counseling astrologer, almost by definition, is probably using one or more shamanic techniques, with or without the mind-altering experiences of the traditional shaman. These techniques are what we will study here.

That being said, I have found it much more useful to first understand the nature of traditional or classic shamanism, and take what we can from that, than to try to take from "Core Shamanism," which is already an extract. In other words, we can each make our own core shamanism by absorbing as much as possible from those parts of traditional shamanism that make "sense" to us, that fit our personal experience. That is the approach being followed here.

What is Astro-Shamanism?

This section is about the shaman's spiritual crisis. The traditional shaman does not choose to be a shaman. Shamanism of this kind is the result of a series of psychological visions or experiences whose very nature estranges one (at least for a time) from conventional society and the normal way of seeing things. The shaman is somehow, against his (or her) will, thrust outside of how everyone else sees life, and into a space and view that is markedly altered and mostly non-communicable to the society around him. They become invisible in that society cannot see where they are at.

The shaman, usually through a personal psychological or spiritual crisis, has become aware of the inner sequence of the life processes typically hidden from society by their very obviousness, processes that are thus somehow "self-secret." This propensity can come about through having a near-death or life-changing experience, mind-altering drugs, or somehow becoming psychologically separated for a time from conventional societal consciousness.

Not the Same as the Vision Quest

The shamanic experience has some similarities to the Native American vision quest, but, unlike the vision quest which is generally voluntary, the shaman's own internal psychological chemistry thrusts the future shaman beyond convention and into an altered state of consciousness until such time as he (or she) can manage (often through what is sometimes a life/death mental struggle) to find a balance, stabilize, and return to normal society. The shaman cannot communicate what he (or she) sees to others, because society is not able or prepared to understand it. They often are viewed by society as a little bit crazy. Society in general (by the very definition of conventional) has not had the experience needed in order to understand the shaman's view. The shaman by virtue of his unorthodox experience is just "out there" on their own.

Unlike organized religions, shamans act alone and are "self-chosen," rather than appointed, in that the intensity of the shaman's own internal experiences separates him or her permanently from the other members of society. They are outsiders not by choice, but by the nature of their own inner experience and awareness, permitted to see and experience realms of the psyche the average person does not.

Typically, shamans may take years to stabilize the vision or mental experiences that they are thrust into, often struggling against mental unbalance and even madness. The shaman can be distinguished from a madman because he (or she) learns to control and understand what has been experienced. He masters those altered states of mind and rejoins society, but with a permanently altered view. The shaman always exists in conjunction with and in contradistinction to his society. Since shamans are defined in relation to the societal conventions they live in, without that society they have nothing to be measured against. Shamans are the original outriders, literally defining the edge of conventional time and mentality.

A One-Way Street

It is generally agreed that once a shaman, one is a shaman for life. There is no going back, and, no matter what other career or work the shaman may undertake, the function of shaman always takes precedence and is their heart function within the society. It just happens.

In other words, shamanism is not an avocation, something one chooses. We do not choose to become a shaman, but the very intensity of our own inner experiences determines a vocation as a shaman, and to what degree we are a shaman.

As my teacher used to say, "We are all initiates to life, but the question is: to what degree?" Although in some societies, shamanic powers can be inherited or run in a family, in those cases it appears to be more a product of sharing a similar mind-set and training, with the parents initiating the children. However, as pointed out, most shamans are "called" or chosen by their own internal experiences and awareness. They come to know what others do not know and cannot know. And this change in view is permanent – a realization. They cannot forget what they have seen, and it is this knowledge of altered states that makes them valuable to society.

All societies have shamans or their equivalent, because shamanism is something that happens to one, rather than something that can just be learned or passed on. In any society, there are always a few members whose personal inner experiences are such as to separate them, at least for a time, from the group. Knowledge gained from this separation then gives shamans an alternative view of life that makes them of use to the community. They alone understand other members of the community who become estranged for one reason or another and their shamanic experience allows them to communicate with those souls who fall through the cracks. It is pretty much axiomatic that the shaman can only help others in those areas where he or she has personally had a similar experience.

Shamans Are Not Priests or Ministers

As pointed out, shamans acquire special knowledge or abilities through their own life-changing experiences, and they are distinct from the rest of their society by the very intensity of these spiritual experiences. In this sense, they are more akin to the mystic. The shaman, as author Mircea Eliade puts it, "is the great specialist in the human soul; he or she alone "sees" it, for he or she alone knows of its "form" and its destiny." The shaman knows the story or journey of the soul. In a very real sense, the shaman wakes in these realms, while society sleeps. They are the watchmen and protectors of the community soul.

Shamans are to be distinguished from priests or ministers and other members of organized religion who work cooperatively with one another to inform and shepherd the entire society. For the most part, shamans are independent, solitary, depending only on their own internal experience or revelation, and they seldom work in groups or attempt to convert all the members of their community to their view. Instead, they assist the stragglers in a community, those who, for one reason or another, have fallen out of the conventional mindset, and are somehow temporarily spiritually estranged.

Shamans acknowledge other shamans, but seldom group or come together. You would not expect to see a shaman conference, at least of the traditional variety. They are for the most part loners, and their knowledge is personal to themselves; it serves to separate them from their particular group or society. The idea of a shaman convention is pretty much an oxymoron.

Societies and Brotherhoods

Shamans also differ from secret societies or esoteric brotherhoods in that they typically are not part of any particular lineage or organized group, and, as mentioned, do not attempt to shepherd or initiate the entire society, but, instead, only initiate or work with those like themselves, those who have the propensity to sustain ecstatic (out-of-the-body) experiences, that is: those who find themselves in an altered state of mind. In other words, shamans guide and inform particular members of their society who are in spiritual flux — those who have somehow fallen through the societal cracks.

As mentioned, there is no attempt on the part of the shaman to convert the larger community to his or her vision, a vision which in the shaman's view is a calling, an exceptional state of mind. Shamans are psychic healers and stand watch over society to protect the integrity of the human psyche. They are the shepherds of the human soul in its journey through time.

The Shaman Is Not a Doctor

Although many shamans are also healers of physical ailments, medicine men or women, this function is distinct from their role as a shaman, at least in this material. The shaman is primarily a doctor of the soul, not of the body, and administers to the psychological and spiritual realms rather than to physical symptoms. The Medicine Man is very much a vocation on its own.

Although the shaman may also use various medicines and can be a healer or doctor of the physical body, he or she is primarily a healer of the psyche, a master of ecstatic (out-of-the-body) experiences. The shaman works on the psychological and subconscious level, seeking out the soul of an individual in distress, identifying with them, and directing them away from their current struggle or mental suffering to the next level or stage: the so-called afterlife. He or she is an intermediary between the visible and the invisible (or not yet visible) worlds.

The work of the shaman does not pertain so much to our physical death at the end of life, but to the many smaller deaths we each die in life, climacteric events (rites of passage) in life that find us dying to one phase of life and struggling or not-yet-born into the next phase. One seeks out a shaman because one is temporarily lost, and the shaman somehow can see both the realm in which we are leaving and the new phase which we are about to enter. Sound familiar? It should, because the public seeks out astrologers for very similar reasons.

Shamanism in Astrology

In this material, we are not going to try to pursue shamanism as it relates to personal totems, power animals, or to any of the more exotic practices that we might read about in books like those of Carlos Castaneda, and other worthy writers, although these are, of course, very legitimate interests. We are not going to skin animals, dig (or take) herbs, draw magic circles, or perform any of the many rituals that you might find in a book on traditional shamanism. Here we are looking at shamanism within the tradition of astrology itself, in particular the role of the modern astrologer as a ferryman or guide to the inner states of the mind and life.

In this sense, most astrologers perform (at least to some degree) this function of the shaman, that of the ferryman from one phase to another. Because of this fact, the counseling astrologer may find shamanic astrology of particular interest.

The shaman helps others to accept their changes or deaths on one level and obtain rebirth and develop familiarity on other and new levels. It is written that the shaman restores the road between earth and heaven, a road that has been temporarily lost or has become unclear or uncertain. Another way to say this is that the shaman knows the way from one state of being or chakra to the next state, and is able to guide or prepare the initiate for that journey. The shaman often guides the would-be-initiate from an unstable or dangerous state of mind to stability and future productivity.

In the esoteric literature, the shaman traditionally escorts the souls of the dead away from their corpses and dying places, and on into the next world. The shaman is capable of entering and holding an altered state of consciousness at will, and can act as an intermediary between the known world of the would-be initiate, and the supra-natural or "next" world.

The shaman does not have to enter an altered state, as in 'somehow' going there. His or her experiences are forever fresh in their mind and they react spontaneously to the psychological distress signals coming from any person they encounter. It is automatic, and does not require any ritual or preparation. It just happens. A shaman can appear to those in need at one moment, point out the way, and be transparent or invisible the next, as if nothing ever took place. This happens all the time, and we may find ourselves shaking our head to make sure we saw what we did see.

By knowing both worlds, the shaman is able to predict or control the future of the would-be initiate, who does not yet know their way around these future worlds. This is a fancy way of saying the shaman can converse or reach one who is lost in an unconventional state of mind, make contact, and guide that person out of their situation to higher ground, so to speak.

Dead and Alive

The shaman is said to be dead in the land of the living, but alive in the spiritual worlds, and therefore knows the future for those living now, who must one day make the same transformation (or death) that the shaman has already taken. The shaman has, in some sense, gone to the next plane or world before other members of their society, and can reveal that world to those who themselves are about to cross over to it, or who are crossing now. The shaman is, therefore, above all, a guide to these other worlds. The shaman has a certain power over time, actually possessing the ability to "make time," and to penetrate between the seconds of clock time to touch on the timeless or eternity — the space beyond or within time.

To repeat: the shaman is one who has already gone beyond, who has him or herself crossed over into the next world or level, has returned with knowledge of these adjacent or other worlds. He or she can then instruct or prepare others for their forthcoming initiation into these other worlds. Above all, shamans mediate between the world of the living and the dead, between one phase or level and the next one. Those with a propensity for shamanism (out of body experiences) often apprentice themselves to an accomplished shaman, through the process of mentoring and initiation. The shaman is an initiate and thus an initiator. This, then, has been a brief introduction to the traditional nature of the shaman. Sound a little familiar? It should, because most counseling astrologers practice the shamanic techniques we will be presenting below.

Out-of-the-Body Experiences

Before we turn to looking at astrology and shamanism, let us be clear about what we mean by ecstatic or out-of-the-body experiences, which is the especial province of the shaman. Shamans, as part of their initiation, are by their own life experiences somehow thrust out of the body of normal conventional societal experience into an altered state of consciousness, what can only be called unconventional. Because these altered states are unconventional, then, by definition, they will not be understood or easily grasped by conventional means and conventional minds. These have been called altered states of consciousness or out-of-the-body experiences.

Everyone, each of us, has out-of-the-body experiences all the time. Consciousness is not some static state, but ebbs and flows, constantly. We are always going out of the body and back into it. However, what is missing for most of us is the awareness of this process. We tend to ignore and not recognize what our mind is doing, and don't often register when we are more in or more out of our body. Instead, we assume our consciousness is stable and more or less the same each moment. In fact, most of us struggle to keep it stable. We don't want to go out. We don't want to be that different. When the waves of change wash over us, most prefer to take a little nap and just ignore what is happening. Usually we are not willing to witness our own birth and passing on the various planes. That is mostly left to the role of the shaman.

If we have not, as have traditional shamans, been forced to look at our mind from an altered state, then, if we want to learn something more about shamanistic states, we will have to study and become familiar with learning to recognize the various states of our mind, the map of our mental states. This is part of what we will study here. Lacking life experiences that force us into an altered view of life, one can learn about the mind through various forms of meditation, in particular, what is called insight meditation or Vipassana meditation. There is not room to go into that here, but there are many books and teachers available on this topic.

The Astrologer as Shaman

Astrology can also be used — and often is used — as a shamanic tool. In other words, astrology is used to guide individuals who are lost or stuck in one area of their lives, introducing them to the next or to a different realm. This is a common practice. How that can be done is what will be presented here.

This material could be presented in a wide variety of ways. Here we will present it as this writer (and his teachers) understands it. It should go without saying that from these descriptions, each of you will find your own way of understanding this, and fashion your own shamanic astrological coat. In no way is this author trying to be dogmatic. It is just the only way I know of this knowledge. You will find your own words, please.

Are Astrologers Shamans?

This book is about the use of astrology in a shamanistic way, not how to become a shaman. True shamanism, as pointed out earlier, is an inner calling, not an avocation, and requires sensitivity gained from life experience not found in the average person. That being said, any astrologer with a successful counseling practice is probably performing some shamanic activity, and has had experiences in his or her own life that were preparations for the better understanding of others. It is my belief that most astrologers already have some form of heightened sensitivity or they would not be pursuing the study of astrology. As mentioned, any counseling astrologer is, to some degree, probably already performing a shamanic function to one degree or another. This book may help you become more aware of what you are already doing.

What I hope to do here is to point out to you how astrology can be used as a shamanistic guide. It will be up to you to determine if there is a connection and if what is written here makes sense and is useful to you.

Seeking The Shaman

The shaman, unlike the priest, does not seek out or try to share his spiritual knowledge with the general community. Members of the community who are suffering in one way or another seek out the shaman, who then agrees to see and work with them. This is not much different from the way the average astrologer receives clients, often by word of mouth.

There is much written about the shaman taking special herbs or substances to enter into a heightened state in order to communicate with the client, but this is not often necessary. The shaman already exists in an altered state, one altered by his or her own internal experiences. The shaman does not need any mental enhancements; he or she already has them.

In astrological shamanism, the shaman, who has previously had initiations or personal life experiences related or synchronous with the client, is able to reach and connect with the client by virtue of already having knowledge of the general psychological landscape the client is going through. The shaman is able to attract and flag down the attention of the client, establish communication, and provide the client with signs that the client will recognize, signs that signify to the client that the shaman has had similar experiences; that is, that the shaman knows where the client is at through personal experience. Once mutual trust and recognition are established, clients allow the shaman to guide or lead them out of the situation they are stuck in and on to another area of the mind, what amounts to their next or future stage of life.

Altered States

The shaman, who, through virtue of his or her personal experience in altered states, can somehow speak the language of the client, can converse and establish communication. The shaman, due to having had a similar experience, is able to answer questions the client may ask, and satisfy the client's fear of being misled by someone who does not actually understand their state of mind.

In summary, the shaman is able to get the attention of the client by displaying signs of experience that the client can recognize and acknowledge as true. Once clients understand that he or she is not alone, and that the experience of the shaman in fact encompasses their own experience, they can submit to allowing the shaman to lead them out of their current predicament and on toward another place, one hopefully more comfortable for them. The act of realizing that they are not alone, and that someone else has had similar experiences, is often a key step for clients in this process.

Beyond Convention

The client, typically, has somehow wandered into a state of mind that effectively isolates him or her from the rest of the society, if only temporarily. Their society has no answers for them and, by definition, cannot but exclude them from their own consciousness. The isolated person thus is cut off from the nourishment of the community until they can resolve their unrest, and stop disturbing society. This is where the shaman comes in and why they are sought out. In many societies, any person with mental instability or a wavering consciousness is told to seek out a shaman, either to be cured or to take up shamanism themselves.

The shaman, who is already permanently outside of the conventional community in some sense, is capable of grasping the degree and nature of the suffering of the client. He or she already has this experience of isolation, and can measure the degree of separation of the client from the community, and guide the client to make adjustments.

The shaman calms the client, assists in his or her stabilization, and eventually restores the client back to the community as whole and usable once again. The role of the shaman is to guide the client from one state of mind to the next obvious state, and help him or her to stabilize. As astrologers we do this all the time. This book will present a variety of esoteric shamanic techniques of interest to the astrologer.

The Inner Meaning

Astrology of the Heart

In this part of the book, we will start by examining the astrological planets as they relate to the system of subtle internal energies called the chakras, a branch of esoteric astrology. Also called occult or secret astrology, esoteric astrology is by definition somewhat difficult to study. It is occult (hidden) or secret, not because it is some deep dark secret, and not because someone or some group is trying to keep it from us, but because it is, by its very nature, subtle and hard to grasp with the mind. It might be more helpful to say, as the Tibetans do, that it is self-secret. It hides itself from us. We can't grasp it.

And this knowledge is hidden or secreted in the one place we might never think to look and that is: in plain sight. In other words, the secret heart of astrology (esoteric astrology) is hidden by the fact that it is so obvious and present to us that we have no way to grasp it or keep it in mind. Although it is with us and present all the time, our mind has trouble grasping or maintaining an awareness of it.

Self Secret

An example of something that is self-secret would be consciousness itself. Try using your consciousness to look at itself. Take a moment right now and look at who is reading this page. Who is that? See what I mean?

This subject is, by its very nature, hard to grasp and thus is "self-secret," which is what mind training or meditation techniques are all about. If you just tried the little experiment mentioned above, you have some idea of how difficult it is to point out the nature of the obvious, yet that is our task here.

Although esoteric astrology of this type is very subtle and hard to grasp, it is very much worth our efforts to understand it, and has very practical benefits. To rephrase this: Unlike our day-to-day world, in the realm of esoteric astrology even the tiniest bit of increased vision or progress can radically affect how we see things. What separates the initiate from the uninitiated may be only the width of a hair in terms of understanding, yet this difference could be all the difference in the world. It could be the difference between ignorance and vision.

Esoteric Teachers

I have been studying astrology for more than forty years. During that time, although I am considered quite technical by my fellow astrologers, my primary interest has always been on esoteric astrology, what astrology means, refers, or points to. I have had the very good fortune to be instructed in esoteric studies by a number of fine teachers. It is to their credit that I am able to present any of this information here.

In particular, I trained for a number of years with Andrew Gunn McIver (a traveling Rosicrucian initiator) who was born in Scotland and later settled in Canada and then the U.S. It was he who introduced me to some of the inner workings of shamanistic astrology, the esoteric or hidden side.

There have been a number of other fine teachers that I have been lucky enough to meet in this world. One such teacher was Iotis Wilder, a Unity minister from Detroit. In recent years, since the early 70s, I have been working with Tibetan psychological methods of mind practice, in particular with Khenpo Karthar Rinpoche, a Tibetan lama. It was Khenpo Rinpoche who introduced me to the Eastern view of esoteric knowledge. I have made two pilgrimages to Tibet and China, one with my teacher.

In these pages, I would like to share with you various esoteric ideas. I am not claiming to be any great expert in all of this, but I do have a sincere interest in the subject and am happy to examine and discuss these ideas with others. My wish is that this discussion may be of benefit to readers and to astrology in general.

The Planets as Chakras

The chakras, vital force centers within the body, are much discussed in the esoteric literature of India, not to mention all kinds of New Age publications. I imagine that most of you reading this have seen illustrations of a yogi sitting in a meditation posture, with a vertical line of colored spheres (the chakras) running up and down their spine. These diagrams, while accurate in themselves, don't tell the whole story, and can be misleading in that they suggest that the chakras are, somehow, only something (points of light) within your personal physical body.

While the chakras or planetary force centers can be said to be within your physical body, as in the diagrams mentioned, these seven centers within our body are but pointers to chakras also outside our body in the world itself, vast areas of life through which each of us live and wander. Or, another way to put this is that the term "physical body," in the esoteric sense, does not just mean your personal body, your arms and legs, but the physical aspects of all life, the physical body of the life in this world -- the world itself as our physical body. We are all wandering in *that* world.

The Chakras in the World

In other words, our physical body (shamanistically speaking) is also the entire world out there. While it can be somewhat difficult to grasp the chakras as spheres of light along the spine, it is not so difficult to see these same chakras in the world around us, and to learn to use them in astrological counseling. That is what this section of the book is about, learning to use shamanistic techniques for helping yourself and others, particularly through the counseling process.

Here, as mentioned, we will not primarily be focusing on the planets as physical points or centers within our particular personal body. Instead, we will examine the idea that the planets (chakras) are vast areas of consciousness and life within the larger body of our existence, the external life of the outside world in which we each wander and learn. We are concerned here not only with the chakras as states or "places," but also in the process and journey each of us makes from one to another of these chakras.

Reflected In the World

So, let's put aside for now trying to find the seven planetary force centers or chakras along our spine. You can't see them in the mirror and, although you may be able to sense something about them from meditating on their qualities, there is a much easier way to learn about these sacred centers, as projected by ourselves onto the world around us. We each have a built-in projector within us.

As astrologers, we are already comfortable with associating celestial events (planets, aspects, houses, etc.) in the heavens with corresponding events personally here on Earth, so we can extend that kind of understanding to the chakras. These areas along the spine correspond with the vast planetary centers in the world around us.

We are familiar, from day-to-day life, with the idea that the mind controls the body, and that if we can learn mental control and stability, the body will usually follow along. If nothing else, we know that what we see and feel in our mind psychologically can affect how we view life outside ourselves, which in turn can affect us physically. We project our inner view onto the outside world, and then proceed to live in that outside world, colored by our own inner psychology, by what we believe and see. If we are still more experienced, we know there is no absolute difference between inner and outer, no hard line --subject and object are one.

We live in a world of projectors, and every person projects their inner world on the screen of life around them and then lives in that world. The phrase "when worlds collide" takes on new meaning in this context.

Then it should not surprise us to learn that the chakras, these great planetary centers, are also vast areas of our mind and life where we exist and live out our lives. If we want to think of the chakras as areas within our body, then we should understand that we are speaking also here of the entire body of existence -- our life.

The World is as 'We' See It

Yes, these centers are subtle energy centers, a part of our mind, but that mind, for better or for worse, very much controls and colors (projects) how we see and act in the outside physical world. In other words: there is no outside physical world that is not filtered or first colored by our mind, by the view in-here from which we see that world out there. 'Out there' is in here projected to a marked degree. Inside and outside are hopelessly interdependent. If we change our mind, we also change the way we see the world. This is not a new idea.

That having been said, it remains to point out to you how to identify and experience these inner planetary chakras in the world you are now living in, and this is not that difficult. So far, I have indicated that you will be looking outside in the world around you for these subtle planetary chakras, and not just within your mind, in the sense that we tend to think of the mind as connected to our head or our personal body. The chakras are also magnified areas of the mind projected in the world around you and quite easy to see.

Living in the Chakras

Although we all have seen diagrams of the seven chakras or sacred force centers within the human body, these diagrams are hardly very useful without a lot of instruction and practice. As pointed out, it is misleading to think that the chakras are limited to a series of glowing spheres along our spinal cord within our physical body. We don't see them in the mirror, and without a lot of training, we can't really sense them within our personal physical body.

As pointed out earlier, more useful to most of us will be to learn that these chakras are more practically understood to be vast areas of our mind (and therefore our life) through which we wander, a journey each of us takes through life, one that lasts as long as life itself. In other words, at any given time, each of us is centered more-or-less in one chakra or another, and I don't mean looking at a little glowing sphere along our spine. We are out there in our life in the midst of the chakras, always, like: right now. The question for most us of might be: which chakra are we in, and how can we tell?

Wandering In the Chakras

We are now (and always have been) wandering in the chakras in this vast body of existence that we call our life. When we read in books about spiritually opening the chakras, one by one, or opening them in this or that order, this refers not to focusing on some glowing sphere within our physical spine, but to our life's journey through time and the mind. We move from one chakra to another, in a very slow progression that will take our entire life. Recognizing this fact can make understanding the world of esoteric astrology very much easier.

At any given year or time in our lives, we tend to be centered or "living" in one particular chakra, one particular life area, and we very gradually move or progress from that chakra to the next one in line, and usually in a given order. That order is the same for most of us, but it can vary between individuals. The opening of the chakras for each of us is the story of our spiritual awakening, our spiritual journey beyond time.

Successive Chakras

It can take years (or a lifetime) to move from a particular chakra or planetary sphere to the next one in succession. And, in general, this process is irreversible. In other words, once we have made ourselves at home in (and mastered) a planet or chakra, we move on. We don't go back and live in the previous chakra, but we do remember how to get around in that chakra. We know how it works and how to use it. It becomes part of our personal spiritual toolbox.

It is important to understand that when we speak here of moving from one chakra to the next, or moving through the chakras, this concept can be misleading. We are not really going anywhere and we don't ever get anywhere, other than the right here and now. Both the past and the future are always accessed from the present, that is: right now.

All of our previous changes, all of the chakras we have been in are with us now, and not somewhere left behind or discarded. And this is true for any future chakras we may inhabit. When we master a chakra or planet, it does not disappear, but it no longer challenges or interests us to the same degree. We are the master of it, and can handle it from that point on, without thinking, automatically, much like when we master steering a car; it becomes automatic for us, part of our expertise. That is how to understand how we move from one chakra or planet to another, in our spiritual unfoldment.

Planetary Landscapes

Each chakra or planetary sphere has what amounts to its own particular landscape and series of rules or laws that govern life in that chakra. We gradually learn to find our way around in each chakra; we learn those rules, and master how to live there. It is not unlike going to school. If we take chemistry one year and graduate, we move on to studying physics. We don't have to take chemistry again, we are not studying it now, but we do remember how to get around in a chemistry book. We can use it. It is a permanent part of our education.

In this life as we live it, nothing vanishes or just goes away, because everything is a part of life. Each stage of life we have passed through, and each chakra, is still right here with us, and other people are now living in chakras where we once lived. It is not behind us, just because we passed through that stage. In other words, passing through a chakra means knowing how to get around in that chakra, how to work it, not leaving it behind.

When we learn to breath, we don't stop breathing, but we keep breathing automatically as long as we have life, but we no longer focus on breathing. That is a better way to conceive of chakras and our journey through them. We never really get anywhere else, but we do learn to handle these parts of our lives with skill and understanding. We master them. We become Initiates.

Mastering the Chakras

What follows will be explained in great detail later on, so don't panic if this does not make perfect sense right away. When we clear out of a chakra, master it, and graduate to the next chakra, we are no longer motivated by what first motivated us within that chakra. It is no longer new for us. We have moved on to the rules and complexity of the next chakra, and are now motivated by what may be a completely new set of rules, and are working within a wondrous new landscape. Each new chakra is somewhat like a new or completely different world for us.

The previous chakra or area of our lives is still with us, but is now void of interest to us. It is empty for is. We have been there, done that, and we continue to do that (whatever is related to the previous chakra), as needed, from this point on. We have mastered it, like steering an automobile. We drive on.

An important point is that the essence of each chakra we are currently in, the essence of the rules for that chakra or planet, is always the next innermost chakra, that particular chakra or planet that is "inner" to the current one. For example, if we are alive and living in the Saturn chakra, the essence or key to that chakra will be the planet that is next innermost to Saturn, which, of course, is Jupiter. The orbit of Jupiter is next inside (toward the Sun) from Saturn. Jupiter therefore is the esoteric key to Saturn, the key that unlocks how to use and master Saturn. This is true for each of the chakras, in turn. Mars is the key to Jupiter, Earth is the Key to Mars, and so on, in to the Sun. More on this soon.

I am sure this is sounding a bit too mysterious, but as you will see, it is quite simple and easy to understand. What we want to know as shamanistic astrologers is: in what chakra are we now living? Where are we? If we are a counseling astrologer, we need to determine what chakra our client is in, and what are they seeing and experiencing? Once we know what chakra they are in, we can direct our clients or ourselves in a variety of useful ways.

Background: Digressions

Before we get into the specific chakras and how to recognize each of them, let's take one step back, and make sure you have all the background you need to understand what I am pointing out here. This will be a digression, but hopefully a very useful one.

In fact, let's even digress one step further and talk for a moment about the process of initiation into the esoteric mysteries, what has been called holding or obtaining the "view." And this might be important to understand

Beginning students of esoteric astrology, although they acknowledge they know little about the subject, can't help but already have formed in their minds some idea of what this subject is all about. Otherwise, why would you read this book? Although preconceptions are common, they are seldom helpful and, by and large, having a pre-formed opinion about a subject is most often the first obstacle any teacher or mentor must overcome, the fact that the student "thinks" he or she knows what the teacher is going to point out to them. Of course, if they did know, they would not be a student, and the teacher, who would see that the student already gets it, would not be trying to point out the topic.

Expectations Can't Define

Now let's introduce a more important factor yet, and that is: the truth of any topic is seldom what you expect, almost by definition. Expectations can't define, and you can't expect to find what you expect. Expectations usually don't help a situation.

Students tend to assume that there is something to get at, some thing or object of knowledge that the teacher will point out, that they can then get their hands on or their mind around. In esoteric studies, there IS nothing (no thing) to get to, anymore than there is a particular end to get to in life, other than the physical end of life, and few of us are in a rush to go there.

What I am trying to say here is that learning about esoteric concepts is more about preparing the student to have the right attitude or view, than it is about getting "at" something. If all it took was telling the truth, then the sages and philosophers throughout history have already told us everything. If we didn't "get it," so to speak, it is because we were not prepared to receive it, and did not have the right mind set. Our mind was not set, like a receiver, to gather it, to take it all in. We couldn't tune in. That is what I am working on here.

Backpedaling

So, what frequently can appear to the student as endless backpedaling on the part of the teacher, endless digressions (like this one here), and putting off getting to the point, is simply that there is no point, no such hard and fast thing like a "point" or fact when it comes to these esoteric studies, in particular. And that is not a bad thing. The teacher has to break this news, to discourage the student from looking for the "point" or preconception that the student has pre-formed in his or her mind, and, instead, gently help to orient the student to receive and experience the actual idea, an idea that, by definition, the student does not know, and has not yet experienced. It is more like setting the sails on a boat, often nothing more than an adjustment of attitude or approach. The student does not yet have the correct or right attitude. They are not properly oriented.

In fact, in most cases, students come with a linear attitude, looking for something they can imagine down the line, the next step, so to speak. Often, what is given is not a next step, linearly speaking, but a change in attitude that enables a fresh view of the same old world. In fact, if you think about it, that is what most of us need, a new way of handling what we already have.

This is not unlike the task of the midwife, who on occasion has to turn the baby around in the womb until it is oriented properly and can be born; same idea here.

In other words, the teacher has the unenviable task of turning and tweaking the student's mind to receive knowledge, and here "to receive knowledge" means to be able to experience and thus "get" for themselves what the teacher is pointing out. Real knowledge is not a "thing" to get or understand, but a knowing, an experience we each need to have for ourselves, and after which we don't need a teacher on the subject.

The teacher points it out, the student tries to get it, and the teacher questions the student for signs that the student got what was being pointed out. If not, the teacher continues to try to adjust and position the student's mind further, and then repeats the pointing out instruction, and this process goes on and on, until the student gets it or gives up.

Intellectual Understanding

In the realm of esoteric knowledge, simple intellectual understanding is not enough. We each must experience for ourselves what is being pointed out, if we ever hope to be able to point out to another what we have learned. Pointing out or understanding, intellectually, what we read in a book is just rote memorization. Learning must be a life experience we have, not just some words on a page.

So, to recap: teaching or pointing out esoteric knowledge is more like setting the sails on a boat, and waiting to see if the student catches the wind, and heads off in the direction desired. The teacher adjusts the attitude of the student, and gradually gets him or her in a position to see or receive the knowledge. It is all about receiving the knowledge. There is no "knowledge" per se, nothing to "get" all at once, but there is the act of knowing, the experiencing for yourself what the teacher is pointing out. The teacher tweaks the view of the student, until he or she gets it, and has the experience themselves, AND could then point it out to someone else. This process is part of what is called mentoring. It is also an integral part of what make lineages so important. And that is the end of this digression.

Approach Is Everything

This last point is so important, let's go over it one more time. In shamanic or esoteric astrology, approach is everything. Your attitude or approach, how you take it, how you are oriented "toward" is most crucial. If you come at it wrong, you will see and experience nothing or very little of what I am writing about here. And here, I am not just talking about understanding this material, per se. I mean being aware of the content of this book in your life. With the wrong approach, you just won't get it, and you will pass right through life and never know these experiences were there. You won't be aware of them.

It happens to countless people all the time.
It is my job here to tease these ideas out in the open for you, to turn your mind around until you can receive them, until you get it. That is why I have been telling you that this knowledge is not something for you to "get," not an action you must perform, but rather an attitude or approach you must assume or take -- reception. The key to esoteric astrology is to be passive and receptive, to prepare your mind to receive and take this knowledge in, like a satellite receiver --a big dish. You can be active in your passivity or reception, but you must be passive in your action. Don't push on, but give, as in "give way."

We Sail Our Ship Alone

I am trying, here, to tune you like we might tune a radio receiver to pick up a music station. The music is playing all around us, but you can't hear it unless you tune in. And tuning in is all about receptivity, and preparing your mind to get it. The analogy of setting the sails on a ship, so as to pick up the wind, is a good one. We have to work with the rigging, and set the sails. There is no doubt that the winds of change will come, and if our sails are set right, we will begin to move through the chakras, to feel the changes I will be describing.

The point here is that shamanic knowledge is not only conceptual, not merely something for you to understand, but rather an experience you must have. As an intellectual idea, shamanic knowledge is more or less just obvious, but as a living experience, it is profound. I am doing my best to prepare you for that experience, and to help set your sails.

Figure and Ground

Now we need to spend some little time painting the background for all of this, giving you a picture of how all of these thoughts fit together. I don't expect you to get it all at once. This is subtle stuff, and anyone who studies esoteric astrology learns to see the chakras in and against the landscape of life. It is a little like one of those pictures you first look at and see nothing. But suddenly a new image pops out. It is a question of figure and ground. If it were not, this would not be esoteric knowledge, but public knowledge. Everyone could see it.

Pointing Out

In a subject so subtle or esoteric as shamanic astrology, the reader can't be expected to get all of these concepts right away, much less have experience with them, and certainly not at first to expect much realization of them. So, what I will be doing here is pointing out important concepts, some of which may not seem to make very much sense at first.

Here is how I suggest you approach this: I will point out an idea or concept that is important to grasp, and in most places, I will tell you I am doing just that. Here are the traditional steps:

Understanding

Your initial task is to understand what I am saying, to make any kind of sense you can of my words. But intellectual understanding is only the beginning, the first step in the process and, by itself, is not going to take you that far. Understanding is just that, developing an intellectual or conceptual idea of what has been pointed out. We do that all the time.

Experiencing

Once you feel you understand what has been said, the next step is to develop some actual experience with the idea, to look in your day-to-day life for living examples of the ideas that have been pointed out, to observe. It is your responsibility to test these thoughts against reality, and to determine if what is being pointed out actually makes sense to you. Making some kind of sense is what this stage is all about, developing actual experience from the understanding, something you can feel and use. Experience has its ups and downs, and is the story of your embodying the concept with meaning through your own investigations.

Realization

And the last step is to accumulate enough experience with the concept until it becomes a permanent and living part of your life, until you realize it. Realization does not have ups and downs, but marks the point where your experience stabilizes and there is no more change taking place with what has been pointed out. You get it and you get it 24-hours a day, 365 days a year. This is also the point when you will realize the emptiness of the experience for yourself.

Three-Step Process

Understanding, experience, and realization mark the three-step process that you will ideally undergo for each concept and for every idea I will be pointing out. This is not to say that this will happen with every concept that is pointed out, or that the process will be an easy one. It may be enough, at first, to just get a rough idea of what is being said, and perhaps a glimmer of a feel for what it might mean in the world around you. No problem, but don't confuse understanding with realization.

With understanding, you have intellectually taken the concept in and can paraphrase it. With experience, you have actually grounded the idea that was pointed out in reality, and developed a real feeling for it that is sometimes present and sometimes absent. With realization, you become the living proof of the concept, and can empower yourself and others with this knowledge. With realization, there is no change in the experience. For your own sake, it is best not to confuse these three steps. The most common problem is to mistake understanding for realization. As my teacher used to say to me, "Michael, some day you must become the book."

The Monad: Divine Astrology

Monad: The Sun Is Shining

I am assuming here, since this is a more advanced book, that you have some basic knowledge of astrology, knowledge of the Sun, Moon, and the traditional planets, what they mean or stand for.

There are a couple of other main concepts that we will go over very lightly here, just enough to make sure you are aware of them. We will go into much more detail later on, but for now I want to introduce you to the concept of the solar system as a living process, and this is often called, in the history of esoteric thought, the Monad. And second, we need to talk a bit about Saturn and the Saturn Return that each of us experiences at around thirty years of age.

The word Monad comes from the Latin word for unit, and prior to that from the Greek word "monos," which means single or unique. There are many uses for the word monad, but here we are using it to mean a single entity or process that is self-enclosed, recursive, and eternal or infinite — beyond time. The monad is self-existing, the "I Am That I Am," and for no other reason.

In this study of esoteric astrology, the monad here refers to our entire solar system, with the Sun as the center, as a single living entity or life. In other words, astrologically the "monad" is the Sun, as a life-giving process. The Sun is now shining in the darkness of space, spewing forth light and life, a living being. It seems unfortunate that the overreach of science has colored everything with the paintbrush of materialism, until the only way we can conceive of the Sun is as molecules and atoms. Yet, we have no problem identifying the soul of life within ourselves. We are quick to acknowledge that "we" are alive and have a spirit or soul, but that which gives *us* life and light, the Sun, is to us nothing more than bricks and mortar — soulless. This is what is called a "miss-take."

How can that be? It does not make sense. At the very least, the Sun should share whatever consciousness, spirit, and soul we have, since it supports and provides for it. I hope you get the idea here: how can we be so concerned about our own consciousness, and assume that our great Sun is soulless? It boggles the mind, and it was not always so, and it will not always be so. This is materialism to the max. It might be useful to make a note of this particular materialistic viewpoint.

The Astrology of No Time

This next point is a very important point:

Most of modern astrology, as I hinted in the above, is presented only through the measurement of time, Saturn or Satan. Satan or Saturn is only one of the planets although, as the Christian faith clearly states: Satan is the prince of time and of the material world. We should be very clear to realize that awareness (spiritual realization) is (and has always been) described as the overcoming of time (or Saturn) in the experience of eternity and everlasting life —the larger life we all share, call it enlightenment or what-have-you.

The planet Saturn, however, only governs our physical form and the laws of time itself. It is unfortunate, as mentioned, that most of modern astrology is so materialistic that all of the planets are seen only through the prism of time and the physical, that is: in their material or Saturnian aspects. In the esoteric or mystic tradition of the planets, only the planet Saturn relates to the physical. All of the other planets each have their own plane and sphere that, while interdependent with the physical (Saturn), are also separate from the physical. Think about this with care. We will get into this very important point, gradually.

Let's take the time here to at least describe what the monad, the Sun and solar system might be like, without the domination of the materialism we have just pointed out, sort of a divine astrology, and we can even allow ourselves to get a little biblical, while we are at it, since those kind of words fit the reality here. Here is what a non-materialistic astrology would be like:

The Solar System as a Tree Of Life

Non-Materialistic Astrology: The solar system as a whole or unity is an endless Tree of Life, and Saturn or time is only one portion or planet in this whole process, although dealing with Saturn (in the world's scriptures) has been said to be crucial to knowing God (developing realization or spiritual awareness). Overcoming Saturn or time has ever been the first key to real awareness (knowing God, spirituality, etc.) and entering eternity — going beyond time.

As mentioned, before we start to work with Saturn or time, with which we should all be familiar at this point in our lives, it is important to give you at least a brief feeling for the concept of what we could call a non-materialistic or "Divine Astrology," that is, an astrology free from or beyond time, where time is but one part. Here is a more biblical way of putting this. Please excuse the prose.

A Divine Astrology

The Tree of Life of our solar system is a tree of endless life, pouring forth life forever, like a great cornucopia. This life is ever present and always new. It is all ways fresh and continuously happening, and this continuousness lasts, and it IS an everlasting life. This life of the solar system can never die or end, but is living now new, as it always has been living, and as it will continue to live. This endless life is what we have to look forward to and we have it here now.

The Tree Of Life

Astrology is one description of this Tree of Life. The Christian Book of Revelations has a very clear way of expressing this concept. In Revelations (22:1), we read:

"The Angel showed me the River of Life rising from the Throne of God and the Lamb of God and flowing crystal clear down the middle of the city. On either side of the river were the Trees of Life ... which bear TWELVE CROPS OF FRUIT IN A YEAR, ONE FOR EACH MONTH, and the leaves of which are the cure for the unbelievers ..."

And further:

"Happy are those who have washed their robes clean, so that they have the right to feed on the Tree of Life, and can come through the gates into the city."

If we do not realize this Tree of Life now, it is somehow (as it is written) because we have not washed our robes clean. In Genesis (3:24) we read "He banished the man, and in front of the Garden of Eden he posted the Cherubs and the Flame of a Flashing Sword, which turned all ways to guard the Way to the Tree of Life .. "

The Flame of a Flashing Sword

The Sun is the symbol of this everlasting life, and it is the center or throne around which all else revolves. The Sun and the Moon, are what are called, astrologically, "The Lights," and for good reason. The Sun is the 'Flame of a Flashing Sword' which turns all ways to guard (not block) the way to the Tree of Life. The Sun is the living sign of the "Lord of all Creation."

This same Sun is the deafening blast of nature living that we call silence. This endless blast of creation is our Sun endlessly sending forth and generating light. This radiance is the trumpet of the Lord of Creation endlessly blowing through our mind night and day.

The Four Beasts

This is Revelation (4:6): "In the center, grouped round the throne itself, were four animals with man's eyes in front and behind. The first animal was like a lion, the second like a bull, the third animal had a human face, and the fourth was like a flying eagle. Each of the four animals had six wings and had eyes all the way round, as well as inside, and day and night they never stopped singing: HOLY, HOLY IS THE LORD GOD..THE ALL MIGHTY...HE WAS, HE IS, AND HE IS TO COME."

This endless radiant song pours forth day and night its never-ending life in a continuous process of generation. To use a metaphor, this fountain of life rushes forth unceasingly from itself in an unending fountain of water that, spewing straight up into the air, reaches the height of its column and, unable to rise higher, opens from the center of its force equally outward in all directions and, arching, it falls back around itself, enclosing within itself, the main stream out of which it emerged.

The First Generation

This generation is a continual process. As the Sun, in shining, throws off light all ways, thus does that generation process perpetually husk itself — forever renewing itself. And this newness throws off what came before, like the snake shedding its skin. The Sun is the archetypal sign or identity of all creation and generation.

There is one and only one generation, and this is the process of constant generation — overflowing life. We are all of the same generation for: it still is. We are only one generation old. The so-called generation gap is but the failure to witness this fact of one generation and, witnessing it, to remain aware of the fountain of youth and everlasting life. Generation is continuous and of one age. We are all of one age and that age is: AGELESS.

So much for the poetry.

The Mystery of the Seven Seals or Planets

To begin with, we are concerned here with the historical bodies: the Sun and Moon, and the planets Mercury through Saturn. We will get around to presenting the outer planets somewhat later in this book. As for the Moon, that is the subject of another book ["Mother Moon: Astrology of the Lights"] and does not figure into a chakra-oriented approach.

The Seven Seals (Biblical) or centers of force (Chakras) are the seven solar system bodies from (and including) the Sun out to Saturn: Sun, Mercury, Venus, Earth, Mars, Jupiter, and Saturn. These are what are called the traditional astrological bodies, the seven centers of force or levels of being in the process of the whole life of eternity — the infinite solar-system process of life around us. The seven seals are created or made in a certain order (as we mature) and, in most (but not all) cases, these same seals are revealed or opened in exactly the reverse order, after our Saturn return at 30 years of age. This book is mostly about how the seven chakras or seals are opened, the process of spiritual awakening.

Formation of the Seals

When we study how these seals are created or formed, we are studying the planets, with the Sun as their center, moving outward to the limit of time or form, Saturn, at about 30 years of age. This is the study of the birth of a child and the formation of the physical body, as we age from that birth through our Saturn return around our 30th year (29.4 years, heliocentrically). Contained within that physical body of Saturn's cycle are, of course, the completed cycles of the other traditional planets: Mercury (mind), Venus (love), Earth (Self), Mars (emotions), and Jupiter (career).

Opening of the Seven Seals

However, when we study how these chakras, centers, or seals are opened or awakened, we study them in the reverse order, from Saturn (the physical) or outer shell, inward toward the Sun. In that process, we study the process of our psychological awakening and spiritual awareness. In other words, each of us experiences in our personal lifetime first the formation (growing up), and then the opening of all seven of these seals or chakras. We all experience our physical body forming and maturing. These are literally our formative years. It is the awareness and realization of this entire process that is more rare and that constitutes what we could call spiritual work or spiritual awareness. It is this awareness and the process of awakening that we are most concerned with here in this book.

Formation of the Seven Seals through Time

Let's look at the nitty-gritty of how this process works in a nativity. Examine the following tables (below) very carefully. It is the measure in time of exactly when in growth (during each child's personal existence) the various planets complete one whole revolution of the Sun (their first) and pass on to repeating themselves. This concept of zodiac repetition is a very important one.

From the moment we are born, each planet continues in its orbit around the Sun, degree by degree. As time passes, one by one, the planets complete their first circle of the Sun (and the zodiac) during our lifetime.

First Mercury, at about three months, then Venus, Earth, and so on. These complete revolutions are the first in the life memory or experience of each child, and after that first revolution, the planet continues on in its orbit, but begins to go over ground (degrees of the zodiac) that it already has covered since the child was born. There is a repetition.

Repeating Itself

Whatever we can agree that each planet represents in our astrology, after that first cycle each planet ceases to introduce anything "new" to us, but turns or falls to repeating itself within our personal life. It circles or cycles, and in some fashion becomes a constant part of life. As each planet, in turn, begins to repeat itself, we are freed to pick up on or monitor the next most outer planet, the next planet which HAS NOT yet completed a revolution. In other words, when Mercury completes its first revolution and begins to repeat in our memory at three months of age, we have that, and start to pick up on Venus, and then Earth, Mars, Jupiter, and finally Saturn, which completes its return at about 30 years of age.

Saturn Is the Timekeeper

Saturn or Chronos is the planet of physical form, the timekeeper of the zodiac, and when it completes its first cycle at 30 years of age, our physical form is complete, and no further growth is forthcoming or can be expected with our body. You get the idea.

A complete revolution of a planet seals or separates the infant from the one non-manifest state out of which he or she is being born into this world of time. There are traditionally seven seals including the Sun (which is timeless) out to Saturn and, with each seal, as the child grows, the rule of Saturn or time takes a greater hold on the lifetime. This is how we incarnate. Here is the list:

Mercury

Mercury returns at about three months of age. In studies of child behavior, we find that after the third month, the child's basic awareness and vision approximates that of an adult and he or she begins to see in color. The child's motor responses switch around this time from reflex to voluntary.

Venus

Venus completes an orbit of the Sun at about seven and one half months. Studies show that, around this point, the child perceives the mother as separate from itself, and begins to become strongly attached to the mother. The child can now distinguish and vocalize both pleasure and displeasure. In other words: a separation or duality occurs that allows appreciation – Venus.

Earth

The Earth completes its orbit of the Sun in one year, and we all know that this is usually when baby steps out into the world on his or her own two feet.

Mars

Mars completes its orbit of the Sun in a little under two years, and any parent is familiar with what has been nicknamed the "terrible twos" — when baby discovers emotions and struggles for independence.

Jupiter

Between Mars and the next planetary orbit is relatively the most-vast change, as measured by time or relative space between any two planets. Mars makes six revolutions before Jupiter completes one at twelve years. In between these two planets is the great asteroid belt filled with countless particles. The six year molar occurs as Jupiter reaches his half way mark and opposes himself, but more important, around 8-9 years the child passes from the more eternal or expanded time concept quite rapidly to the adult perception of time's passage.

After the twelve year molar and Jupiter's return, the child expands into adolescence and begins to pick up on and to monitor the next and most definite set of cycles, that of Saturn. At Saturn's opposition, puberty has set in, and time or Saturn moves to complete its cycle at around thirty years, after which point, spiritual awakening or unsealing of the Seven Seals proceeds, and at an accelerated rate.

Major Planetary Aspects

Below is a chart of all major planets' aspects to their own natal horoscope positions, as they transit to complete their various cycles, for a period of 85 years. What should be clear in a careful study is the bunching of important aspects at certain points and years in any lifetime. Space prevents elaboration here, but examination on your part will show you how and when the 'seven seals' are formed, as well as how they open or come apart.

Any good dictionary will list certain crucial years under the term "Climacteric," but not as linked to the cycles of the planets. The most well known are the years: 30, 42, 63, and 81, but you will as an astrologer recognize these years as well as important: 7, 8-9, 13-15, 21, 29-33, 36, 50-51, 59-60, 66, and 72-73.

Current Age and Major Aspects

Yr	Jup	Sat	Ura	Nep	Plu	Yr	Jup	Sat	Ura	Nep	Plu
01	045					21	300		090		
02	090					22	315	270			
03	120	045				23	000				
04		060				24		300			
05	180					25	045	315			
06						26	090				
07	225	090				27	120			060	
08	270					28	135		120		
09	300	120				29	180	000			
10	315		045			30					045
11	000	135				31	225		135		
12						32	270				
13	045					33	300	045			
14	090	180	060			34	315	060			
15	120					35	000				
16	135					36			090		
17	180					37	045				
18		225				38	090				
19	225	240				39	120	120			
20	270			045		40	135	135			

Current Age and Major Aspects

Yr	Jup	Sat	Ura	Nep	Plu	Yr	Jup	Sat	Ura	Nep	Plu
41	180			090	060	61	060			135	090
42		180				62	090	045			
43	225					63	135	060	270		
44	270	180				64					
45	315					65	180				
46						66	225	090			
47	000	225				67	240				
48	045					68	270	120			
49	060	240				69	315	135			
50	090					70			300		
51	135	270				71	000				
52			225			72	045				
53	180					73	060	180	315		
54	225	300		120		74	090				
55	240	315				75	135				
56	270		240			76					
57	315					77	180	225			
58		000				78	225	240			
59	000					89	240				
60	045					80	270				

Major Planetary Aspects

Our physical life process as measured by time follows a very regular pattern of growth, sustaining, and aging. The physical body is not independent from the spiritual, but reflects the spirit, and vice versa. Our physical body is the ultimate charm or talisman. It is the sign or signature of spirit, however much it may fail at any point in time to reflect our intentions. As the adage says, "The road to hell is paved with good intentions."

The Planets as Chakras

Inner Key to Outer

The entire process we are about to describe here refers to the process of our spiritual birth or awakening and, for most of us, this does not occur until after our Saturn return (or just prior to it) at 29.4

years of age. What follows here has to do with the opening of the chakras, what has been called the process of spiritual awakening or self-discovery.

In each case, in order to reveal, open, and use the outer, we learn to take from within, we ourselves must go within. It is a personal journey. Each planet (from Saturn into the Sun) is the entire essence and key to the planet just outside its orbit, which brings us to what might seem at first to be a paradox:

The key to this external world is not found outside in the external world itself, no matter how hard we may search, but can only be found within us, by looking inside, and by going within. We have all heard this concept. The religions of the world have made it a constant refrain: look within. The process of how this is done, step-by-step, is what will now be presented. This is the mystery of the seven seals or planets.

The Planetary Key

As for the astrological use of this information, what follows is a simple planetary KEY to personal horoscope interpretation that any counseling astrologer can use with confidence. The natural ordering of the planets outward from the Sun to Saturn and then back in is literally a description of their function and use. In this book, there is only one key thought necessary in order to use the planets in your own natal horoscope and that is: the inner is the key to the outer.

The Inner is the Key

To repeat, the KEY idea presented in these pages is that THE INNER IS KEY TO THE OUTER. We must learn to take from within ourselves, discover and bring what we find there out, and manifest our good intentions (inner) in this world. We go in to get out.

Learning to take from within, to look within, is what we are studying here. It is something that can be understood, learned, and realized. It requires that we stop only looking outside for answers, and learn to look within ourselves for direction and support. How we do that is what we are presenting in this book.

Most astrologers would agree that, in our personal horoscope, we can look to Saturn in our chart to see just how we will be tried and tested. Saturn is time and the test of time. Saturn represents form and limitation, and is the limiter. In this approach to shamanic astrology, the key to overcoming and working with our Saturn or limitations will always be our natal Jupiter, and meditation and study on this part of our chart (Jupiter) will gradually help us to succeed in rising above and handling our Saturn. Jupiter is the next planet within Saturn's orbit, so we can look within to that planet.

Again: In this approach, the inner planet is the KEY to the planet outside its orbit, from Saturn into the Sun. The outer planets (Uranus, Neptune, etc.) follow another pattern, which will be discussed later in this book. "God helps those who help themselves," but from within.

When doing astrological counseling, we use the same concept: the key to the outer is the inner. For example, the key to Saturn in the chart will always be the planet Jupiter, the next inner planet, and so on. Now let's look at all of this in more detail.

Saturn: A Formal Definition

Most of you are already familiar with the astrological nature of Saturn, but let's go over it again:

Saturn or Chronos rules time, form, and the physical in all its aspects. Saturn is limitation, and thus the great limiter. Saturn (sometimes called Satan) has been said to be the prince of the material world. Saturn is the very narrowness that makes the way felt, the raceway or spillway through which course (Jupiter = the course) the waters of life. Jupiter is the pathway through which the blood courses, the "way we go," but Saturn is the course walls of the arteries, the resistance that allows pressure to build to something definite, to real "feeling."

Saturn the Shaper

Saturn is like a wood shaper that is adjusted to produce a certain piece of molding. Any wood presented to this shaper has no alternative but to pass through, and then only where it conforms to the desired or possible shape as set by the limits. All other wood is shaved away. In this analogy, Saturn is that limiter and we are the wood, like the force of gravity. As my teacher said "We don't break nature's laws; nature breaks us."

Eternity or truth dictates the limits, and Saturn is the shaper or test of form. When we talk about "getting straight" or "getting in line" or "in tune," we are talking about getting within the control that already is. In this sense, Saturn helps to determine the shape of things to come. All of these Saturnian laws working together: form.

Saturn: Walls That Make Homes Possible

Saturn is most simply the system of natural laws, the functioning of which determine what is possible in this material world (such as the law of gravity) — the laws that hold things in place, the walls that make homes possible. Saturn is the laws that govern the forms things take, as well as (simply put) the form things take. The forms things take is only the form things are taking (the process). Saturn represents those laws to which we will be physically determined. Saturn is the form to which we each must submit before our evolution or unfolding may take place. Without that form, there can be no unfolding.

Saturn is the laws against which we may ram our head until such time as we learn, by feeling our way, to walk around or even to build upon them, to count on them. Saturn is literally where we are bound to learn. It is simple as mentioned: We don't break nature's or Saturn's laws; they break us if we go against them.

The Test of a Lifetime

Saturn is the test of a lifetime and equally a lifetime of test. We are subject and tested by these laws until such time as we learn to use these laws in our own behalf, and put them to use working for us. We rise above Satan or Saturn in proper use and obedience to the physical laws. "Render unto Caesar that which is Caesar's." Handling Saturn is the province of Jupiter, the lawyer and guide through Saturn.

Saturn is where you come to grips with yourself and first learn of spirit. It shapes the end to which we are tending, but also affects how we tend to get there.

"Call what carriage as you may your hearse," for Saturn holds you together, as much as it may appear to hold you back. That is the general idea of Saturn.

The Seven Chakras

The chakras are paired with the traditional planets, from Saturn in to the Sun, and that would be Saturn, Jupiter, Mars, Earth, Venus, Mercury, and the Sun. The Sun and the Moon, the Lights, are not directly used here, but will be covered elsewhere. The traditional seven chakras, using their Sanskrit names, are:

Saturn (Muladara Chakra) Base of Spine Jupiter (Svadisthana Chakra) Genital Region Mars (Manipura Chaka) Navel Earth (Anahata Chakra) Heart Center Venus (Vishuddha Chakra) Throat Mercury (Ajna Chakra) Third Eye Sun (Sahasrara Chakra) Crown of Head. Let's go over them one by one.

Saturn (Muladara Chakra) Base of Spine

Chakra: Saturn (form, circumstances)
Key to Chakra: Jupiter (career, life path)

The Saturn chakra represents the physical world of form and the process of time that created that form. As we grow to complete our Saturn return around the age of 30, we each gradually come to grips with the rules, laws, and limitations of Saturn.

The Key to the Saturn chakra will be to invoke Jupiter, and without activating the Jupiter chakra, life would be very, very difficult in the Saturn chakra, as we will describe later on.

Jupiter (Svadisthana Chakra) Genital Region

Chakra: Jupiter (Career, life path)

Key to Chakra: Mars (Meaning, Union, Marriage)

The Jupiter chakra is the key to Saturn, and has to do with the life path or career, the particular way to pass through Saturn or form. Jupiter is the way we go through life.

The Key to the Jupiter chakra will be to invoke Mars, which has to do with the directionality or the meaning of life. Once the Jupiter or career is functioning and we have our head above water (making a living), the next chakra, Mars, has to do with "But what does it all mean?" and this is the chakra Mars, which leads to marriage and union.

Mars (Manipura Chaka) Navel

Chakra: Mars (Meaning, Union, Marriage)

Key to Chakra: Earth (The end of meaning, what it all means)

The Mars chakra is the key to Jupiter, and has to do with what life means, the sense life makes, and this leads to some sort of yoga or union, marriage being the most common form of yoga.

The Key to the Mars chakra will be to invoke the Earth chakra, which is the heart of what it all means, the Self, or simple existence itself. Earth is where we are all trying to get to and where we ultimately live.

Chakra: Earth (The End of Meaning)

Key to Chakra: Venus (love, compassion)

The Earth chakra is the key to Mars, and has to do with simple existence, being the end of all meaning, the point we have been striving to reach.

The Key to the Earth chakra will be to invoke the Venus chakra,. As the literature of the world has told us forever, the key to life on Earth is love, loving kindness, and compassion.

Venus (Vishuddha Chakra) Throat

Key to Chakra: Mercury (Light, Mind)

The Venus chakra is the key to Earth, and refers to love, kindness, and loving compassion.

The Key to the Venus chakra will be to invoke the Mercury chakra, an inner chakra, which refers to the light in our eyes, the mind itself.

Mercury (Ajna Chakra) Third Eye

Chakra: Mercury (light, mind)

Key to Chakra: Sun (life process itself)

The Key to the Mercury chakra will be to invoke the Sun chakra, the innermost chakra, representing the entire life process itself.

Sun (Sahasrara Chakra) Crown of Head

Chakra: The Sun (the entire life process and center)

The Sun is more than a chakra, being the whole process of life itself, all of the planets and their interdependent interaction.

What Chakra Are You In?

As a counseling astrologer, you want to be able to determine which of the chakras your client is currently living and learning in. It is not that difficult, and here are some general rules that have proved helpful to me in figuring this out.

Most of the clients you encounter will be in the Saturn, Jupiter, or Mars chakras, somewhere on their journey to reaching the Earth or Heart chakra, which is where each of us is trying to get to. Those who are in the Earth chakra will not need our help, and these are pretty rare anyway. The type of person who would seek out astrological council will most often be, as mentioned, those in the Saturn, Jupiter, and Mars chakras, one of these.

Forget about the Venus, Mercury, and Sun chakras. These are inner chakras, internal to Earth existence and, while we all aspire to their qualities, you will probably not encounter (or at least not be aware of them) anyone living at this level. In my entire life, I have only met one living person who appeared to be fully in the Venus chakra, and that was a very high lama in the mountains of Tibet, who was fully realized in that chakra, realized enough that anyone in his presence experienced themselves (not the lama) as pure compassion, which is the nature of the Venus chakra.

Identifying the Saturn Chakra

Those living primarily in the Saturn chakra are very easy to spot. For one, they can't manage to make a living, and have not found a way to get through or handle the demands of Saturn, and simply to survive. This would involve invoking Jupiter, and gradually making their way to that chakra, and, once there, maintaining that chakra. By "maintaining," we mean, simply, making a living, surviving and learning to handle their Saturn, keeping their head above water. In other words, they have not yet found a career that works for them. They cannot handle or cope with Saturn.

You will find a great many clients that are in this state, or who wander in and out of the Saturn chakra, trying to learn it, and master it. It is not as if they have anywhere else to go. Jump-starting one's Jupiter is pretty much required to have any sort of life in this world.

Can't Make a Living

So, if the client has no way of making a living, and is constantly besieged by one onslaught of Saturn after another, trying to find a way to just survive in a minimal way, then you have someone in (or mostly within) the Saturn chakra.

The Key to Saturn: You will want to read to these folks from the "Book of Jupiter," helping them to identify what is their particular way to go through life, their career or life path, some way for them to cope. Of course, you can use all the astrological techniques you know relating to career, such as sign, house placement, and aspects for Jupiter, and probably the north lunar node as well. These are all solid vocational indicators. I have found that the best Jupiter-type information are the heliocentric StarType Patterns. See my book "StarTypes: Life-Path Partners" for details.

In general (not always), you may find that until the Jupiter chakra is awakened and routinely functioning, that inner chakras like Mars, which has to do with marriage and settling down, will probably not be very workable. The traditional order of opening these chakras are Saturn, Jupiter, Mars, and not Saturn, Mars, Jupiter. In other words, it is going to be hard to help a client stabilize their marriage (Mars), if the Jupiter chakra is not first stabilized, that is: if they can't first make a living. You have all seen the old movies or read the books where the young man first finds a career and then gets married. This is the normal way these chakras are opened, Saturn, Jupiter, Mars, etc.

Invoking Jupiter

I always work with clients who are lost in the Saturn chakra by helping them to invoke and stabilize their Jupiter (career) chakra, and that stabilization alone is usually enough to bring more stability to any inner chakra, like Mars, if that chakra is already activated, that is: if the client is married. A married client, with a weak or unstable Jupiter chakra, more often than not, will have trouble with the marriage. The first step then, is to strengthen the Jupiter chakra, and THEN work on the marriage. A strengthened Jupiter will already bring help to a struggling Mars or marriage.

Keep in mind that each of us has all the chakras available to us and, of course, we cycle in and through all of them constantly. However, each of us tends to spend most of our time in one particular chakra at a time, and determining which chakra that is can be important in a consultation. What we are looking for and speaking of here is stabilization, practically mastering a particular chakra, so that the client can use it at will, when they need to.

For example, if you have found a career, and know how to make a living and hold a job, that is a permanent part of your makeup. You learn to make a living, and you keep on making a living. It is a constant. At that point, you can operate in the Jupiter chakra, and have more or less mastered it.

Identifying the Jupiter Chakra

Identifying whether the client is in the Jupiter chakra is also straightforward, usually as easy as determining if they have a successful (or at least a workable) career AND are still unmarried. That is the pure Jupiter experience plain and simple: working, but unmarried.

Once the Jupiter chakra is activated and some path or career is discovered and maintained, this is considered sufficient mastery of this chakra. The client is are able to keep a career open and functioning. If they have a solid career and are happily married, you want to be looking into the Earth chakra. Otherwise, Jupiter is where to focus.

Crossing the Gap

The gap between Saturn and Jupiter, between the Saturn and Jupiter chakras, is not great, and most of us are able to come up with some means of making a living, some work that will keep the wolf (Saturn) from our door. However, the gap between Jupiter and Mars (relatively speaking) is very much greater than any other two planets. We could say that it is somewhat of a long journey from making a living (Jupiter) to being happily married (Mars). This is simple statistics. There are many people who have jobs, and fewer people who have a successful and happy marriage. Right?

It is one thing to have sharp career skills, and another to translate those skills into a marriage that is as stable or content. The vast asteroid belt is located between Jupiter and Mars, and there are countless small bodies (asteroids) there that never made it to being a planet, a fact that we will pass over for the moment.

Jupiter's Lightning

Astronomers are even now marveling at the immense lightning storms beneath the surface of Jupiter, the largest such storms in the entire solar system. I mention this, because Jupiter is very much also an intellectual trip, literally using the mind to control matter. Remember, aside from his role as guru or guide, Jupiter is also the lawyer, the one who handles (Saturn), and the law. There often can be a lot of manipulating and not a little conniving, when Jupiter is invoked.

The Lawyer: Skillful Means

Jupiter is the career or life path, but finding that path involves using your head, and figuring out how to get around or at least work-with or handle Saturn. This is the planet of skill, and skillful means, and Saturn requires real skill to master. The legal profession is full of those with a pronounced or highly active Jupiter chakra. On the near side of Saturn, the Jupiter chakra leads to using the intellect to master the law and matter, lawyers, and what not. On the side of the Jupiter chakra closest to Mars, we have more of the guide or guru Jupiter types, leading or guiding others. More about this further on.

To repeat myself, it is a LONG way from the Jupiter skill to the more feeling and intuitive nature of Mars. As we each journey from Jupiter to Mars, we learn to ground our skill (our sometimes too clever minds) in directionality or meaning, that is: to mean what we say, and we learn to say things with meaning. There are many stages and stories on this Jupiter journey, and we will detail some of them in the journal entries in a later section.

Mars: The Key to Jupiter

Here, we will just point out that the Key to Jupiter will always be Mars, and that the point of all our skill and directionality (Jupiter: where we are going in life) has to do with what it all means. Those who are awake and successful in the Jupiter chakra, who are no longer struggling to make a living, will always be concerned with "But, what does it all mean? What is the meaning of life?" They have achieved material (have mastered Saturn) success, but what does it mean? This is how you will know the Jupiter chakra client.

The Jupiter client has mastered simple survival, has overcome Saturn through one career move or another, but where does one go from there? What is the point of a life of simple survival? They are now a free floating agent, freed from Saturn's demands, but have not found love (other than fleetingly), much less taken the plunge, tied the knot, and settled down to a marriage. The Jupiter chakra person is fascinated with what things mean, the sense of things, where do they lead, but they have not followed those meanings down to where they end, in the sense world itself. They are not grounded. The rubber has not yet met the road.

Still Unmarried

We will go into how this Jupiter-to-Mars journey might manifest later on in this book. For right now, it is enough for you to identify that the client has a successful career, would like to find a life companion, but is as yet unmarried. This is the nature of life in the Jupiter Chakra, and is easy to determine, by just asking the client.

For these Jupiter chakra clients, you want to read from the book of Mars or marriage, encouraging them to ground their thoughts and desires in experience, and to make some "sense" out of whatever they can imagine. This can be as easy or difficult as pointing out to them that all their speculation, their interest in what things mean, where things are going, the drift of things, all point to the sphere of action, to taking the plunge.

And the Jupiter-chakra person is invariably caught up in one form of dualism after another, always on one side of equation with some "other" or "negative" forces on the reverse side. Jupiter is always trying to resolve difference or duality, trying to find the One in the Two, trying to make sense of it all -- sense.

All thoughts, to the extent that they have any meaning at all, are only as useful as the sense they make, and "sense" has always to be an experience, an experience that we each must have. Book learning is not enough. The Jupiter type must be encouraged to stop thinking so much, and to act on their feelings, and to more fully immerse themselves in life, to somehow take the plunge, and that plunge is into the realm of marriage or Mars.

Career Problems

If the client has some sort of career, but that career is sputtering on and off again, or is generally unstable, you may want to look to their Mars, for the Mars chakra is what drives Jupiter.

Mars is the meaning and movement or drive of thought, what it all means, where it points to. And finally, all thought points to experience, to action. The meaning of any thought is the "sense" it makes, and thus all thoughts end in experience or action, the sense world. Mars is the planet of action, movement, ambition, drive, urges, urging, anything that motivates us to the sphere of action. Mars drives us to act and experience life. Mars propels us through Jupiter's course. It keeps the career moving along.

The experience of life itself is what life means; that experience is its own meaning, and this, traditionally, is Earth or the Heart Chakra, the end of all meaning or directionality. It all points to experience, the Earth chakra. We will get to that soon.

Identifying the Mars Chakra

Identifying whether a client is actively initiated in the Mars chakra is as easy as determining whether or not they are (more or less) happily married, that is: committed. That is the simple test.

The Mars chakra is all about union or yoga (resolving duality), and the most common form of yoga practiced in the world today is that of marriage, the joining of two persons in one life. A better way of saying this would be the realization that the two are already and always have been one. The Mars chakra is another major initiation, one involving simple acceptance, saying "I do," which is what marriage is all about, the recognizing the "one" in the two persons, a common bond.

We do not have to be married to a physical partner. One can be married to one's work in the word, to whomever or whatever. The point is that in marriage, there is somehow the realization and acceptance of another person or the world, just as they are or it is -- treating another like you would treat yourself. The two (duality) that went before is seen as one, as always already having been one.

In fact, after the first Saturn return, we all are, in effect, married to life, whether we know it or not. We must accept or embrace our personal situation. At some point, soon after 30 years of age, anyone who has not said "I do" to life is living an imaginary separateness, and is just unrealistic – an ostrich in the sand.

The Most Common Form of Yoga

The dualities that we had previously seen and struggled against in our self, and in the world, are, after Saturn returns, somehow now seen as one; the two become one. Where before there were two, man and woman, you against the world, etc., that is seen through to the unity uniting both, the two become one. In fact, the two have always already been one; we just didn't know it. Being married, spiritually, is when we realize just that, when the concept of duality is seen through. As Parmenides said: "Being alone is" or "Being all-one is."

Once we have accepted a partner, whether in the form of a person or the world itself, we enter into union or yoga, a relationship that gradually works through dualism in all its forms, resolving differences into the unity that embraces them. In other words, experience in the Mars chakra gradually stills the rush and roar of the mind, solving its dualities, reducing at last, over time, dualities to stillness.

The Mars chakra follows all direction or meaning to the sense it makes, and this is finally an experience in itself.

Identifying the Earth Chakra

We might think that all of us, by virtue of having been born on Earth, are automatically masters of the Earth chakra, but we would be wrong. In esoteric astrology, Earth is not something we are given by virtue of our birth, but rather something we aspire to, and earn. In fact, masters of the Earth or Heart Chakra are few and far between. Moreover, anyone skilled in this chakra does not normally need astrology of any kind, and will probably not seek it out. We should seek them out.

The Earth of Heart Chakra

Let's review what it takes to reach the Earth chakra. It means mastery of Saturn, and that requires a successful career, one that can be maintained, and is under our control. That is the Jupiter chakra. In addition, it means a successful marriage of some kind, the Mars chakra, and a thorough knowledge of meaning and emotions, an acceptance and resolution of any and all dualisms, which is what would bring someone to the brink of the Earth chakra.

The Earth chakra is pretty much the master of the external world, not in some arrogant or aggressive sense, but in a peaceful and confident sense. As I mentioned, these initiates don't, for the most part, seek counsel, because they have no need for it. They are their own counsel.

Although we might be quick to point out that spiritual adepts (rinpoches, zen masters, enlightened priests, and so on) would qualify, but so would masters of any trade or station in life, anywhere we find someone who is confident, content, and present.

The Chakras Inner to Earth

There are two chakras or planets interior to Earth (aside from the Sun itself), and they are Venus and Mercury. The inner chakras, those inside the orbit of Earth, are just that, inner, ones that we won't find by looking in the outside world, as we know it. They represent something interior to Earth, inner qualities that perhaps we can only aspire to and dimly sense.

Identifying the Venus Chakra

The first of these would be the Venus chakra, that of love and compassion. Poets and bards, throughout the long traditions of song and literature, have always written that the key to life here on Earth is love and compassion. Venus is that love.

How appropriate, for Venus is the next interior planet to Earth and it has always been associated with love and compassion. Venus is the key to Earth.

Identifying the Mercury Chakra

Mercury is the other inner chakra, one that we may perhaps visit on the best days of our lives, but probably not where we live or get to spend much of our time. Mercury (the Sanskrit word is "Budha") is awareness itself, the light in our eyes that we see shining! Again, like Venus, Mercury is an inner quality we all have, and reach for. We don't live there in any real sense.

And the Sun chakra is that about which nothing can be said. I shall be foolish enough to say something, but the Sun (monad) is, pretty much by definition, beyond description or words.

We will go into these inner planets in more detail later on, but for now let's examine the life experience for the chakras Saturn, Jupiter, Mars, and Earth.

The Saturn Chakra

Experience under Satan's Seal (The Seal of Saturn)
In the counseling experience, it is important to be able to recognize if a client is living mostly only in the Saturn chakra or realm. One obvious clue is if they have no career going for them, no way or path through Saturn, and are thus unable to make a living, and simply support themselves. But there are

psychological correlates as well. Here is some prose that should make the Saturn experience more clear:

"The psychological experience under Saturn or time is to know only total fear for our life. The external world sulks, looms ominous, and threatens disaster and accidents at every street's crossing. We are wrapped in the rush of time, tearing at hour's hearts. Every single thing, every outer edge and hard person, only serves to cause us to put off our life, to postpone real living, and sends us scurrying fast into the future, hoping, hoping, hoping — someday, somewhere, to find the chance to be ourselves, to have the time and space to live, and to bloom. Living in this state of fear, we put off endlessly until tomorrow what we find just too hard to do today."

If you have ever been out of work or unable to make a living and support yourself, you have had a glimpse of what living under Saturn's seal is all about. It is about waking up at 3 AM and wondering how you are going to pay that bill. It is about panic, hope, and fear.

The Beautiful Soul

The Saturn experience is somewhat like the "Beautiful Soul" that Hegel describes in the "Phenomenology of the Mind" so exactly :

"This soul lacks force to externalize itself... the power to make itself a thing and to endure existence. And, to preserve the purity of its heart, it flees from actuality and steadfastly perseveres in a state of self-willed impotence to renounce a self which is pared away to the last point of abstraction... and to give itself substantial existence or in other words: to transform its thought into being and commit itself to absolute distinction, that between thought and being."

The Poetry

Life under Saturn is an endless imitation and a rehearsal, boredom, and a long, long wait. The way we tell it asks a lot, and, in all our talk, we hear our own hollowness echoing back upon ourselves to inform us that we still have not begun. We are the prey of time and Satan (Saturn) as this poem only too clearly portrays.

This poem was written in what I would have to say is a masochistic state of mind, the result of having my sails set wrong, taking life in the wrong way, where our life is being taken from us, rather than our learning to take life in our stride.

> **INNER EAR**
>
> What will eager issue out,
> And into us would enter,
> So to stare, to stuff itself,
> To eat itself the center,
> Of what we wait to wither in on,
> After it is all.
>
> It eats us out.
> It only is,
> In every inward eaten,
> The echo of an endless ache,
> That arches heart's hard hearing,
> And opens up each inner "enting,"
> And enters it as out.

The Jupiter Chakra: Guru

The Key to Your Saturn Is Your Natal Jupiter

Life, for one lost in the Saturn chakra, was briefly described above. While most astrological clients who will seek you out may not be so completely lost in the Saturn realm, many will have had or still have some problem traversing that realm, perhaps the most common being difficulty jump-starting their Jupiter function, establishing and maintaining their career.

For these folks, an introduction to their natal Jupiter is what is required, a reading from the Book of Jupiter. Using the concept of the inner being the key to the outer, here is some Jupiter prose, which should help you get the idea:

The Sanskrit Word is Guru

A Sanskrit word for Jupiter is "Guru," so that tells us a lot already. Jupiter is the KEY which unseals and overcomes our natal Saturn. Jupiter is in a very real sense the heart of Saturn turned inside out. It is the guide and light (the guru) that sees each of us through the darkness of time or Saturn — the straight and narrow path by which we are able to pass through Satan's test.

Jupiter is our particular way of going or our religion — our dharma path. It is the way we go or continue, our particular "luck" or solution to time's (Saturn) test. Jupiter is the only way or doorway open to us and through which we may pass through time. Jupiter is linear expansion, because life unfolds or continues at this point. It is here that we find the extension of the present situation: the way through or on. Jupiter is continuity, how we may continue.

Success or Succession

Jupiter is the endlessness of life regardless of the particular form. Jupiter is how and where things continue or happen. Jupiter is an endless round of passage, the lamp or light that will see shadows fail. Jupiter is above all the KEY or reverse of Saturn. It is the recognition or realization and use of Saturn. For, Jupiter is the way we must go through life, our way to go, the recognition that that through which we have to pass is the way we go through life. Jupiter is the way - success or succession through time.

The Vision of Jupiter — Baptism or Rebirth

The invoking or awakening of Jupiter is somewhat of a big deal for each of us. It is how we first awaken from the 30-year sleep of Saturn, learn to take care of ourselves, and begin to find our own way through life. Many will have an active Jupiter long before the Saturn return, for Jupiter takes about 12 years to make a return, so by 24 years of age, each of us has been shown twice how Jupiter can work for us, how we CAN make it through the obstacles of Saturn. From those two complete Jupiter cycles, we should have extracted or at least be on the path to a vocation or career that will work for us, one that will handle our particular Saturn.

Regardless of when that awakening experience is, the opening of the Jupiter chakra, the finding of the life path or career is a major initiation for each person, for at that time we are, for the first time, born above or get beyond Saturn. Here are some details:

Through the two-fold repetition of the Jupiter cycle, thus the invoking of Jupiter in the natal chart, we first overcome Saturn and begin to awaken from within the womb of time itself. Up to that point, we have been wrapped in the sleep of time, Saturn's womb, going through what have been called — aptly called — our "formative years."

Born Awake In Time

When our Jupiter chakra opens (as we start to get the idea), we are still within (or under) time, but we are gradually being born awake, yet still within time, and from that point onward we hold in our hands the key to the unraveling of time. We have figured out how to succeed in this world. This Jupiter awakening to faith is like the crowning (in childbirth) and appearance of the head of an infant, and that first breath of life.

In its own way, this is a baptism, not an immersion, but an emergence in the waters of Spirit for the very first time, and with it, the resulting knowledge and ever-growing faith that we can overcome time, that it can be done: this is the message or 'Word' we hold.

What is faith? In this case faith means that once we have seen the light beyond Saturn, that we can overcome Saturn, we cannot (we will not) ever forget that experience. We will never go back to that sleep, for something within us has stirred. We will ever hold out for more of what we have only now glimpsed.

Faith as a Force

Faith, no longer an endless waiting (or hope) for something good to happen for us, but now a force itself (this faith) more powerful than time, for through faith we end all time. Once in the Jupiter chakra, we begin for the first time in this current life to awaken to our eternal life, call it awareness, our true self, what-have-you, and, although still living partially embedded within the world of time, we have now open eyes (awareness), and this amounts to the proverbial word of God that, when it shall be made flesh, will set us free over time, for all time. It is no wonder that the world's religions value faith. Faith is, fueled by insights, an awakening.

After our Jupiter chakra is activated, we shall never again fall back to sleep in total ignorance, for our eternal memory has revived, stirred, and WE CAN NEVER FORGET. We have awakened in time, for all time. We have time, and not vice versa!

The Sword of Faith

To use the Christian metaphor: with this first seal of the seven seals laid open, we rise above Saturn (Satan) or time as a warrior in the army of the Lord of Life, and can now wield time mortal blows as long as life lasts. We are now, as it is written in the Bible, one of the warriors of God's Word, carrying forth his sword of faith that cuts at time's heart, and always opens Saturn's seal and, even now, today, is forging ahead into eternity. The lightning quick sword of the awakened mind can never rest, but rides from victory to victory over time's rule. Jupiter is succession through all time. Jupiter is succession, continuity — simple continuing, success. Jupiter is the key to Saturn or time.

When we begin to awaken from under Saturn's seal, our mind stirs and we glimpse life in a new way. This is what all those that have born-again experiences are referring to. Our eyes are now open and we cannot close them in ignorance again, but we are still a long way from mastering the Saturn chakra. At this point in our journey, faith becomes about the only way we can cope with our experience, as this poem shows. I wrote this poem.

THE FORCE OF FAITH

The form of force enforcing form,
Finds freedom from that form in fact.
And in fact forced is freed,
A form of force with faith in form,
That finds in fact:
Faith itself a force.

Thus, force finds itself in form on faith.

And force enforcing faith in form,
And form informing faith of force,

Faith is that force in form.
Faith is our form of force.

Experience of Jupiter: Awakening and Trial

The opening of the Jupiter chakra, being the first of the chakras or seals to be opened within Saturn, can be a major life experience and initiation. It opens up, perhaps for the first time, the whole world of spiritual awakening. It is the first breath of life beyond Saturn, and it can be somewhat of a big deal for each of us, although, for reasons unclear to me, our society does not openly celebrate this inner opening.

This whole idea of spiritually awakening in the middle of life, of being, somehow, as the Christians say, "born again," is not a just a passing phase, and it is not just for Christians. It happens to each one of us and this opening is more or less permanent, and although it may take months or years to stabilize this insight, once the awakening has occurred, many (if not most) are at first very sensitive, and so vulnerable. It is like a baby's skin, a skin that is very, very sensitive.

Handling Saturn

With the Jupiter awakening, each of us begins to get the idea of how to handle our particular Saturn, how we might actually be successful working in the world, and just what we can do to be a success. We get it. For most, however, it is a long way from the initial insight or awakening to stabilizing that vision and becoming an experienced person in this newfound world or chakra.

Those of us who are at this point in life older, encounter this every day in the young person who has an intellectual understanding of life, the "idea," but no real life experience. They have all the answers, right out of the book, but they don't yet know what they are talking so glibly about, and they don't know that they don't know. They get the idea, and they think they now know, and that is all there is to life! As we say: they still have a lot to learn. They have the "word," but that word has not been made flesh and yet lived. This is similar to what happens in the Jupiter awakening.

Jupiter Is the Lawyer

In fact, it is a very long journey indeed for most of us, from having an intellectual grasp of what makes life tick, an idea of how we might handle Saturn, to becoming a grizzled old veteran of life, with deep experience, and a little of what we might call 'wisdom'.

Perhaps this can be made even more clear by pointing out why Jupiter belongs to the realm of lawyers and all those who are quick with the mind, those who use the mind to outwit the world, that is: to manipulate Saturn. The Jupiter lawyer handles the law. It is like handling poisonous snakes. This is not intended to knock lawyers, who perform a real and necessary task in this world, but to point out that often their sheer facileness and slickness, while successful in getting around the law, leaves something to be desired in the way of life wisdom. Agreed? This is what I am pointing to. Of course there are good lawyers.

The journey from the slickness and intellectual power of the Jupiter chakra through the search for the meaning and sense-of-it-all in the Mars chakra, to the stability and union of the Earth chakra is for most of us a long and often difficult passage. It is the process of learning what life is all about. What follows is just a brief sketch of some of the possible phases that may occur in that journey, and includes quotes from my own journals of experience in the Jupiter chakra, so if this kind of writing is not your cup of tea, then skip on to the next sections.

Jupiter Phases

After the initial Jupiter awakening, it seems that no step of the way is easy, yet the hardest may to be the test each soul goes through AFTER that first awakening has taken its course, as we begin to get the idea of how we might make life work for us (and not vice versa), and begin to settle down to daily living. Once we awaken and begin to discover or glimpse our inner self, our awareness (whatever you want to call it), we are forever changed in our approach to life, yet we find ourselves still living in (within) the same lifetime and personal habits that we had before our discovery. This is almost always somewhat of a problem.

Our old personality (by definition) is never strong enough to hold the force and power of our new insights and approach to life. Our existing personality, with its bad habits of old, too easily breaks under the strain and demands of this newfound awareness, plunging us into instability and all the possible hells or stages of purgation and house-cleaning. We can see that all our old habits have to be purged and cleaned up, that there has to be some kind of reformation, during which we reform our personality. This holds true until we build a new body-of-personality or life to hold and reflect our new-found enlightenment, our awareness.

The Asteroid Belt

It is astrologically significant that relatively the longest stretch of space exists between Jupiter in to the planet Mars, passing through the wide asteroid belt filled with broken dreams. There are many who awaken to this new faith in life (Jupiter), and of that awakening much has been written. Stories of being "born again" are common. Less writing is available concerning the journey of the soul who has been awakened (who has somehow heard the word, gotten the idea, been born again) through to the realization of the word, idea made into reality, locked into real flesh and solid re-formed habits.

This is the great desert, the guardian at the threshold (of the beast itself) that must be slain and overcome as we each cross this seeming endless stretch of life in accordance with our own personal mistakes or errors. Catholics call it purgatory, and that is a good concept. I can only present to you my own experience to give you some general idea and feeling of this journey. Your story will, of course, be different, but the end or goal for each of us remains the same, regardless of the path followed. Here is one story of that rite-of-passage:

Journal: First Moments Of Jupiter Awakening:

Context: Like the lives of the stars in the heavens above, some burn slowly, some flare outward, and some supernova. There are ways to live and die. I have done many hundreds of one-to-one readings over the years, and can testify that there indeed are many ways to wake up.

For me, there was almost total darkness for most of my young life, and then, one night, in the middle of a bar scene, standing on stage, playing music, it came all at once. This is a rather vivid and poetic account of the Jupiter chakra awakening, in this case a sudden awakening, rather than a gradual one.

> "All I remember is haze — red shifting to orange — as I strained under the infinite pressure of my past, like a baby being born, and then, through the strain of this labor (so intense that time slowed) in which somehow I was involved, and through that slowness like the head of a child in birth, I crowned, and for the first time came I, me, a glimpse of my eternal self — real awareness. I saw myself. I found myself."

"Emerging right up through the top of my head, I was born as through a veil and vale of tears, surrounded on all sides by people living in eternal slowness. Tears stood in all our eyes, for I was them — huge catlike creatures, winking and blinking in the slowness of expanded time. We moved together in this, the rhythm of our birth, rising and falling like the cry of some great beast. Living was so slow that it took forever. We were all, together, one, born out of suffering, born out of and beyond time itself, born through a veil of tears, itself an endless rain."

Journal: It Could Never Happen Twice

Context: Here is more of my own Jupiter awakening from within the Saturn chakra.

> "And I remember one white-hot-flash-like-electric blast that went dead in my mind. I could never have it happen twice. I "was" absolutely not (as if all stopped), and then it started again. And after, I wavered, awash like a flower on the sea — a lotus. And as I found faith in my new awareness, I rose above time in knowledge of myself, in this new awareness. And as I lost that faith, accidents of a deathly kind became very possible. It was not subtle."

> "There was I, born again and living, alive in a world that I never really knew and that knew me not at all. I was still in the world, but I was no longer of that world. Like a newborn child, I searched everywhere for those who would recognize me and welcome me alive. Mine was a back-room birth, enacted in a century that could no longer afford to act out a drama as old as time itself."

Journal: The World Knew Me Not

Context: Awareness, awakening, insight, these experiences are very addicting, as in: we want more of it. We don't want to slip back into the endless sleep out of which we just emerged, and we search through our world for any signs of recognition, to see if any others can verify what we are experiencing. Can I find a witness?

Getting a witness is very difficult to do, and this lack of acknowledgement, lack of recognition, can make life and confidence very difficult. It is very easy to go overboard, trying to verify whether we are just dreaming or really awake in our new vision. Here is a journal entry from that time:

> "The fulfillment of this ancient ritual of awakening and the celebration of it was a bother in this time. The world knew me not, and everywhere all I got were short services, the barest sign of recognition, and then: ignorance. I became my own welcoming committee, born alone above a sea of persons. I wrote:"

> > Ah!
> > Who could let such a bargain pass,
> > As this poor century will allow,
> > On coming in, I'm asked to leave,
> > And when asked to leave, I bow.

> "I never thought to wonder what others might feel or think. I shared my newfound openness with all I contacted, never doubting that they experienced what I was experiencing, and that I was the only Johnny-come-lately. At best, we laughed and cried together, and paused in our lives of time to celebrate some moments of eternity. I wandered where I would, and went searching through the towns and universities for men who shared my realization. I just walked into their offices and caught them in their lives, some too stiff to share, but others wept with joy, and held my hand in encouragement and thankfulness for the grace of life. They had been there too!"

Journal: Eternity's Door

Context: Once the Jupiter awakening occurs, we could not go back to sleep, even if we wanted to, and we become prone to all kinds of highs and lows, in particular: dualisms. And dualism creeps into the picture, as we cannot keep our new eyes open, but, against our will, we slip back to sleep, time and again, only to reawaken, terrified that we have somehow agreed to forget what we found so hard to remember. Here is an entry:

> "Eternity's door lay open before me, and, for weeks I went all through the nights in a celebration of the end of my personal darkness and the return of the prodigal son — awareness itself."

> "I cannot remember exactly where the first doubt crept in as regards other people — dualisms. I guess it came with the realization that the rift of time (this openness) remained open only as long as I endured in a conversation and that, if I let it go, it just closed, and there was no curiosity forthcoming from those around me. I was subtly told that most persons would just as soon I left them alone, that my vision was my own, and was to them painful to behold. Gradually I was ignored."

Journal: Reading from the Outside

Context: Falling backward or wandering into zones of fear and terror can be very much a part of any shamanistic-like experience, where we have entered a new state of mind, but are unprepared to hold it, not able to stabilize ourselves. Stabilization, depending on the degree of awakening, can take many months and years, and is often accompanied by much fear and trembling that we will forget again. Here is an entry:

> "Somewhere along here I tripped, stumbled, and I know now why I have such an intense fear of high places, for I plunged from eternity back into time's hell like a lightning. I doubted."

> "Up to that point, I had been taking from within myself, bearing out the new-found truth, and surrounding myself in an atmosphere or aura, itself protective. But from some point, I began the fatal error of reading from the external — taking the outer as a sign to follow. I began to follow the external, and, without realizing it, I ceased to draw from within myself. I was suddenly cut off, separated from my own well of awareness and self, veiled from grace once again by time, yet unlike before, I had now known what is called by believers the "Grace of God," known something of my true self, and I seemed as a fallen angel separated from all I loved, yet not understanding why. What had I done to deserve my fall from grace?"

Journal: My Trial of Faith

Context: A very common experience in the Jupiter awakening is the sense of having tasted real awareness, only to fall back into where we came out of, but not quite back to ignorance. We are only one mind shift away from grace, but trapped in the past. I call this: to fail ignorance, by a meter or a foot. I could no longer be blissfully (or painfully) ignorant. I wrote:

"We slide through it all, the state of grace I sought to regain appearing and moving in unison beside me, yet now not within my reach. At my strongest moments, I can offer a vessel, hope for more, and yet gnash at what I have. The blood is in us all. And I taste blood when time quickens and I am born again. I smack it inside me and laugh the laugh, insane as it is, that announces my arrival, remembering that I have been here before. I am back. I have found myself again. Then I am happy."

"Try me. Take more of me. Give me again a show of strength and let me learn endurance in your favor, so that I may taste again of my only hope and life."

Journal: The Beast Claims the Whole

Context: Here is more on being locked out of our new state, held to the past by our own bad habits. Spiritual awakening, like a swan looking for a lake, can only rest in a personality that is somehow purified and stable. I am not speaking here of "holier than thou," but the simple fact that a lifelong set of inefficient or "bad" habits cannot be changed by one glimpse of freedom. In that glimpse of awakening, I could clearly see what I had been doing wrong (where I wasted time), but the changes required were vast, nothing short of a great change in attitude, and this kind of change cannot be perfected in a day, a week, month, or even a year. And given that about half the time I ended up off course and causing as many problems as I was solving, it is no wonder that I did no better than one step forward, and two steps back.

I understand that to many of you, this will not make a whole lot of sense. Yet, a few of you will have had or be having similar or related experiences. This is the primary work of shamanism, to catch the stragglers who fall through the cracks of society, let them know they are not alone, and help them to stabilize and rejoin that society. This is why this story is shared. An entry:

> "Without this pure awareness, I am lost, alone, and wait on its coming as on the break of day. I hear it breathing, and know I am often only steps away from the health of the spirit, yet I am bound in my pattern, unable to move the least inch to it, home."

> "It knows this. I am trapped in this form, and yet the form holds all my bid for its favor, trapped so close to the Lord of Life. Yet, it is everywhere perpendicular to myself. If I were stronger, I would come at it, and be forever in its hands. More of it, I cannot but cry for more of it. It breathes and moves under, around, and over all of me, yet I cannot grasp it. It is behind me, then in front, yet I cannot hear it direct. It moves in the corners of my eyes, yet defies my pursuit. I must get back to a clear state. The wolves of the flesh howl for my soul, for the beast in us stands forth at every handout and claims the whole. Way be clear to my heart. Open. Open up."

Journal: The Test of Faith

Context: And, in the beginning, our faith, no matter how strong that faith may be, is tested, because our personal vehicle cannot yet reflect or sustain our new vision. The ensuing instability sends us careening off path, only to wake up days or weeks later, remembering that we forgot to remember. And worse, we can end up in very real and dangerous life situations. Here is another experience, one that came waist deep in the middle of an icy rushing trout stream.

> "Surrounded on both banks with overhanging trees, I rose and fell, step by step along that stream, as my faith was or was not, as I kept faith or lost it. It all came at once. Again and again I snagged (and hopelessly) my fishing line in the overhanging branches. And, as I found my faith, that line would melt like cobwebs, falling back into the water. And, as the experience peaked (and this is no drug experience), I began to lose my footing, and be pulled away into the rushing waters."

> "And as, in my fear, I would open my mind, humble myself, and trust myself, that ground would catch on, hold, and raise me up. You would think perhaps to read this that there was no danger. But the thread of my lifeline was so tenuous during this whole period of conversion, that this entire adventure was lived in like a dream state. I was awake and living in my own dream, and I would fade in and out of the possibility of existence, as I believed or did not believe in myself, as I opened myself to trust, as I had faith. And I did! And after, I took off all my clothes, and dove again and again in those ice cold waters in celebration of my decided life of faith."

Journal: A World That Knew Me Not

Context: Spiritual progress, once an initial opening or realization takes place, is most often very slow, as we struggle to escape our own past. And that we cannot escape. Problems of self-reference, dualisms between our self and others are unavoidable and very painful. Here is a journal excerpt:

> "As an animal trapped in a net struggles in vain until exhaustion, so I struggled against all restriction. The harder my struggle, the more polarized my hell became — the "other," the "they" and the "them" quality. I was born into a world that knew me not, a world that shut me up, that turned me away, ignored me, and it rapidly became for me a world of the devil. And I was to fight for my life in a world hard-edged to cut me off from myself. The joy of my birth was turned to bitterness, as I realized there was no place for me, no room in the "in."
>
> "I just had to get free from the world in which I seemed to be trapped. I wanted desperately to somehow confirm my spiritual insight. The more I tried, the more my world became a living hell."

Journal: Do Not Do a Thing

Context: In the mind's map, one of the most painful places to be is where our own reaction or suffering becomes how we know or recognize that we live, our reaction to others. For instance, I then wrote:

> "They were all around me now, waiting on me, easing my pain. But my pain and suffering were all I had left of my awakening experience, were the only ways I knew I still lived — that I

could still feel, when I could remember. To lose my sense of aloneness or uniqueness might mean never waking up again, becoming average, lost in vanilla."

"And they asked me in every subconscious under-the-counter way to: DO NOT DO A THING. Relax, be still. Do not struggle so. Yet, at this time, it was only in the struggle that I knew myself (great stallion that I was), when there was a "them" and a "me," I against them, me and the devil. And now they wanted me to let go and even cease from that struggle. Not gonna' happen."

"I was overflowing energy, and they came in endless lines like ants to each take a part of my nervousness, my energy. They consumed me, willing (it seemed) to suffer any abuse from my person, but they kept on eating me, taking my pain away."

Journal: I Was My Pain

Context: When we become (identify with) our pain, and if pain is how we know ourselves or remember, then to lose that pain or to let it go is synonymous with dying or falling back unconscious — a terrifying thought and state of mind. Entry:

"And at this point, I WAS my pain. My pain was all I had, all I had ever known up to that point. Pain stood between me and that melting sea of mediocrity, where no difference remained. I did not have the faith that I could let go and still be distinct, still be me if I let go and fell into that sea of silence. I fought all attempts, signals, and messengers of peace."

> "After a life of nothing, of being no one, at last I had tasted real life and was "someone." I had known myself and the joy of overcoming time or Saturn. It was as if I had taken my first breath and was afraid to let it go out, so much did I value it. I did not have the faith that another breath would ever come. This is why they used to spank newborn infants, to get them breathing. Life was kind enough to knock my breath out for me."

Journal: Refusing To Breathe

Context: Becoming attached to our spiritual experiences and clinging to them is another common way to suffer in the Jupiter chakra. We all do it to some degree:

> "Not ever having known the experience of breathing, I was indeed being born, but this infant refused to breathe, refused to accept breath or change — the rising and falling cycles of our lives. Life had to knock the breath out of me to start me breathing. And so it did, and, gradually, I could breathe."

> "I wanted spiritual knowledge and enlightenment so badly that I clung to the high side of each life experience, clawing to get away from the heavier material side of this world until, exhausted, I would fall senseless back into time's arms, only to awake later, terrified, and struggle all over again. It was like trying to climb up out of the center of a deep lake. I wanted out of the body forever. I did not know that all out ends turning in, or returning. I knew nothing yet of the returns of life."

Journal: Roaming Purgatory

Context: Something we all are intimately familiar with, but seldom discuss, are questions of personal power or the lack thereof. Not being able to let go of people and experiences that strike us, and struggles with personal power, the power of the personality are pretty much standard fare, and have to be negotiated on a daily basis. Spiritual experiences and insight, before these experiences have settled into some kind of stable realization, are fraught with all manner of very real problems. For example:

> "And so I roamed the purgatories of my existence, just burning and burning. And rising through this waking dream came the great spinning wheels of Pride, as I attempted, again and again, to lay personal claim to the power of the spirit, to make it "mine." Again and again I would know awareness for seconds or days and yet, sooner or later, I would make the fatal attempt to associate that power as somehow my "personal" power, only to plunge into yet some new kind of hell.

> "And there I remained, in that torment, until I could find some way to surrender, let go again, and to open myself. This was never more obvious than when I was with others. I was, during that time, in total confusion as to who I was. And, if I was who I, in moments, knew myself to be (having had some realization), what did this mean in my personal life? Was everyone like me? Was I the only one? The answers to these questions found me struggling through other persons with my self and my "God."

Journal: Pride's Examples

Context: Pride and feeling superior to others is another very painful state of mind, filled with intense suffering, and one that can take years to work through:

> ". . . As he rises above them, they raise their weapons. As he sinks back, they relax. As he becomes in all his strength, they unite to hold him back. As he gives away his strength, they once again support him. He controls himself = self control. His struggles attract their attention and they seek to ease his pain, to assist him to relax. They guide and direct his energies. They give all they can to him. They take away his pain, his nervousness, and share it with him. They take his pain on themselves. The light of spirit does not penetrate the flesh. They flock to him, because he is dead to this world and cannot hurt them, yet he does not know this yet . . ."

Journal: Self-Reference

Context: At this point in the Jupiter chakra, we can't yet live with our new realization and we sure can't live without it, so we are torn between two seemingly opposing worlds, the world of god and the world of the devil -- push me, pull you. Matters of self reference are thorny, even to philosophers and psychologists. Imagine what they are like to a young person, trying to figure out which piece of the pie might be his or hers. This is when shamanic counseling can be a real help. Journal entry:

> "I left off listening to my inner dictation, and became fascinated and terrified at what I saw

reflected in the mirror of my exterior world, especially through interpersonal relationships. I sweated through moments in total fear for my life, in fear that all would pounce on me, and tear me apart for what I was thinking about them. I knew that all thoughts were a common experience, and that there was no such thing as privacy, but had not yet been able to accept others as I accepted myself, as a reflection of me. I was dualistic, and it hurt:

"I was lost in thoughts about personal power and self-reference, In checking the ID's of every person I met to see if they "knew" what I now knew, when I could remember to know it."

"I became the censor of all persons. I tested them to the quick. I fought to keep possession of my powers, and never even thought that this might be what is called "personal power" — the power of the personality. I became enamored with being a "great" person or genius in my own time:

"You are too much for this century, little man. You bloom embarrassingly along Main Street. You delight to pain and terror the businessmen. You ARE too much. How could they bear you all at once? But a pinch is all they will ever know. You have seized the time, and your grasp froze to life itself. Your happiness, time and again, emerges behind them, yet first. You hold them in a cloud and waft them on to nowhere, hold them back from their future, their fate, and their destiny. You kiss them on the fly, and they are so shocked that they emerge in that moment. A conversation and meeting, and then they fly on over life in their coffins. What woman waits senseless fated for *your* love? "

The Mars Chakra

Journal: I Am Led To the Sea of Love

Context: Trial and error, trial and error, that is how we learn. In time, very slowly, and usually through a lot of personal anguish, we gradually stabilize and do move forward. Our stability is commensurate with our unbalance, with our "sins." I wrote:

> "Gradually, I righted myself and slowly built a vehicle in which some kind of normal life was possible. I gathered around me the whole body of occult literature and searched through endless thousands of pages for the meaning in it all. I was certain that, given time, I could figure it out. The new god which I came to worship was the god of "Meaning" — deeper, deeper meaning, deepest, heavy, grave. Through all of my search, I thought to find the very bottom of, the grave of, truth — gravity. Across this vast intellectual framework crawled I, and became an expert on verbal gravity, the specific density of words and phrases. Gradually I came to this (for me) most shocking realization:
>
> All thought depends on its meaning."

Journal: The Sense of Life

Context: Jupiter maps the vast extent of the mind, of thinking, and complicated intellectual frameworks. It is no accident that the most terrible lightning storms in the solar system occur on the planet Jupiter. The lightning of the mind strikes again and again, but the life of the mind gradually dries up, ceases to satisfy, and, in time, is gladly traded for actual real-life experience. I was finally getting stabilized:

> "The essence of thought was what it means or conveys — the sense of it. The world of thought stretching around eternity all finds its end or meaning in the sense it makes, the sense world — the senses. All thought and thinking only ends in action or simple existence — experience. This was, for me, a profound realization. I would never have guessed."

> "My joy in the life of the mind slowly had dried up, for all my intellectual studies, however refined, depended on what it all meant. Meaning is not intellectual, but sensual. I could intellectually talk about what it meant, but unless I had experienced myself what it meant, I didn't "know" what I was talking about. In other words, MEANING is a simple act of referral, nothing more than a pointer that says: over there is the sense of it. Experience it for yourself. Go and see for yourself. Feel of it. Know it."

Journal: Balboa and the Sea of Sense

Context: Reaching the brink of the Mars chakra is a major initiation, which amounts to getting engaged and beginning, perhaps for the first time, to understand what the term marriage might actually be all about. It is humbling for the intellectual to discover that all thought, all words of philosophy or what-have-you are dependent on what they mean, and meaning is a simple act of referral, a pointer that points out where this can be experienced and known. I was amazed:

> "Suddenly the world of the senses stretched before me, an almost unknown and discarded item in the diet of my life. I had done all I could to avoid physical contact, and had driven myself high into my head to keep from feeling anything "wrong." And now, in all justice, my thoughts (and esoteric studies) had led me (their every conclusion the same) to that ocean of feelings, the senses — the sea of love. I had no idea!"

> "I stood like Balboa before an endless sea of sense, all the sense in the world. All I had to do was to jump in. It was the end of the intellect, for I was about to lose my mind forever, and no longer to mind every last thing that came to pass, whistling through my world, into eternity. I entered this sea of sense like a middle-aged old maid enters a very cold swimming pool, by inches and degrees, and shivering all the time. In my own way, I TOOK THE PLUNGE."

Mars Is the Activity That Generates Space

Mars is the energy that moves us. The kind of energy or activity that we have determines our personal atmosphere or aura: the kind of room or space in which we have to live, our living room. The kind of living room determines how we feel about our life — comfortable or cramped.

Mars is the bringing across of spirit or room into matter, the injection of space into time, of anti-matter into matter. An injection of Mars energy frees things up and creates an atmosphere for things to move and re-form. Mars expands time with space or room. The kind of room or atmosphere in which we have to work determines the way we work — the kind of our action. Mars has come to represent the sphere of action, the kind of way we do things. Mars is our way of working, the possibility of work. Mars is the energy or room that makes work possible.

Mars Is Meaning

Adrenaline, activity (Mars) creates space and space orders (Jupiter) time (Saturn). The room or space we each have to live in — call it our aura — "effects" how we experience life, how life feels to us. Mars is how we feel about life, the kind of "living" room we personally have.

Mars is meaning, or the direct road to meaning. The meaning of something is how we feel about or toward it, like a blind man feels about a corridor. It is an active feeling of a thing on our part, an action or movement. The Martian world is the world of sense and feeling or pushing our way along. How we feel about life is the key to success. Mars is the key to Jupiter.

Journal: The Vision of Mars Is Our Marriage

Context: The following is pretty much self-explanatory and self-documenting, as marriage is something our society does celebrate, but not much is spoken of about the process of engagement, the road that leads to marriage.

When the Mars chakra is awakened, one begins to feel and not think so much. Jupiter is about thinking and calculating, without feeling — handling the law. With Mars, one learns to feel and not always think. The world of feelings and the senses is the path to actual experience, and experience leads to knowing.

Marriage is a change of life or perspective as natural as the physical change at puberty. The vision that leads to engagement and marriage, union, and yoga is a major initiation in any lifetime. Some take another person as a sign of their marriage, and others are married to their work in this world. Any way you spell it, marriage is the end of personal affairs. Mine was like this:

> "It was that fast! One minute I was talking to another person that I had just met, and the next saw me through her person standing in eternity. Bells rang and lights went on, just like I was always told. I finally got the point. After having spent years at constant attention and worry that I might miss my wife in the shuffle of life (pass her by in an awkward moment of non-recognition or inattention), the reality was ironic to say the least. How could I have ever missed her, for she was to be my very wife. In fact, there was no way in the world that I could have avoided HER."

Journal: Marriage Is Quite an Affair

Context: The discovery of the unity in all dualisms marks the point of engagement with the actual physical body of life itself. It is the end of living only in the mind. By "unity in all dualisms," I simply mean that after a lifetime of dualistic thinking (you versus an other), you realize that in fact that the two are already (and have always been) one. Here is an example of how that might come about:

> "The actuality of the moment of marriage was nothing like I had anticipated. For years I had sponsored an impression that marriage was like the joining or fusion of two spirits into a union or 'One'. The great spirit that I had come to recognize as my real self was looking for another "great one," with whom to join together in a marriage of the two. But, that was not it!"

> "What WAS totally clear when I met my wife, for the first time in my life, was that there were no two spirits to be found. We were already, everlastingly ONE. There is one and only one Spirit. Not some spirit over there in her body tying up with my spirit here, but one Spirit and two bodies. My "alone" had become "all-one." I was "one" with my wife. We were already one and not two. Or as the great Les McCann tune puts it: "Compared to What?""

Journal: Dewdrop Slips into the Shining Sea

Context: The bigger the front, the bigger the back is an old Macrobiotic axiom. I suppose that "the bigger they are, the harder they fall" says the same thing. That's what falling in love is all about, once you tip over the top and start to fall, it is one heck of a ride. There is no going back! Responding to another person is the key to the Mars chakra.

> Journal: "My overriding experience was one of response, response to her person, and not to her spirit. Not another spirit. For the first time in my life, I responded and cared for another person as much as I did for myself. I

> responded to, rather than resisted, her personality, and in the opening of that second was swept away a lifetime of fear of OTHER persons.

"The dewdrop slips into the shining sea."

> "So this is what that dreaded word "responsibility" really meant — my ability to respond or love. After a lifetime of pushing forward, I was at last responding, and all I wanted to do was to endlessly care and provide for the unfolding of this person before me. I felt protective for the first time, and wanted to forever serve and assist in the care and the fulfillment of the one spirit. And this particular person just happened to be the one through which I first realized this experience. I took it as a good sign, and she became my wife. I was never to fear persons and the power of persons again, although the purification process was to go on."

And so far, so good. As of 2009, we are looking at our 38th wedding anniversary.

Journal: Why Marriage Is Like a Funeral

Context: As we move out of the intellectual sphere of Jupiter, where handling a problem was more a matter of manipulation (how to handle it) than understanding, we increasingly engage the experience of life itself. Where before it was "us or them," now we are beginning to see, in reality, it is "us and them," and search for a unified solution. Once the dualistic concept of two becomes one in our experience (when we are engaged), we have no more enemy "out there," and have to change our behavior. Entry:

> "Marriage is the end of our personal existence. I had been a warrior of truth, wielding the sword of the mind (Jupiter) and cutting any excess to the heart. I spared neither persons nor institutions, but went from victory to victory over time in my mind."

> "Marriage is the union between subject and object. The two are seen to be, in fact, one. No more "enemy." I was out of a job, so to speak, in that, by the fact of marriage, I chose to "lay down my sword and shield... down by the river..." of life and to study war (Mars) no more."

> For I had become one with the Martian sphere. It was the end of life as I had known it. It was like being at my own funeral."

Journal: Relieved Of Duty

Context: When we begin to get beyond the reach of time or Saturn, that is, after we are about thirty years of age, we gradually lose the push and rush of time that drove us all these years. If we do not know to look for it, to expect it, this experience of peace can be frightening, as this entry shows:

> "To be relieved, finished, the one thing I had never expected. Maybe at life's long end of eighty or ninety years, sure; it might make sense. But now, in the prime of my powers, in the middle of my life? To be relieved of duty? Are you kidding me?"

> "No one ever told me about it. I heard no talk of it. I didn't read about it anywhere. Am I the only one? Am I to remain silent? Who

is even interested? No one seems to notice."

"Relieved of duty in the middle of the war, I must be a traitor. I must have made some terrible mistake, to be relieved. I mean, I looked forward to a life long-filled with searching and suffering. And now this, this terrible guilt of non-involvement, of really not caring like I used to care, and I would rather die than not care. Caring did not mean love to me; it meant worry and suffering continued. To be carefree, this I never thought to ask for. I had lost my edge, my suffering."

Peace Terrifies

Context: When time stops at thirty years of age, we begin to enter the "silence," as it has been called. It is easy to fall into the view that we have lost something, and that we are of no use, when in reality we are just beginning our voyage of spiritual discovery. Here:

"It is like someone turned off the engine, as far as we personally are concerned. All at once, this great silence and sense of peace, and when you first begin to hear the silence, it terrifies. We can now see younger persons still driving and pushing their birth, yet we don't feel that old drive as we once did."

"There is the feeling that we are somehow washed up, finished. We have lost that old drive or "thing" which made us, ourselves. And all of this unspoken about, unmentioned in public conversation, simply ignored. As I can see, many just cannot accept this change, and wander stunned in a stupor and state of shock for years, or fill their lives with noise and activity — anything to drown the sense of silence and rest that they feel."

"Lifted out of our life's sorrow, we refuse to acknowledge the incredible and obvious lightness of being we now feel. Unburdened, enlightened, we feel no gravity or weight. Up until now, life beckoned and lured me running fast through time's meanings. What does it mean? What does it all mean? Where is it all leading to? What exactly is the point? And then, this: Silence."

Journal: The Shell of the Self

Context: What is called the middle-age crisis can come much earlier than that, and many who experience this make all the noise and busy-ness they can, in an attempt to cover up the sense of inner peace and silence they now feel coming over them. For myself, I struggled hard against it, with all my might:

> "I tried desperately to get back into my old self, to get into other people, into my work, anything but face what was actually happening. I was forced to continue living in the shell of a body, the life of which had now passed on into the hands of younger persons who cared for life now like I used to. I simply wanted to be alone, and to not be disturbed In this, my terrible loss. It was like a funeral, and I was in mourning.

"Perhaps more than anything else, I was mortally embarrassed that, after all my years of fierce aggressive intent, of meaning well, better than average, 'BEST!', to be now caught short, found empty. Me, who had always been so full, now empty. I did not have the heart to continue on in my life's direction, which had suddenly just evaporated.

"There was no "more" out there. I turned aside, hoping to lose myself in hard work. I had no plans, no future, no "more." But I was to discover that I could not even rest in peace in the grave I had made for myself. After some extended period of time, disturbed by every passing thing, I at last gave up "giving up," and resigned myself to return to the world to do what I could.

Awake In My Own Dream

Awakening to the Martian or emotional sphere is the end of ignorance. It is like rising from some torpid dream, rubbed awake by our attention's endless demands. We wake from our dream of ignorance, much like when, in our daily sleep, we dream of getting up and getting ourselves a drink of water. Again and again we get up and drink that water, yet we are thirsty, for we are still asleep and cannot raise ourselves to the physical act.

Spiritual awakening, at least after that first flash, is like that. We try to shake off the irritating demands on our attention, so that we might dream on undisturbed, but these demands become increasingly sharp, until we are literally rubbed awake in response. This constant nagging at us is just plain annoying, and at first we attempt to get rid of it, to quickly attend to these irritating demands on our attention, so that we can return to our sleep. Yet, they only increase in strength, and in the end, their persistence is stronger than our ability to sleep. We find ourselves forced to wake, and reluctantly respond more and more of the time, until our entire life seems to be one of complete response to the demands and questions of our person or of other persons. Our action has become passive or receptive.

A Life of Response

And many come to this, the ability to respond, very slowly. For most younger people, "responsibility" has long been something to be avoided and put off. Yet we soon find ourselves identifying more strongly with our waking state of perpetual care and attention to life's demands, than for our once-longed for dream of more sleep. One day it strikes us that we are now living what we had only dreamed about before. We have made our dreams real or have somehow awakened in our own dream. We are now taking care of ourselves, like we would take care of a garden of flowers, giving constant care and attention to whatever needs and demands present themselves for our attention. In this state of constant attention, we discover the heart of all meaning to be: simple existence itself. We are waking to the Earth sphere and the Heart Center chakra.

Journal: Awakening In Response

Context: When we cease to struggle with our newfound peace, and allow ourselves to fall to rest, to simply accept… all the remains of our previous life, what has been held down, what we could call our subconscious (or placenta) begin to rise to the surface and has to be looked at and dealt with:

> "Bobbing at the surface to bloom. Opening now. Letting go. Letting it go. Letting it go on. Allowing it to go on. As if I could stop it anyway."

"My acceptance and cessation of struggle against the world released all of the material that I had repressed or ignored through all of the years of my intellect's domination. All of the unrealized desires began to present themselves in an endless procession before me, each with its very plain demand. The world of sense, of the flesh and body that I had ignored for so many years, came to mind. A phrase that my teacher had told me over and over now began to make sense. He said, 'Michael, the student closes the door. The teacher never closes the door, and the day will come when the winds of change will blow that door wide open, and there will be nothing you can do to stop it.'"

"I had no alternative but to look. I feared that, as I started to look I would be swept into that sea of sense, never to be heard from again — tormented by lust and unfulfilled desires, a pornographic idiot staring till doomsday at all the bodies that he wouldn't let himself see enough of before."

Journal: Take a Good Look

Context: Whatever we have pushed back or under in our past, that which has been subconscious until now, is free to rise to our attention, and cries out to be taken care of, once and for all – orphans of our mind. As we take an ever-increasing embrace of life, we are no longer clinging to the top of the pyramid, but begin to accept more and more of the raw stuff of life that we have put out of our mind (and experience) previously:

"The corner of the eye glance became: "TAKE A GOOD LOOK FELLA." All of this came to a head as I was led into the sea of senses, or should I say: at this point I lost my head forever. I was at last losing my minding of every last thing. My head had roamed far in front of my heart for many years, and my heart found it very hard to carry out all of the dictates or orders from my head. It became clear to me that just because I was ahead (a head) of my times did not mean that I personally felt like carrying all these ideas into effect. It became a choice between a life lived in slave labor to ideas that I did not feel like or have the heart to follow, and sacrificing some of my ideals of conduct to get the sense of it, some feeling."

"It seemed preferable for me to perhaps die several years earlier (and perhaps from a worse disease), but to have enjoyed my life in the fulfillment of what I personally was able to do, that is: to have relaxed a bit, than to live to be a hundred and yet be totally uptight in discipline — a curse to myself and to all who had to know me. I guess you would call my new reasoning: moderation in all things, including moderation. I was to have a little excess."

Journal: Out to Pasture

Context: Along with whatever else from our past comes up or rises to our attention, our own personality is at the top of the list. Even with a new vision, there is only so much we can do to retrofit and modernize our person. We have to learn to care for it as we would a stranger:

"The metaphysical point I am elaborating here is simple: I turned my personality out to pasture at this point. I began to care and love and give it what it needed to be happy, what it needed to fulfill itself. I did not give it what my intellect thought it should have (to be strictly correct), but I gave it what it needed in order to feel some sense of relaxation. I let my person do more or less what it felt like doing. I respected its needs as I would those of a stranger's needs under my care. I began for the first time in my life to put on a little weight, to get over my fear and avoidance of money — to enjoy myself. I had steadfastly refused everything of a physical or sensual nature for so many years in some vain attempt to deny my materiality."

"You would be wrong if you interpret this as indicating that I thought the dictates of my intellect were not true. I know they are very true. I still plan to take all the changes that my head can see, only gradually, as I am able to feel like taking them, and not just because they are there or possible. And I can see some changes will remain for my children to take, that I may not get around to feeling like enacting. I have learned that we must be able to feel our changes as well as see them. I have nothing to offer my children, if I cannot give them a whole, full-feeling and joyous father. It is better that I have all the vices of my century, but have love for my wife, children, and this creation, love not just in my mind, but acted out, in the flesh and with feeling."

Clearing the Subconscious

Context: Opening up our own past subconscious is not something we have any choice about, if we want to have a clear mind. Opening our mind means allowing whatever we have kept out to rush in, and everything that we have kept in to rush out, and so it does:

> "I have too little space to present here all of the material that I feel should be reviewed in approaching the opening out of the subconscious. The psychic world or world of our subconscious is just that: sub or beneath our consciousness, beneath the ground of our conscious mind. By definition, we cannot take our conscious intellect into this sphere, but must leave it by the shore of the senses and proceed farther by feeling our way, very much like you might feel around for your shoes in the dark. For many of us, learning to feel our way around without thinking (to experience life) takes a whole lot of bravery and practice. It is like learning a whole new sense, and it takes years of experience to become confident in what you feel. I want briefly to mention some of the material we might encounter when we first accept our feelings, actively experience them, and permit them to rise into our consciousness, after perhaps years of ignoring them."

The Sewer

First, it is very like taking the seal off a sewer, in that there is in most modern consciousness a lot of rotten material that has spent years stagnating and dying to come up. So, don't expect a beauty parade when you first begin to feel and experience this material consciously. This is not something you can just do in the privacy of your own home, but, once you begin to relieve yourself, it is something that will happen wherever you happen to be. You will be in everybody's subconscious as well, with all the cesspools in the world at your fingertips.

What do I mean by cesspools? I mean the countless strangled desires, thoughts, and dreams that were cut off by the tyranny of the intellect or conscious mind, or that society insists we repress. All of the bodies that were never looked at, never felt, never loved — all of the gentle wishes that were shoved out of realization to become twisted caricatures of themselves, all of the many parts of yourself that you have ignored or that your society and upbringing ignored. All of this material desperately needs care and attention or at least the last rites, if not complete resurrection — all of the anger, frustration, horror, and hells we have repressed ourselves to live in.

Open Subconscious

The subconscious, first viewed, can be like a raging beast, openly realizing all the wounds of a lifetime. We cannot personally realize all of these broken dreams. Many of our desires will have been so twisted that it is very hard to find any way to bring them out to relief. What we can do is to look directly at them, recognize them for what they are and, in this realization, put them to rest, one by one, forever. We can trace our feelings down through all this frustrated material to find the source itself, the fountain from which all life and feelings flow, and redirect this flow to good use and a new life. It is like water that muddies when stirred. The stirred up mud will flow off and there will, in time, be just clear water in its place.

In summary, through the Mars chakra, we learn to "feel" all over again, to feel pure and true. When we say all parts of ourselves, we mean to say that this extends to all persons, to everyone, for we are it all. We all share the same subconscious, which is little more than the product of our times, a social convention. There is nothing weird about subconscious work. It is all too ordinary, all the obvious that waits for someone to recognize and care for it — a great shadow. Only those who can respond to their own feelings and subconscious content can pass through this great shadow to know the light of the heart within.

Journal: The Poetry

Context: What is left after the subconscious (which is nothing but our own personal past) is clarified is quite clear, a free-floating consciousness, like a lotus, riding on top of the flux of life. It can be put into words:

> "No matter what you think about me, about my person, I know in time you will learn to recognize me as yourself, and you will love me, as I have learned to love myself, as I have learned to love you, like it or not. My person has not changed. How could it, truly? For person is the product of time, and my person — like a freight train — rushes on at the future. It always has. Only I, stepping off my person, am with you now."

> "I am myself. I turned off time's endless matter at thirty. I dropped my body or sense of gravity. It proceeds on without me or rather: with my perpetual care and love. But I am not only my person. I am, as well, one with the creator of my body, of any body."

"My faith informs me. Each day's passage frees and reveals my past, 'presents' my past, and clears it open. Where before was but an endless accumulation, layer on layer, is now removed with every passing day. And as the layers lift, it is clear to me that there is nothing there worth worrying. All the past lives I have are presently living, are become clear. Nothing to go back to, no place to hide, no cover."

"I am born free, held awake by all that lives. Where before I could not keep my eyes open, so now I cannot shut or close them. No closure. From my subconscious pours my past. Cloudiness clearing, it is my present. My placenta is being born, turning out all of that which nourished me."

"I can clearly see all that clouds this stream of consciousness is but a searching, is itself but a frowning, a looking to see, a pause, a hesitation that, caught and unfurled in the eddies of time, finding nothing, becomes clear and, laughing, I leave it go clear and turn from a darkening or dimming of my mind to light. And it came to pass, and I let it pass."

Journal: Awakening of the Earth or Heart Center

Context: After our Saturn return, we can float above and just beyond time, held aloft by all that is. This is not something that requires any action on our parts, but just the reverse: we must learn to sit back and ride, pushed forward by all the changes of life around us.

"The morning's brightness lights the day. And when that day is gone, the quietness of evening here approaching settles to sleep this restless world. Hard can I hear the frantic rush, as I turn away from the edge out into floating rest am I. It is not *my* conscious direction doing this, but as a head down-turned all life now turns up a blossom to the night, the night of time urges me open, at last a flower too, open to life. Already the dawn."

"Still, around me, urging caution, a retinue of persons set my spirit, like a jewel is set, in time. But where before my worry, now my rest. The tide rolls on beyond me. Ever changing, it rocks me now asleep. And in my sleep, awake am I, so clear a bell is ringing."

"The smart of persons lash and crack to drive me at time's edge. My personal ties are slipped, as floating out, I'm gently tugged. Too long have fought to force my thought, and not, at ease, arising like some cloud to pass. My work undone, yet done, I rise. Drifting through strains, I sieve, and pass myself, open out to nothing thoughts to touch back not once more.

A clear sleep is soft, its ever blooming sound is silence. Now to find my way among the slips of time. And slip I will, now lost to striving, and lounge in this room of emptiness. To lie back in time, behind its edge, and ever look eternally. No way to pass this on. This is: passing on. Slamming against the walls of time, I shove off into eternity, and spread open a flower, so wide."

The Earth Chakra

The Earth Is the Heart of Meaning

The Earth or Heart Chakra is the KEY to Mars. Mars is feeling, directionality, and meaning, and the Earth is the essence of what it all means — the heart of meaning. Earth is itself what it means, where it all leads to. Meaning, motion, and Mars is ever referring itself onward. Earth is the end of that referral, where the buck stops.

Earth is its own meaning. This is where we are, the Heart center of Buddha, the Christ Center itself, the "I AM THAT I AM," and for no other reason — simple existence. On the planet Earth, we stand between the inner and outer planets, the balancing point, the middle way, the Son, the communion between the Father and the Holy Spirit.

We cannot see with our physical eyes beyond the earth center, for all that is visible is the blinding Self or Sun of the eternal union between matter and spirit. The Sun is shining! Beyond the earth (Sun), veiled behind this flashing Sun, is the mystery of the godhead itself.

The Earth sphere is where the crucifixion takes place, what has been called by poets the "terrible crystal." The personal ties of time (the dragon), in this center, lose their hold and merge with the divine will.

Journal: Everlasting Life

Context: The concept of the Monad, very briefly presented earlier in this book is that of the entire process of the Sun endlessly generating life, tended by the souls who happen to be spiritually awake at any given time, as this poem portrays:

EVERLASTING LIFE

What will in words not wake,
Clear sleeps,
And clear, sleeps on
What wakes stands watch
to see that sleep as sound.

What wakes will serve to set a sleep
Inset a sleep with standing words,
That wake, if ever, last.
And on that "last," in overlay, our life.

Yes, to lay at the last
A life that over lives,
To ever last that "last" of life,
And in ever "lasting" life, everlasting,

We have a life that lives at last.

Journal: The Consummation of the Marriage

The Child or Heart Center

Context: Reaching the Earth or Heart Center is what our life's journey is all about. We cannot know peace or rest until we have achieved this, until we have taken possession of Earth, our heritage by birthright. At this point in our journey, we have come a long way. Our awakening within Saturn, and the struggle for simple survival and to somehow find a way through life, the province of the Jupiter chakra, is behind us. We have mastered that.

Our search for something more meaningful, through the Mars chakra, has led to our embracing (accepting) all of life, just as it is — marriage. We accept life as it is, because that is how it is. It would be foolish to do otherwise.

All of this has led us to the very center of our self, or as Hegel said so well:

"We go behind the curtain of the Self to see what is there, but mainly for there to be something to be seen."

The opening of the Earth or Heart center is what follows, which involves holding life within us, as we would hold a newborn child. Here is how it was for me:

> "The birth of our first child was heralded by a spectacular series of visions and revelations. It was like waking up repeatedly from dream within dream. The finale at the fireworks display is stunning!"

> "I had accepted our pregnancy in the traditional way: I hoped for the best and prepared for the worst. It never occurred to me that childbirth was a sign of deep change in my spiritual nature, or that it meant anything more than the physical act of learning to care for a child."

Journal: Childbirth

Context: Some notes about the coming of my first child.

> "What did I know about kids? I knew nothing of children. I avoided them, like I avoided every other part of my life that commanded my attention, and whose attention I could not command. I had seen children around, in the

outskirts of my life, but never where they could get at me, never where I had no choice. I guess in my accustomed style, I prepared myself for the worst, and yet hoped for the best.

As a matter of fact, childbirth has changed me in deep and real ways, changed me beyond recognition. It is change. I now understand why the world has a population problem. I was not (perhaps) married when I married, but I did become a father when I had a child."

"As if my life were not hectic enough, I had no job. My wife and I knew little better to do with our time than to fight with one another. Our dog was pregnant again, and again, against our will. And now a child. I guess I had all of the typical thoughts about children, of the cynical variety, that this was the living end of our freedom, that we had really done it this time, had finally done something that we couldn't easily wriggle out of. Along with this programmed variety of thought came others of a more uplifting nature, basically an acceptance of the fact as a sign of its necessity. As I like to tell myself: It was permitted."

Journal: Looking Out the Window

Context: More on the opening of the Earth or Heart chakra.

"And there was an ever growing joy (at first hard to feel) that this was really the most important thing that had ever happened to us in our lives. This last idea grew, shattering the

> shells of all the others before it, and progressively overcame us with the steadiness of love."

> "Our child was conceived in a rare moment of deep tenderness and openness between us. As the pregnancy moved along, it drew us together and gave us something more substantial to relate to than our own endless differences. This pregnancy was a very happy time for both my wife and me, a time during which we enjoyed each other more than we had ever before. And time after time would find us sitting — during those last days — like high birds looking out the window at: absolutely nothing at all."

Journal: Through God's Looking Glass

Context: More on the opening of the Earth or Heart chakra.

> "I had an interesting experience one evening, while visiting my brother and his wife who had a newborn little girl. This was not long before we became pregnant. And as I was talking to him, I noticed he was not really listening to my conversation. I turned to see what could be more important and found him looking into his little daughter's eyes like he was looking out an open window from a stuffy room. It was at that instant (unconsciously perhaps) when I realized that there was more to having a child than a headache. I believe I wanted one too."

Journal: A Midwife of the Spirit

One very important event that happened just before our child's birth was our meeting a Unity minister, a Black woman in her fifties, who was to be our teacher in so many ways. I don't think there is an easy description for what she was or did. She was a very strong believer in what she called "Divine Love."

I thought nothing out of the ordinary when I first met her, until she began to retell an account of how she had removed a tumor from her own body. I went on with my own thoughts. It was part of a radio interview of which I was a part of. There were several of us listening. When she had finished her account, everyone gathered around remarked at what a powerful story they had just heard. At this point I realized that, although I had felt the power in what she had said, I could not remember one single word of it. I had not been listening to her words at all. Instead I had been looking deep, very deep within her at her feelings or emotional state — her subconscious. And, as I gazed, I saw that she was so deeply expressive and so careful not to let the world know how deeply she had been hurt and had suffered."

Journal: My Heart Went Out

Context: This entry has to do with how we can recognize when we have found a mentor or teacher.

> "My heart went out to this soul, for certainly did I understand the state of her being. I understood so very well indeed. I felt that I could help this person to become stronger and to bear her inner sufferings out into the world. She had so much love inside her, if she could

only realize that the ideas and thoughts that she presented to others, that she felt so important to maintain, were not important at all. The sheer immensity of her very presence dwarfed anything her intellect had to say about it."

"This is how I met one of my life teachers, and need I tell you that it was many, many months before I could stand to realize that much of what I saw in her was just my own self, reflected in her long-gone mirror. She was able to reflect in its entirety my whole personal drama, without a ripple of confusion, and I saw inside myself how it was with me, although I thought I was seeing her and how it was with her."

"My wife and I saw a lot of this woman directly after our meeting. She would drive all the way from Detroit to our house in Ann Arbor, time after time. At first, I insisted on ministering to her, and giving her my readings of her problems, but in time, as I realized that all I was seeing as her was but my own reflection, I ceased to feel obliged to lecture her, and took up actively the contemplation of this great window of eternity."

"And, for those interested, this is one of the primary ways one knows when one has encountered a mentor or life teacher, by reflection. Real teachers reflect not their nature, but our own, and we are not used to seeing our own reflection clearly through others. We think we are meeting them, but we are finally meeting ourselves. Watch for this."

Journal: The Heart Center

> "One morning, not long after meeting this teacher, and after a particularly unsatisfying long night of conversation with an occult scholar, I awoke feeling as if my head were encased in cement. Then something very different occurred. I found myself (without thinking) dropping to the floor and going through quite automatically some very odd contortion-like exercise."

> "And as I worked, my body began to shake and nauseate me, and slowly I worked over my head — like pulling off a sock inside out — and cast off the heavy sickness of feeling that had occurred from the night before. I was shedding my mental skin just like a snake. With this experience came a symbol to my mind that expressed this process and it has become the symbol we are using in our work here. [See the book cover]"

> When I told my teacher about this strange exercise, she laughed, and told me the name of it, and that it was one of her exercises. This was the first of the many truths that came to us through her, quite unconsciously on my part, almost by a system of osmosis. We continued to work together for many years, and my wife and I have spent some of our dearest moments with this woman."

Journal: The Valley of the Shadow of Death

Context: Opening up the Earth or Heart Chakra.

> "The weeks before our daughter's birth were one continuous waking vision. I was breaking

finally through the end of my Martian sphere and opening into the Earth or Heart Center. Together, my wife and I consciously walked into and through the valley of the shadow of death. Not death itself, for there is no death, but the shadow or shade we fear and call death. This great cleft opened, like the Red Sea once opened, parted, and, arm in arm, we walked through this valley and into the light beyond and behind all appearances. The entire world of wincing pain and personal suffering was laid open in our vision."

Journal: Hard Thoughts

Context: Looking to look pain and death in the face brings its own rewards.

"Up to that point in my life, whenever a painful thought or "bad" feeling had occurred, I always turned inward and experienced that thought alone — took it personally. Now my eyes were open and, as I watched people in their daily intercourse, I saw that all experienced these painful thoughts at the same time. They were like waves that swept through a room — energy."

"And that, as a hard thought arose, everybody winced and turned inward, each taking this thought in his or her way, each taking it personally, as their own fault or problem. All turned inward until the thought was absorbed, and then, all opened out again as might some plant or animal that had stopped to digest or absorb a piece of food. All opened out again at once, like flowers, and conversation went on as if nothing had ever happened. But something did happen."

"No one seemed to be aware that this had been a common experience. Each thought it was their separate problem and sorrow. And in those moments of pain (or whatever we can agree to call them), I looked on through the experience into life itself. It was simply a moment of truth or growth, like a plant might shoot forward suddenly in a spurt of energy. What we call psychological pain is, for the most part, simply the fear to share the thought — the loneliness of not sharing the experience."

Journal: Pain Is Fear

Context: More on awareness of pain.

"Parting Is Such Sweet Sorrow."

"The experience I witnessed was not intrinsically painful in itself. It simply was exactly what it was. The experience of pain was the fear to share the thought or feeling in common and to acknowledge a common life. Fear itself was the pain. Each took privately what they feared to recognize together. We all agree to forget what we find so hard to remember."

"The growth process of life itself is like some great amoebae growing, separating into two, and flowing together once again. The pain of separation was simply the process of knowing the Self, splitting into one — endlessly dividing to join again. We could call the pressures of this process not pain, but tone — feeling our self. It was simply the process of physical growth, separation, and greater union endlessly going on."

"What astounded me was that practically all the pain and suffering was man-made. It was the pain of being alone, of taking these changes inwardly or personally. The pain came from ignorance of the common life and communion, not from the life process itself. Needless to say, this was a revelation for someone who had come to consider pain as a necessary evil."

"This endless life process was the trumpets of the Lord of Creation forever blowing our mind. It was the tree of life set in paradise, and although my mind is not conscious of this revelation most of the time, I have never been as afraid of life since."

Journal: The Vision of the Heart Center

Context: We have mentioned earlier on about discovering the silence, as we move beyond the grip of Saturn, around thirty years of age. Beyond the Saturn return comes the experience of what is called "Entering the Silence," which is what this entry is about:

> "The silence had been there all along and was especially present since my marriage. Yet, as I have previously written, I ignored it or, if unable to ignore it, I viewed it as the end of everything I had known, which in a very real sense it was."
>
> "I began to accept this vision at a birthday party for my two-year-old niece, just for family. The adults stood around the room's edge, while the children played in the center. I suddenly saw

the children as a radiant source of life energy and the adults as shells or relative ghosts on life's periphery. When we went home that night, my wife and I had to shake our heads to be sure that we had ever even gone out that evening. It was like a dream."

Journal: Could Care Less

Context: More.

"With the next night came the main load. I had been a performer of popular music for many years and, although I had lost my interest in performing music at the same time I got married, I still, on occasion, would perform. I had been invited to sing a few songs at a local benefit and together, my brother and I got on stage — just like we used to, a team."

"My whole singing career had been one of intense concern for the quality of the music and its expression. I never ate before a performance. I never was satisfied with any performance and, almost without exception, when I had finished a set, I was ashamed of the reality of what had gotten across compared with what had been my intention and my vision. I invariably could not look anyone in the eye after singing or else would endlessly apologize for what I considered to be the faults of the performance. I felt like I was wearing a scarlet letter and glowed red with indignation that the circumstances could affect my intent."

"Well, this night was to be very different indeed. We got up and did a few songs. The rush and flurry of the evening (and the fact that we had not played together for a time) made some of the songs come off very poorly. Poorly, in that they failed to reflect in justice the potential beauty of the songs. But as I sang these songs, instead of looking down to dig deep and find my meaning, I just sang and looked out at the sea of bodies before me. I just sang the songs. And a friend came up to sing with us and, when she stumbled in her delivery (as it sometimes happens), and turned to me for some kind of company in her "misery" (which I had always been good for), I just looked at her and I did not care. I understood what was happening."

"It was not that I was glad that she felt bad or that I would not help her. I already was doing all I possibly could to make the music as good as possible and more than that I could not do. I was not going to worry that it was not what it should have been. I accepted it for what it was."

Journal: The Silence

Context: Beyond the Saturn return comes the experience of "Entering the Silence."

"And when it was over, I got up, stepped down, and walked into the crowd with no apology whatsoever. I went up to another performer friend of mine and the "old" me started to apologize and managed to stammer out something about how it had been "up there" on the stage. My friend looked me straight in the eye and said "Yes Michael, it was exactly what it was!"

"There was nothing and nobody to whom I need apologize, not in the whole world. And that entire night, in the mad wild atmosphere of that bar, I experienced complete calm and silence. Silence. It was as if I was the only one there. I don't mean that I was high above it all and somehow untouchable at that time. I mean there was no resistance of any kind at all. I had to snap my head to see if I was dreaming. It was so very silent there."

"And that is how I first began to enter the Silence. I was in the world, but I was no longer of the world in the same way. I am living in and getting used to my Earth or heart center and open to learning something of that next planet: Venus, not the planet of physical desire as some think, but of love and compassion. And so here my personal story ends for now. For me it is always still the beginning."

The Inner Chakras

Venus Is the Key to the Heart or Earth

Well, there you have it. I am afraid the best I can do is point out, as best I can, the chakras from Saturn into the Earth/Sun. I am still struggling to stabilize my own Earth center life. After all, that is where we were born and where we live, on Earth.

The planets within Earth's orbit are just that, inner planets, and they are in fact our inner life. They shine within us as the Sun itself shines within us. I can't say that I have any experience in these inner realms, but I have studied them, so let's go through them, at least in outline.

Venus is the essence of the heart and the key to Earth. Venus stands behind the veiled Sun of the Earth or Heart Center and there is no material here. Venus is a rendering or loving of all that is — irrespective of the personalities. The idea to understand here is that Venus is beyond the material world of Saturn, and beyond Earth.

Perhaps the best I can do is to point out what all of the great poets and artists, throughout the centuries, have been telling us about Venus, and that is: the key to life on Earth is love. Love is all there is. The wise men and philosophers have said this repeatedly and forever. Love is the key to life here on Earth or as we might say here: Venus is the Key to Earth, being the next planet within the earth's orbit. It is that simple.

There is no way to grasp through our material senses what Venus represents. We can only experience it as we come to know our own mind, as we find awareness within. Venus is all the love there is, the Holy Mother, and Immaculate Conception, for it endlessly conceives in love all that is. The Holy Mother or spiritual force has not ever, is not now, and never will "matter" in this world, for it is itself beyond the reach of matter. It is the support or womb of all matter. It is the uncreated or unborn cornucopia out of which all life endlessly pours itself, forever immaculately conceiving all life.

The Bodhisattva

Matter or form resides with Saturn, and learning to find our way around in form is what Jupiter is all about, our path. Feeling beyond that took us through the Mars journey to find meaning all the way to Earth itself. Don't expect for your inner life, life within the Earth chakra, to matter materially. It never will. It "matters" spiritually. Beyond Earth, it is all about love and light, no matter how twisted these concepts may appear in life. Behind or within the form is the love and the light, Venus and Mercury.

Venus is the Bodhisattva, pure compassion, which is total appreciation or love. This planet is the key to our earth life and to our natal horoscope. It is the essence or divinity itself from Earth's viewpoint. It alone is the key and mother of Christ, forever giving birth to the Christ within us. It is for divine love that we pray and worship, for this love is the key to our life. Venus is divine love and compassion.

Mercury Is the Light of Love

The same is even more true for Mercury, a planet or chakra that is within Earth, within Venus, and very close to the Sun-source itself. Mercury is even less physical.

The Sanskrit word for Mercury is "Budha," awareness. Mercury is the key to Venus, the very throne of God or spirit itself. Mercury is the light of love, the divine light of eternal truth, the eternal corona and radiance of the Sun center itself. It is the Voice and direct Word of the Father itself sent forth — god's messenger or consciousness and awareness itself. Mercury is the light of the mind, the light we see shining in each other's eyes.

The Sun Center Itself the Whole

The Sun, the center of it all, is more than just another planet or chakra. It is the source and creator of the whole system, and the entire system of moons and planets that hang on the Sun. Sure, we can say that the Sun is the Key to Mercury, but also to all creation. It is the center itself and only nothing can be said here. It was in the beginning, is now, and ever shall be.

We do not simply mean the Sun as we find it in our horoscope, for that is the representative of the Earth/Sun/Moon relationship. Here we mean the Sun as it exists in itself (timeless), itself the eternal messenger of all time.

> I am round and such so:
> A treading finally and letting go,
> As spreading circles open so,
> An even inward outward flow.

The Moon

As some of you may have already wondered, where is the Moon in all of this? That is a good question. For the most part, this book is about the larger-scale life of our solar system, with the incendiary Sun and the planets bound in orbit to it. The Moon is really part of the Earth system. In fact, the Earth and Moon are such a binary system that the shared center of gravity of the Earth-Moon system is actually located within the earth's surface. It is located about 1,060.68 miles beneath the surface of the earth. Does the Moon not have an esoteric side and meaning?

To be sure it does, and a very important one at that, one that would require and deserves a whole book of its own. [Mother Moon: The Astrology of the Lights] This study of the chakras is not the place for such a work. However, it may be helpful to point out some general guidelines when considering the Moon from an esoteric perspective.

First, when I speak here of the Moon, it should be kept in mind that I am speaking of the Moon-Earth system and, actually, the Sun-Earth-Moon system, for most references to the Moon, such as the lunar cycle and orbit involve the phase angle of the Moon with the Earth, and this requires the Sun's position as well.

It is an interesting astronomical fact that, from Earth's perspective, the relative size of the Sun and the Moon in the sky as seen from Earth are about equal. This is what makes total eclipses of the Sun possible. In fact, there are all kinds of facts about the Moon, the lunar orbit, and its relationship to the earth and the Sun that are interesting and call out for us to explore their more esoteric meaning.

The Lights: Sun and Moon

In the tradition of astrology the Sun and Moon are called "The Lights" and, as we mentioned, we need to read that as Sun-Earth-Moon in every case. The Earth's place in all of this is always assumed.

Looking at the esoteric meaning of the Sun and the Moon has to be distinguished from the use of the Sun in the chakra system, where it represents the peak or crown chakra. In the chakra system, as I have presented it in this book, the Sun represents the entire solar system as a single entity and the process of interdependency between the planets and our fiery star. Esoterically, this process and state is called the Monad, and I have given some information about its meaning earlier on. In a similar way, where we spoke earlier in this text of the Earth chakra and the Heart Center, we were referring to Earth as a planet in the chain of planets that make up our solar system.

However, when we speak here of the Sun and the Moon, the astrological "Lights," we mean the Sun as the Earth, in the same way we consider Sun signs astrologically. My telling you that I am a Cancer sun sign actually says that Earth (which actually is in Capricorn) sees the Sun in the zodiac sign Cancer. It is the earth that we really mean, when we say the "Sun and the Moon." We mean the "Earth and the Moon" as a unit, but in relationship with the Sun.

In this section, therefore, we are leaving behind the concept of the Sun as the monad and all that we might have to say about that, and are looking at the relationship of the Sun-Earth axis and the Moon. Please make this distinction. Here the earth is not being looked at as a chakra, but as part of the Earth/Sun-Moon pair, "The Lights."

That having been said, the esoteric story and meaning of the Lights, the Sun and Moon, offer a different perspective and rendition of the same material covered in the chakra sections, the same story, only with a somewhat different view. All of this will come into focus for you by my just jumping in here with some specific esoteric concepts.

The Moon as Our Mother

In the history of astrology, again and again, it is said that the Moon is a mystery in that it is both a mother and a child. The Moon is our mother, because (similar to the womb of Saturn) everything and every body issues forth or is born from it. The Moon represents the subconscious and unmanifest regions from which all life, literally all "stuff" comes forth. Like an endless cornucopia, the Moon mothers forth.

The Moon is our support system, all that nourishes us, in the sense that we literally form ourselves and arise from within its womb. There are all kinds of historical paintings, drawings, and text images about life (bodies) arising and Issuing forth from the womb of un-manifestation, from out of the great void. In this sense, the Moon is our mother. How then is the Moon our child?

The Moon as Our Child

As each of us is born from the Moon stuff, we draw around our spirit whatever kind of form or body appropriate. We individuate or extract our self from mother Moon and take on our individual form. We are no longer part of the great matrix or womb from which we came, but at some point have been born and begin to separate from the mother. We are an individual, now separate from our mother, and living on our own.

The Moon then, once separated from us, is something we can remember or look back on. In fact, we can see by the light of the Moon, by the sunlight bouncing off the Moon and illuminating it so that it can be seen. Otherwise, it is lost in the darkness of the heavens.

And as we gaze on the Moon, we are looking at where we, ourselves, came forth from, looking at the past where once we were. And here is the point:

Life is a process. As we separate from the Moon, the process of the Moon giving birth does not end. The Moon is the womb from which all things emerge, aside from the place we came. Looking back on that Moon, we see other souls, much like we were, now being formed, and in the process of extracting themselves from the womb, just as we did.

In the Western esoteric texts, the Moon can also overcome or suffocate us, if we cease to individuate and move onward, but instead fall back into her arms. I remember Robert Heinlein's science-fiction novel "The Moon Is a Harsh Mistress." Yes, she can be.

I am trying to paint here a word picture, and the point is that we not only push forward in our lives, always extracting ourselves from our Moon. In addition, by the light of the Sun, we also often gaze upon the Moon. We look back at ourselves, as we once were, and see younger souls (souls like us) who are now being born, just as we once were. By the light of the Moon, esoterically speaking, we can see ourselves young. The process is ongoing and continuous.

In this way, the Moon is our child, because we are no longer of the Moon, but we came from that Moon. We remember back to then, and the Moon is all about memory, about the past, and about where we came from.

Perhaps this will be clearer, if I give an example: As kids, we tend to group together. Those of you reading this who have been through what is called "Middle School," the intermediate levels of school, like the 6th, 7th, and 8th grades know well what a fierce rite of passage that is. At that age, we are socially more a pool or a group than we are yet individuals, and individuation is just what starts to happen in those years. As puberty is reached, the first Jupiter return at 12 years of age, but more physically the opposition or halfway point in the first Saturn cycle (15 years of age), we begin to lose our childlike and group-clinging tendency and start to take on some of the characteristics of an adult, facial hair, menstrual cycles, and so on.

The intense peer pressure that rules the group mind of the early teens begins to break down as the more independent souls struggle to leave the group and become individuals. The image that many sculptors have worked with of an amorphous mass of clay, out of which individual figures are emerging, should be familiar.

Perhaps you can see in this image where the idea of the Moon being both our mother and our child comes from. We each go through this birthing process and we end up as individual adults, sooner or later. We emerge from the group mind, differentiate ourselves, and can look back not only at where we came from, but also see others there now as we once were. We are gazing at "our" Moon. If we fall back, if we get too close to the past, to the way we were, we run the risk of getting caught in the Moon mass and stifled.

When I was younger I used to return to see my parents, wanting to show them all of the progress I had made, I would often slip-up and get caught up in my old habits with them, resort to stupid arguments, and having them tell me: "See, you have not changed." This is what I mean when I say the Moon can suffocate or pull us back into what we have struggled to get out of by individuation.

The Sun

Now we have looked a little bit at the mystery of the Moon, but really we have only presented one half of the equation. If you remember, it is always Moon-Earth-Sun, and we need to bring the Sun into this discussion.

Just as we pointed out that our life here on Earth needs to keep an appropriate distance from our Moon, less we fall backward, the same is true with the Sun. We cannot get too close to the Sun or, like Icarus, we will be burnt up by the solar rays. The Earth is always somewhere between the Moon on one side, and the Sun on the other, located at just enough distance from the Moon to remain an individual, and just enough distance from the Sun to feel its warmth, but not be burnt up by the solar rays.

If the Moon represents our mother and where we came from, then the Sun represents the father principle and where we are going, what we will become. In the tradition of astrology, the Sun represents the father, the mentor, the one in authority, what we look up to, what we hope to become, and, in general, our future. We come forth from the Moon and we go toward the Sun.

The Sun is also said to represent the Self, and everything about us that is future oriented, what we will become when all is said and done, how we will turn out. When we have finished taking all the changes possible to us, the Sun (our Self) is what remains, our potential realized.

By this point, you should have the idea that this Moon-Earth-Sun relationship is all about how we are balanced between our past (the Moon) and our future (the Sun), not too far and not too close. We are strung out between the past and the future, the Moon and the Sun. Our life on Earth is always somewhere in the middle of these two extremes. We keep our distance from each one. That distance makes life possible.

When the Moon is strong, we remember and are pulled toward our past, perhaps getting caught up in reverie and old habits. If the Moon is too strong, we lose out on our future, and remained mired in the past. When the Sun is strong, we put all that behind us and surge toward the future, coming ever more into our own, but perhaps risking burnout, if we move too far, too fast. The balanced or middle way is the way of even growth.

As astrologers, you already know how to examine the positions of the Sun and the Moon in the chart, their angular separation or phase angle, and measure how strong or weak these two bodies are in the nativity. Is the Moon so strong that it keeps one from the future? Is the client drowning in their past? Or is the Sun too strong and scorching the every attempt to get ahead before it can amount to anything? These are examples of how this esoteric knowledge of the Sun and Moon can be used to advantage. For those interested in more information on the Lights, there is the book I mentioned earlier.

The Outer Planets

Saturn and the Outer Planets

There you have the story of the planets from Saturn into the Sun, and my attempt to point out how the very order of the planets themselves can be a key to how they may be used, a key to our own inner journey of discovery. But what about the outer planets, the planets beyond Saturn: Uranus, Neptune, Pluto and any others still waiting to be found?

It may be helpful, before reading through this article, to understand a little about how I view astrology, which is above all as an oracle. Astrology, in my understanding, speaks to us in its own language. There are many approaches to astrology, and thus many languages or ways to make astrology speak. It is what astrology speaks to us *of* that I consider important, not the words themselves, and not astrology, per se.

We have also to be prepared to hear or listen.

The Transcendental or Outer Planets

What is presented here is most appropriately part of what we could call Shamanic Astrology: initiation and tales of the soul's journey through time. My approach is not meant to be dogmatic, but like all astrological techniques, this is but one of many to better understand our life and life's journey. Please accept it in that tone.

We will now look briefly at the planets that exist beyond the realm of Saturn or time. These external planets are beyond the physical or material (on the outer or the far side), just as the inner planets are beyond the physical on the inside or within Saturn's orbit.

These outer planets are Uranus, Neptune, and Pluto, and the three together have been called the following: Out-of-Body Planets, Transcendental Planets, Metaphysical Planets, After-Death Planets, Planets of the Unconscious, Spiritual Planets, Impersonal Planets, Psychic Planets, and other names. Why these names? What are these outer planets all about?

We could push the limits of language and say that the outer planets are not about anything, not about any "thing," for they are by definition beyond the physical, beyond Saturn. Yet they have a very important message for us and, although this book is primarily about the traditional planets, I will briefly try to present here an overview of the outer planets and how they might be used in counseling.

One reason to include them here is that these outer planets represent in yet another way the same life initiations or rites of passage that we have looked at elsewhere in this book, initiations as seen in the planets or chakras within the sphere of Saturn. These outer planets are the eternal witness and awareness of all that is — the revelation. In other words, these trans-Saturnian planets serve to reveal and emphasize the nature of the inner planets. This will require some explanation.

The Meta-Physical

From the point of view of Shamanic Astrology, the outer or transcendental planets (Uranus, Neptune, Pluto, and any trans-Plutonian planets yet to be discovered) are not stations or experience beyond our physical life in the sense of some next place to get to or land. These outer planets are not physical in the sense that Saturn is physical, for — as pointed out — Saturn is physicality or form itself. The outer planets are by definition beyond Saturn, and are therefore formless or meta-physical.

Because these outer planets are beyond form or Saturn, they are (and can only be) part of the 'revelation' of the physical or internal planets we have already looked at, the planets within (and including) Saturn's limits. The outer planets can but reveal the nature and importance of the inner planets. This is the extent of their power, but as we shall see, this is power indeed.

Pointing Out: Saturn Is Form

It is important here to grasp that Saturn is the realm of form and time, the planet of all physicality, similar to the form of our body that contains all the organs, and in this case all the planets within Saturn, including the great Sun, which of course is not a planet. Saturn is this physicality and form.

Just as we know that Mars has to do with drive and energy, Jupiter with direction and path, so Saturn has always been the planet of form and the physical. It is not enough to simply nod your head that you understand this concept and move on. If it does not deeply register, then what follows is not going to make much sense to you, the fact that the outer planets are not physical, are not physical places or stages. In the context of Shamanic Astrology, these outer planets are beyond form and the physical, thus: meta-physical, the measure of the physical, the sensing of the physical – a mirror.

Astrology here is but a language. We are not talking about putting a space probe on Pluto and sampling soil, but instead we are using astrology here to point to the esoteric meanings of the planets, in this case the outer planets, Uranus, Neptune, and Pluto. Astrology is only a language we use to point to something happening in our lives, and not itself much of an end. Shamanic astrology does not have to correspond exactly to other forms of astrology or to science. There are many astrological languages, and the point is to make them articulate and speak to us.

Saturn is the Physical End

Saturn marks the form and physical end of things. It always has, throughout the long history of astrology, East and West. That physical form contains within itself the great Sun, and all of the planets out to Jupiter. Beyond Saturn, beyond form itself, we have the outer planets, which are by the above definition, formless and non-physical. What can they mean or point to? What is their use?

I have mentioned elsewhere in this book that each of us is born and grows our personal body over time, and in time. Every body is mature and complete, physically, when Saturn returns at 29.4 years of age. There is no more physical growth from that time forward, unless you want to include middle-age spread, but that is not what we mean here by growth. The physical body is finished growing by the Saturn return. It has reached its physical peak and is mature. This is what we are speaking of here. At that time, the physical body is not going to get any better. There will be no "more."

The Prime of Life

Beyond maturity or the prime of life, it is downhill for every body. There is not a higher peak of physical prowess to be obtained. Like the trajectory of a missile, our body (if exercised and cared for) will reach a peak, maintain its form for a while, and then eventually begin to fall and fail. We all know this is true. It is true for every body, human or otherwise.

Therefore, the planets beyond Saturn, beyond the physical, will not bring us any more physicality or form. They cannot. If we are looking for more of that, then the outer planets can only testify or prove to us that there is no more increase of form to be expected. By this same definition, we can say that these outer planets will reveal this fact as a natural by-product of getting to know them, by using them as an oracle. And in this regard, the outer planets are indeed very oracular. Astrology, at heart, is an oracle, albeit a complex one. It speaks to us.

If we are used (during the first 30-year cycle of Saturn) to something always being added on in the form realm, to there always being something "new," then we will not find (physically speaking) any more "new" as we move beyond that 30-year Saturn cycle and begin to pick up on the cycles of the outer planets.

Straight Lines Curve

If we have been caught up in the exposition of Saturn, as it makes its first cycle after our birth, which ends at 29.4 years, we may have become used to thinking of time as linear, as a straight line or linear journey that we have been on. This is a common and quite natural mistake that most of us make.

When Saturn completes its return, and turns to repeating itself (going over the same degrees of the zodiac for the second time), that linear sense starts to fade in our minds, and the idea of a circle begins to dawn for us. The straighter the line, the finer the curve.

Before and through the Saturn return, most of us are used to conceiving our life along a time line, in a linear format. Time in this view stretches on into the future, with birth at one end and death at the other. This is the common view, a time line from birth to death.

But with the Saturn return, this linear sense of time begins to be challenged by the essential circularity (cycles) of life, the tendency for all things to repeat or cycle. This is for most a major initiation, and a source of great confusion for many.

The Straighter the Line, the Finer the Curve

I am not suggesting here that this is a sudden realization. For most, it is not. In fact, this altered sense of time, as a cycle or circle is very, very gradual for most, and apparently non-existent for some, at least awareness of it. The ingrained time as a "straight line" theory is slow to give way to the reality of time as returns, and returning — cyclic.

Yet, beyond the 30-year Saturn return, time stops as we have come to know it, and begins to repeat itself, to go over the same ground (zodiac-wise) for the second time around. This is what we might term a climacteric event, one with far-reaching implications, and one that should be studied in a section by itself. Here, we will just touch on the main articulation points, but I have gone into this in much greater depth elsewhere in this book.

The Physical End of Life

At our Saturn return, we as a thing or body are complete, and we (our body) are launched beyond time itself for the first time. Time as we have come to know it up to that point just stops. Let's take a quick review of what this kind of time suggests.

Up to this point throughout our life, Saturn or form has been positing or declaring itself zodiac degree by zodiac degree. Over the course of our formative years, the activities of the inner planets, which complete their initial circle or cycle around the Sun, one by one, have caught our attention, each in their turn. This too is explained elsewhere in much greater detail.

But after our Jupiter return falls to repetition at around 12 years of age, we can perhaps begin to pick up on Saturn's story. And the second Jupiter return, around 24-years of age, marks a real turning point for tuning in to what Saturn is (and has been) laying down all this time. We could mark these first 30 years as the track or line of time (as we mentioned earlier), this almost unavoidable sense of linearity, of time seemingly stretching endlessly toward the future – going on forever.

The Bewildering Display of Time

Keep in mind, here, that all during our first 30 years, Saturn is developing or positing the form or physical experience that we have up to this point. It is all that we have known, and it is captivating. It would seem that each of us is fascinated, if not entranced, by the seeming-endless (often bewildering) display of form and new experience. As I pointed out, there is a quite natural assumption that this stream of new experience will go on forever, and that this is just the nature of life. Like the proverbial deer in the headlights, we are caught up in this bewildering display of time.

When Time Stops

It is my contention here (in the esoteric sense) that time literally stops as Saturn reaches its return and turns to repeating itself, as it begins going over a section of the zodiac for a second time – around thirty years of age.

This is not an "Aha!" experience for us. Most don't get it all at once, and some never seem to get it at all. Instead, as Saturn falls to repetition in our experience, that sense of something new as always appearing at the "present" point of our timeline fades. It falls away. There is nothing further physically forthcoming. There is no more "more." You have it. This is it! There is a great silence that sets in.

For most people, this is not easily recognized, but mostly at first somehow intuited. They "feel" different. Something has changed, but they don't know what it is just yet. Some part of their deeper consciousness is monitoring all this, and they sense a gap or change in their experience, but can't quite put their finger on it, Dylan's "You don't know what it is, do you Mr. Jones."

Entering the Silence

In the Western esoteric tradition, this has been referred to as "Entering the Silence," for the great motor of time has been turned off for the first time. The rush and roar of time that has been there all our life fades to silence.

My esoteric teacher, who was a traveling initiator in a Rosicrucian order, had his own way of explaining this concept to me, and I will pass this on to you, since I found it totally helpful myself.

He spoke of this whole Saturn-return transition as being like the launching of a rocket into outer space. Our time within the Saturn cycle, until we reach its return at roughly age 30, is the time during which we can work on and build our own personal space capsule. We are still grounded, so to speak, and have all the tools and resources we might need to construct as perfect a vehicle as we can manage.

The Vehicle is Launched

At the Saturn return (29.4 years heliocentrically), that vehicle is launched, ready or not, well-built or not-so-well-built. Literally, there is no more time after that to work on the vehicle. The physical growth or development has reached an end. For better or for worse, our vehicle is finished and launched as we enter the space beyond Saturn or time, what we could call here: outer space, the space outside what we had been up to that point enclosed within — a major initiation.

Our journey beyond the realm of time (Saturn) to a very great degree depends on our vehicle, how it was constructed, how well it was made, and so on. We are literally floating out there, beyond time, floating in that space beyond time, if that phrase makes any sense.

One Generation

If you are older than thirty years of age, you are already out there beyond time. For many people, this transition is not consciously registered and seemingly not a great problem. They are oblivious to it, or so it seems. However, for others, this transition can be very problematical. In particular, those who begin to awaken to this experience (and try to put all the pieces together) may not understand what they are going through, and even become fearful, frightened.

And it is this group that can benefit from some form of shamanic astrology, some spiritual handholding and guidance. And there can be so many questions that occur to those making this transition. A spiritual friend or guide to these regions can be a friend indeed, and serve us in good stead.

The Outer Planets

And thus the whole concept of the outer planets, the planets outside Saturn's grip, comes up. How are they to be understood?

Of course, we have quite a long history now of using these outer planets in astrology, so I am assuming you already have that. What is being presented here is not in any way contrary to that material, but rather our focus here is on what shamanic astrology can bring to the picture. Let me try to describe this.

Using the linear sense of time we discussed above, as we hit our Saturn return at 29.4 years of age, it is like driving out of town and hitting the outskirts. Suddenly, there are no more houses, no more stores, no more "town," and we are looking down a line of highway that is empty, and perhaps, we hope, going somewhere. To our eyes, it appears to stretch out toward what we have always viewed as the future. It is what we are used to. It has always been something like this for us, time as a line going somewhere.

A One-Way Street

Now imagine that as we drive out from town along this straight highway, we encounter three signs, much like those of us who are older used to see as a series of signs for products, like the old Burma Shave slogans of the 1950s, that had one phrase on each sign, things like:

> A guy who drives,
> A car wide open,
> Is not thinkin',
> He's just hopin',
>
> Burma Shave.

Sorry, but I had to do that. Well, in our case there are just three of these signs at this point, in the order Uranus, Neptune, and Pluto. We can add more, as more trans-plutonian planets are added, but they will ALL tell the same story. And what is that story?

That story is as simple as that there is nothing more out there, no place to get to or go to, AND you had best turn around or at least take a look back over your shoulder at what you are leaving: all of the planets and bodies within Saturn's orbit. If you do look, this is what is called "discovering your inner life." If it happens all at once, it has been called "discovering your Self." It is the physical point of no return, and, therefore, a major (perhaps THE major) turning point in a life.

The esoteric principle here is that the only thing to be seen when you get out of the body is the body itself, just as we gaze at Earth from the space shuttle. Out-of-body experiences are a vantage point only and not a place to get to.

Sidebar: Out of the Body Experiences

So much has been made (and is still being made) about out-of-the-body experiences, astral travel, and related experiences. And this is just what we are describing here, ecstatic experiences, how we exit the body, and pass from that body to a more subtle experience of all things.

There are scores of books about out-of-the-body experiences. And although these books appear quite exotic, for the most part, if you read them with the concepts being presented here, they will make more than a little sense. Out-of-the-body experiences are not uncommon. In fact, they are ubiquitous and universally experienced by all of us, all of the time. Our consciousness is always moving in and out of our body, but starting with our Saturn return, many of us begin to consciously experience this and remember those experiences. What may have been rare up to this point (the Saturn return) is an awareness of what we all experience, this passing beyond time and the physical, to the metaphysical — beyond the physical.

Somewhat of a Big Deal

This trans-Saturnian view is not a minor piece of information for most of us, those of us who have been assuming that there IS something out there all those years, that there is much more of something waiting for us along this linear road of time, and especially perhaps something for us at the end of that road, like heaven or hell. The usual scenario: we are trying to proceed along our straight timeline, as we always have up to that point, and here are signs that are telling us to "Go Back!" What are we to think?

I hope by now you are beginning to get the general idea. These outer, transcendental, planets are not physical, in that they are (by definition) beyond Saturn or the physical. They have been called the meta-physical planets, and rightly so. They are not going to manifest in a physical way. They are meta-physical, that is: beyond the physical.

However, these outer planets can (and do) reveal the physical, perhaps in a new light. They are planets of revelation, and the only thing tangible (physical) they can reveal or render is the physical world and all that is within it, the same old physical world we are used to, but now viewed differently. And this is what they, in fact, do.

Revelation and Rendering

What do we mean by "revelation?" Revelation is just that, a true revelation, and in the biblical sense: a revealing of the true nature and sheer importance of the Sun, Moon, and planets out to and including Saturn.

And what do we mean by the statement that the outer planets "render" the inner planets? We are using the word "render" here in its sense of "to give back" or "hand over." The outer planet initiation can give back to us that which we have come to take for granted and perhaps lost an appreciation for, including our entire sense of the Self.

By saying that the outer planets are the revelation of the inner planets, it is meant that the outer planets are the realization (growing awareness of) of the absolute value of the inner planets. The outer planets, like a rear-view mirror, are really all about the inner planets, the value of which is being pointed out by exposure to the outer planets. We learn to value what we formerly took for granted. With one foot firmly on Earth, we might think to step out with the other off the Earth, but we only sink back into Earth, because there is no other place to step to. We are stuck with the Earth and thus begin to see if differently.

The View from Earth

When astronauts leave Earth, what is it that they see and most commonly photograph from the trip? It is not the dark and starry cky beyond the earth — the relative emptiness of space. No, it is Earth itself, that great blue and white planet that looks so awesome and peaceful from a distance. That is what we all look at and see. This is key.

In the same way, when we emerge beyond our Saturn return, the most important thing for us to see is not outer space, but inner space, the space within, including the Sun, planets, and Saturn. We discover not what is out there, but what we just left or are leaving. There is nothing out there, but we now know it. This is just common sense.

Saturn represents the physical form of things, and planets beyond Saturn are beyond the physical form and are non-physical. As my teacher would say to me, they are "transcend dental," and he would snap his teeth together, literally beyond the dental or physical. It may take time to understand this, but it is time worth taking. These outer planets will not add one iota to the physical world, because, as pointed out, that is the domain of Saturn.

The outer planets are the realization of the rest of the solar system, the Sun and all the planets, their production and the presentation. We indicate this in that, for the most part, these outer planets are by age (return) longer or beyond the personal experience. We each of us don't live that long, so they are what we have yet to fully know, even through death. They mark the aura of the solar system, and point back to the Sun center, and not beyond to deep space. They reflect.

Lineages: Outer Planets

In a very real sense, these outer planets' cycles are of a duration longer than an average lifetime. For sure, the 84-year cycle of Uranus is now within range of the average lifespan, at least here in the West, but that was not necessarily true when it was discovered. Neptune and Pluto's orbits are, of course, well beyond any one person's lifetime. We don't personally live that long.

This fact, itself, is of interest. We could say as fact that a single person will not manage to encompass all the degrees of the zodiac these outer planets cover within their personal experience in a lifetime, and that, because of that, in a real sense we do not and cannot personally "know" the whole nature of these planets.

I suggest that this may very well be why there are groups, brotherhoods, and lineages of an esoteric nature. Some of this information, which we cannot experience ourselves, may be passed on from mouth to ear, above ground so to speak, and may not travel through the womb-birth process. This is pure speculation on my part, but something that makes a certain amount of sense. Does it not? There are indeed many whispered stories of what is beyond life.

Outer Planets in the Chart

One common question that we can clear up right away is: If the outer planets are not physical in the sense that Saturn and the planets it contains within its orbit are physical, how can we use them in the astrology chart? That is: if the outer planets' only purpose is to reveal the true nature of the inner planets, then what do they mean in themselves? Do they have no intrinsic meaning?

First, most of you are already using the outer planets in the chart, and nothing you will learn here will alter that fact. The point to grasp is that, since we can agree that Saturn rules the physical, the outer planet meanings will still be communicated mostly through the physical, through some form or another, which is all the touchy-feely-ness that we know in this life.

All form comes or is expressed through Saturn, of course. We could equally say the same thing about Mercury, Venus, Earth, Mars, and Jupiter. They do not represent or rule the physical, but are revealed to us through the everyday physical life each of us lives. When we get physical, we are speaking of Saturn (perhaps interdependent with another planet), and if we want to examine the physical effects of planets like Mars or Neptune, then Saturn (form) will be involved in some way. This, again, is by definition.

How Do Outer Planets Manifest?

So the question to ask is how do the outer planets (Uranus, Neptune, and Pluto) manifest to us, physically or in any other way? And the answer is: just as they already are manifesting, and have been manifesting in our astrological charts, since their discovery.

We are not replacing any experience we might have with these outer planets, but just enhancing (or fulfilling) that experience. Here we are showing how these outer planets can be used to tell a shamanic story, a journey each soul takes. That is what we should take away from this presentation: that aside from separate planetary concepts, these outer planets describe or point out an inner journey of discovery we all take, that we all are taking. It is that journey that we are pointing to here, and that story is part of any Shamanic Astrology. For clarity's sake, let's summarize what has been presented here relating to the outer planets.

As we pass the age of 30 years, our sense that time is a linear line running from birth to our death at old age begins to fade. When we are past our physical prime, there is nothing more physical being added on. We stop growing physically. In the physical sense, we have nothing more to look forward to.

Up to this point, we may have intellectually thought about this fact, but we have not known it through experience. Now we begin to experience it. Suddenly we are past our prime, however marginally this might impact us at first. This fact may be unspoken, but its silence speaks volumes.

Suddenly the life line we have been on does not have the same kind of future it did when we were growing up, when we were within Saturn's orbit and grip. We are looking at decline and eventual failure, not at growing (physically speaking) any more or better. This fact gives us pause. No longer does the linear line of life point onward toward "more." In fact, it points onward toward less, and to ever increasingly less. Most of us are not in a hurry to go there.

In fact, perhaps for the first time in our lives, we pause and perhaps even turn around and begin to look back, back at where we came from. We can't go back into what we came out from, but we (most of us anyway) begin to view our past with more appreciation. Nostalgia of some sort usually sets it. Where before we always looked forward toward the future, now we begin to look back at the past, but with a new understanding.

The three outer planets, Uranus, Neptune, and Pluto are waypoints or markers on that linear journey we have been on up to this point. Rather than adding something more on, these transcendental planets take something away, if only our ignorance. In turn, they gently (Uranus and Neptune) and then not-so-gently (Pluto) inform us to "go no farther" in this linear direction, but instead to turn or circle back on what we came from, and to cherish that.

If all the earlier years we thought that we were going somewhere in our line of life, the outer planets reveal to us ever increasingly that there is no place to go to other than where we have already been. Another way to say this is that the place we have to go to is to value and cherish what we have already been given. We will be given no more, other than that information.

Uranus, Neptune, and Pluto bring us that message, at first through this insight described here (Uranus), then through acceptance of the fact (Neptune), and finally through direct experience that life is circular or cyclical and not linear (Pluto). A whole book should be written about this outer-planet journey. Here we will just briefly say something about these three metaphysical planets.

The Outer Planets: A Step toward Interpretation

Although this section is not primarily material on outer-planet interpretation, it would be a shame to leave you without a quick tour of that realm. Here are some keyword-style interpretations for each of the outer planets, and a just a bit of their shamanic story.

The Uranus Journey

Uranus Keywords: "To see eternity in a grain of sand."

Uranus represents our keyhole beyond day-to-day reality into the future, and has to do (so modern astrology tells us) with discovery, invention, and insights. "To see eternity in a grain of sand," that is Uranus, finding new uses for everyday objects. It has come to stand for anything out of the ordinary: the unusual, eccentric, unconventional, novel, and innovative. It also brings independence, rebellion, and revolution. It is the opposite, reverse, or undoing of Saturn.

Uranus is the first planet beyond the Saturn cycle, and it brings the first glimpse of the breaking up of the saturnine grip on us, with flashes of insight and recognition, brief glimpses of the more general awareness that is to come.

Through Uranus, each bit and part of Saturn's physicality becomes a lens through which we can peek and see a glimpse of eternity, the eternal process of awakening that awaits each of us beyond time or Saturn. Uranus is ever the planet of inventors and inventions, of lightning-fast insights, of discovery, and new ways of seeing things. Makes sense, does it not?

When Saturn releases its hold on us, and starts to break up, when we begin to glimpse or see through the chinks in time's armor to what is beyond time, that is the function and sign of the planet Uranus. It is the lightning insight, where physical time itself becomes the lens into something beyond time. "To See Eternity in a Grain of Sand" as the poet William Blake put it; that is the work of the planet Uranus.

Every grain of Saturn, every physical part and form, in and of time, becomes a window for us into eternity. At first, there are just lightning flashes that light up our awareness for brief moments, glimpses into another world, the timeless. But these flashes, as time progresses, as time fails to hold our gaze, become longer and light up more and more of our inner sky, until at long last the great Sun dawns, and we have constant light. It dawns on us. We get the idea. Our spiritual life begins. This constant light is the province of Neptune, which we will get to next.

The Neptune Journey

Neptune Keywords: "The dewdrop slips into the shining sea."

Neptune traditionally represents compassion, acceptance, unity, and universal love. "The dewdrop slips into the shining sea," is what this planet is about, anything to do with communion, and non-separateness. Neptune rules the imagination, dreams, mysticism and inspiration, including music, movies, film, and anything related to our ideas and images.

If the Uranian experience involves flashes of insight, then experience of Neptune dawns slowly and evenly. Neptune is more like the finale at a fireworks; it ever-increasingly lights up our entire inner sky. Through Uranus, we break through Saturn and began to discover our inner life. With Neptune comes the dawn, and it is like the Sun coming up. With Neptune we can at last get our arms around the whole idea, in this case the whole world. Our process of self discovery has gone beyond counting mere glimpses and insights, and into a cacophony of light. We finally get the whole idea, that beyond life as we knew it, we find that same life, alive and well, but now within us — our inner life. As Sir Edwin Arnold so aptly put it, "The Dewdrop Slips into the Shining Sea." Neptune is the archetype of the "big picture," the Grand Trine illumination of the planets.

With Neptune, we reach the point where we not only realize that we are now outside time or Saturn, but that we have (and we have always have had) an inner life, and that the same hard-edged life we grew up in and through is now something to be cherished and cared for.

Neptune embraces life, and with no exceptions. It is pure compassion, and everything is valued equally. In the Buddhist hierarchy, Neptune represents the Bodhisattva, the one who vows to care for and cherish all sentient beings until every last one reaches enlightenment.

The idea here is that what we discover in the planets beyond Saturn is not something out there beyond Saturn to "get," but the true fact that there IS nothing else out there. This is what we can call the turning point, and as we turn, we discover the life we left and grew up in and through, to be the only game in town. As the philosopher Parmenides so eloquently put it: "Being alone is." In other words, there are not two, but only one. Neptune is our finally discovering that one.

Uranus provides insights and flashes into this fact, and Neptune illuminates our inner sky with full daylight as to this truth, which leaves Pluto.

The Pluto Journey: Identification is Circulation.

Pluto Keywords: "Touch me if you are!"

In the tradition of astrology, Pluto points to deep inner change and transformation, always touching the raw nerve, just where we are the most sensitive and vulnerable. If we can't stand to look change in the eye, Pluto brings it about by force, if necessary. For many, this has to do with our thoughts of death, dying, and what rebirth is all about.

Thus far, each planet beyond Saturn brings home the point to us that looking outside or down linear time will never work. Uranus and Neptune point out that we must turn around and look within to find what we are looking for. Therefore, speculation about finding more and more planets beyond Pluto, whether they be large or small should be tempered with the fact that we cannot hope to get any different message from them, even when they are found.

They will all tell the same story to us, and that is: Look no farther out there. Turn around and begin to look within, embrace what you already have. It is precious. That is the key. Of course philosophers and poets have been telling us this for centuries. Regardless of how many more bodies will be found out there at the edge of the solar system, their meaning will all be the same: look within.

Pluto represents that message more clearly than the insights of Uranus and the embracement of Neptune. If Uranus is breaking out, and Neptune is turning back and embracing all that is, then Pluto is the knowledge that this whole process will repeat itself, endlessly. It is one thing to discover our inner or spiritual life (Uranus), another to embrace it fully (Neptune), but yet a very different thing again to grasp that we will do all this again, and that we don't only go around once, as the beer commercial would have it, but we go around again and again.

Pluto is the planet of reincarnation and that experience, not as an abstract idea on the pages of a book, but as a vital realization of the nature of life. Pluto is the experience that all life, all people, and all sentient beings are us, and that when we look into a young person's eyes, we are seeing ourselves, not as an abstract thought, but seeing ourselves in the (and through the) eyes of a child. That is Pluto, daring to see that the "them" out there in the world is you. The light in the child's eye is you looking at yourself. Pluto has only recently been discovered (relatively speaking), and its message is still being sorted out. I associate Pluto with the rise of modern psychology and everything that this entails. This planet is still somewhat hard to put into words.

All of our life we have been the center and the light shines from our eyes outward – radiance. The Pluto initiation is that we see the light shining from other's eyes and we have become the radiance. Think about that. A reversal.

Uranus is pretty clear by now, as to its meaning in astrology. When our Saturn construct (physical body) begins to self-destruct and to fall apart (and it does for each one of us), Uranus has to do with the holes or chinks in time's armor through which we peer and glimpse a larger reality, something beyond time.

Neptune has to do with the state when the peep holes in Saturn's grip are larger than what remains of our linear sense of time. When there is more light than shadow, the dawn comes and that has to do with Neptune, and the cherishing or embracing of all that is. In Neptune, we are outside and able to embrace our inner life, to savor each moment and fact. Yet up to this point we are still dealing with subject and object, self and other — whatever you want to name it.

Pluto carries us beyond the experience of cherishing, the experience of Neptune where we are the subject and the world and other people are the object of our care.

With Pluto, the distinction between subject and object is lost forever and the experience of our own inner light is identical with the light looking out at us from eyes of a child. Perhaps the best keyword for Pluto is "identification," to identify yourself with another, without the dualism of subject and object.

And being now beyond the grip of Saturn, younger folk are not going to see the Sun in us, but only darkness or, if we are realized somewhat, they can see their own reflection in us. That is what a teacher is all about.

All these words here are very abstract and fail to communicate the very direct experience that Pluto provides us, the in-your-face presence of complete identification of "I am you" and "You are me." As you can see, words fail, which is as it should be.

Let's just say by way of Pluto that "identification is circulation," the lifeblood of the cosmos knowing itself through us, through our eyes. Identification is nothing more than the circulation of cosmic knowledge, and the Pluto experience is as close as we come to realizing this fact. It is through constant identification that the universe we live in communicates with itself and continues to cohere or exist.

There you have a brief introduction to the outer planets, from more of a shamanic point of view.

The Fixed Stars And Beyond

The Fixed Stars

The space beyond the outer planets is not empty, but filled with all kinds of matter: stars, nebulae, quasars, black holes, and other deep space matter. Although there is a lot of matter scattered out in space, it is not evenly distributed, not even remotely so. Most of the matter in the universe beyond our solar system is severely grouped or clustered in just a few areas of the heavens. In fact, clustering is the rule, not the exception with stellar matter.

Stars tend to occur in small groups. These groups are themselves part of still larger groups and, as the size of the groups increases, it is clear that they cling to one another to form vast stellar planes. The most obvious plane is the plane of our local galaxy. When the galactic plane is overhead on a summer night in the Northern hemisphere, it is a blazing mass of stars, packed together in a single narrow zone.

As mentioned, stars are not randomly placed out in space, but hang out together in a group. Even stars that appear as singletons are usually just stars so near that we can't pick up on the group to which they belong. We are right in the middle of the group ourselves.

Everything out there in space is all about stars, about their lives and deaths. Stars, like people, are born, live for a while, and then fade out and die. Even exotic stellar objects like black holes, quasars, neutron stars, and supernovae are simply stars in one stage of their lives or another. And the vast gaseous wraith-like nebulae are nothing more than clouds of gas in which proto stars (young stars) are born. It is all about the life and death of stars. That's all there is. Period. What else did you expect?

In our inner and esoteric sky, the fixed stars that shine are what serve to guide us through the dark hallways of life. Here there is not space for a thorough discussion of the fixed stars and other deep space objects. I wrote a book on this deep-space astrology that was published in 1976, called "Astrophysical Directions", and more detail can be found there. It has been republished as "The Astrology of Space" and is in paperback on Amazon.com.

If you have read this far in the book, you must have some general idea as to how to approach getting at the esoteric meaning of exoteric facts and signs. Let's give you a test. In what follows, I will present a rough description of the fixed stars, along with their life and death cycle. I will stick more toward the scientific facts about these bodies. Let's see if you can follow the life story of the stars and apply it to your life, based on the chakra-based material given earlier in this book. I will give you some hints as we go along.

The Life and Death of Stars

Once born, each star must live and die, much like us. The death of stars is inevitable and the life process is often conceived as one of thwarting or putting off of this inescapable death and thus prolonging life. The most fascinating aspect of a star's life is the intense struggle between the forces of gravity and contraction on one hand (so called outer forces — Saturn) and the internal forces of radiation pressure on the other (solar). As long as there is radiation coming from within, the forces of gravitational contraction are resisted or balanced, and stellar life as we observe it continues. The star shines. In fact, the entire life of the star can be conceived of in terms of a continuous conversion process.

Within each star, these two archetypical forces form the stellar shell, which is well below the actual surface of the star itself. The thickness of this shell as well as its position near to or far from the inner stellar core suffers continual change and adjustment throughout the life of the star. In the end, the inner comes to the surface and is out.

The incredible weight of the many layers of gas first initiates and then continues to contain and maintain the radiant process — a cosmic crucible. This pressure and the inevitable collapse that must occur in time is forestalled and put off by an incredible series of adjustments and changes going on within the core of the star. First of all, hydrogen burning (initiated at the birth of the star) continues for around ten billion years. This constitutes a healthy chunk of the stellar lifetime. Our sun is about halfway through this stage at present, and we can expect the sun to continue as it is today for another five billion years or so.

However, the eventual exhaustion of hydrogen signals the onset of drastic changes in the life of the star and brings on the next stage in that life.
The radiant pressure of burning hydrogen within was all that held back the initial contraction of the protostar, and when this is gone (like with the Saturn return) the star's core continues to contract. It then has no material strong enough to stop this contraction and the core again shrinks, causing increased pressure, density and temperature. When the temperature at the center of the star reaches 100 million degrees, the

nuclei of helium atoms (products of the hydrogen burning stage) are violently fused together to form carbon.

The fusion of this helium burning at the stellar core again produces a furious outpouring of radiant energy, and this energy release inside the star's core (as the star contracts) pushes the surface far out into space in all directions. The sudden expansion creates an enormous star with a diameter of a quarter of a billion miles and a low surface temperature between 3,000-4,000 degrees — a red giant (the Jupiter Chakra). Born again.

In about five billion years, the core of our sun will collapse, while its surface expands. This expansion will swallow the earth and our planet will vanish in a puff of smoke. Red stars like Antares and Arcturus are examples of this stage and kind of star.

This helium burning stage (red giant) continues for several hundred million years before exhaustion. With the helium gone, the contraction process again resumes and still greater temperatures, densities, and pressures result. At this point, the size or mass of the star begins to dictate the final course of the life. For very massive stars, the ignition of such thermonuclear reactions as carbon, oxygen, and silicon fusion may take place, creating all of the heavier elements. These later stages in stellar evolution produce stars that are very unstable. These stars can vary or pulsate in size and luminosity. In certain cases this can lead to a total stellar detonation, a supernova.

A star may end its life in one of several ways. When all the possible nuclear fuels have been exhausted, all conversions or adjustments made, the inexorable force of gravity (the grave) asserts itself and the remaining stellar material becomes a white dwarf. As the star continues to contract, having no internal radiation pressure left, the pressures and densities reach such strength that the very atoms are torn to pieces and the result is a sea of electrons in which are scattered atomic nuclei. This mass of electrons is squeezed until there is no possible room for contraction. The resulting white dwarf begins the long process of cooling off.

Becoming a white dwarf is only possible for stars with a mass of less than 1.25 solar masses. If the dying star has a mass that is greater than this limit, the electron pressure cannot withstand the gravitational pressure and the contraction continues. This critical limit of I.25 solar masses is termed the Chandrasekhar Limit after the famous Indian scientist by that name.

To avoid this further contraction, it is believed that many stars unload or blow off enough excess mass to get within the Chandrasekhar Limit (middle-age crisis). The nova is an example of an attempt of this kind. In recent years it has become clear that not all stars are successful in discarding their excess mass, and for them a very different state results than what we find in the white dwarf. We have seen that the electron pressure is not strong enough to halt the contraction process and the star gets smaller and tighter. The pressure and density increase until the electrons are squeezed into the nuclei of the atoms out of which the star is made. At this point the negatively charged electrons combine with the positively charged protons and the resulting neutron force is strong enough to again halt the contraction process and we have another type of stellar corpse: a neutron star.

We have one further kind of "dying" star. There is a limit to the size of star that can become a neutron star. Beyond a limit in mass of 2.25 solar masses, the degenerate neutron pressure cannot withstand the forces of gravity. If the dying star is not able to eject enough matter through a nova or supernova explosion and the remaining stellar core contains more than three solar masses, it cannot become a white dwarf or a neutron star. In this case there are no forces strong enough to hold up the star and the stellar core continues to shrink infinitely! The gravitational field surrounding the star gets so strong that space-time begins to warp and when the star has collapsed to only a few miles in diameter, space-time folds in upon itself and the star vanishes from the physical universe. What remains is termed a black hole.

It should be clear at this point that all of the many kinds of stars and objects in space could be ordered in terms of the evolutionary stage they represent in the life of the star. Just as each of us face what has been called the "personal equation" in our lives, so each star's life is made possible by the opposing internal and external forces. In the end, it appears, the forces of gravity dominate the internal process of adjustment and conversion that is taking place, just as in our own lives the aging of our personal bodies is a fact.

And yet fresh stars are forming and being born, even now. The process of life or self is somehow larger than the physical ends to the personal life of a star or a man and our larger life is a whole or continuum and continuing process that we are just beginning to appreciate. Some of the ideas that are emerging in regard to the black hole phenomenon are most profound and perhaps are the closest indicators we have of how the eternal process of our life, in fact, functions. Hint: true teachers are like black holes.

In conclusion, a very useful way to approach the fixed stars, as pointed out above, is to determine what stage in stellar evolution a particular star may be. Is the star a young, energetic newly formed star in the blue part of the spectrum or an old dying (red colored) star? Are we talking about a white dwarf or a super dense neutron star? I have found this approach to the endless millions of stars to much more helpful than ascribing particular characteristics to existing stars and objects, most of which are too new to have any history in astrology anyway. As mentioned earlier, learn to read the writings of science from a personal or esoteric astrological perspective. It is very instructive.

The Solar Mysteries

Our Self and Sun

In this modern era, the esoteric traditions of the West and the East are being examined and compared. For the most part, Western thinking is becoming aware of Eastern thought and, rightly so; we are going to school on that. This difference between these two views, East and West, is perhaps nowhere clearer than in the concept of the Self.

Here in the West, the concept of the Self has been, and still is, considered important, if not central to our thinking. I would vote on "central," and it is very much a love-hate sort of thing.

On the one hand we are, from childhood onward, exhorted to get to know our Self, to find or discover our Self, and above all to "be" our Self. At the same time, we are told by almost every spiritual and religious persuasion to not be selfish, to not think of our Self too much, or not think only of our Self, but rather to think of others. In fact, we are asked to put the needs of others above those of our own Self. And then we wonder about schizophrenia. What is this all about?

In modern Western astrology, virtually in all traditions, the identifying of the Self (whatever we might agree that is) with the Sun is standard. The Sun, at least in standard geocentric astrology, is considered synonymous with the Sun. A legitimate question might be: are we talking here about the Sun as in "Sun Sign" astrology (where Earth sees the sun in the sign opposite where it is), or are we speaking of that great fiery orb, the center of the solar system?

The answer from my understanding is: both. The Sun as the Self is a standard correspondence in Western astrology. This is not so in the East, and we will get to that in a moment. For now, let's say more about this Western astrological identification of the Sun as the Self, and the Sun having to do with self development and the like.

The Sun, so most astrological definitions go, is who we are in essence, our very Self. It is also our goals, who we are aiming to be, what we will become in the future after we finish going through all our major changes. We will end up there. The Sun is as much into the future as the Moon represents the past. I won't spend a lot of time on the common definition of the "Sun as Self," as most of you already know this or can Google it in a few minutes.

I want to return to this dichotomy of the Sun as being who we are in essence, or the essential Self we will (or are trying to) become, and the endless admonitions on every side to not be selfish. How can we be asked to find or discover ourselves on one hand, but to not be "self-ish" on the other. Which is it?

Well, the answer, of course, is both, and this is the source of the confusion here. It would seem that, no matter how we try to be unselfish, every road of inward discovery leads to our Self. It is our Self that is somehow "in there" and stands like the proverbial guardian on the threshold. When we try to find our selves, and to look inward, we come across no other than our Self. That is what we have been told to find. And yet, we are told not to take our Self too seriously, not to get too enamored or attached to our Self, and to try to put thoughts of our Self out of our mind, or at least on the back burner. Hey, don't be so selfish!

I THINK I AM

I have gone to paint the sunrise in the sky,
To feel the cool of night warm into day,
The flowers from the ground call up to me,
This Self I think I am is hard to see.

The Self in the East

Now, let's take a break and look at the Eastern concept of the Self. For the most part, there is none. The Self does not play a prominent part in Eastern astrology or, for that matter, in their psychology or philosophy. Moreover, where it does appear, the Self is pegged straight away as an illusion, something that has no substantial reality — a phantom.

Instead of being told not to be selfish, in the Eastern philosophy, we are told, instead, to examine the Self and to see what it is. For example, Buddhist poetry is filled with images to the effect that the Self is the only cloud in an otherwise cloudless sky, and is the single greatest factor in our not seeing the true nature of the mind. In this tradition, in a very real sense, the Self is equivalent to ignorance — to our ignoring the true nature of the mind.

In Eastern psychology, the Self is considered but an illusion, what these philosophers call a "composite," meaning it has no true existence, but is (roughly speaking) a particularly ingrained collection of mental habits that we become attached to and continue to identify with. It is this habitual identification or "identity" that here in the West, we call our "Self." Only here in the West, although self-examination is often advised, there is no methodology as to how this might be done. It is more like a punishment, than a direction.

In the East, they don't identify. This is not to say that they do not have the experience of what here in the West we call our self, but rather that this "self" is considered not only "nothing substantial" in itself (so to speak), but only a stepping stone to actually discovering the true nature of our mind, albeit a rather large stone.

Here in the West, this same self is considered by many somehow the goal and point of all our inner searching and discovery, that is: Self discovery. We seek to find ourselves. There any number of books out there on how to find ourselves or how to find our true Self. Self discovery is way more than just a cottage industry. It is a way of life, spiritually speaking, here in the West.

Seeing the Self

I assume that we can agree on how here in the West the Self is enshrined on the one hand, and banned (love of self) on the other. I covered that earlier. Let's look more closely at the Eastern view of the self as a composite, as something that has no true existence. This lack of existence of the self has some more important ramifications when thoughts of life after death are involved, and if a composite self can, by that very token, have no personal future. This has to be one of the stumbling blocks that keep the concept of a Self so close to us.

As written elsewhere in this book, it is a real misfortune that the idea of meditation here in the West amounts to something like relaxation therapy, while in the East meditation is a very precise journey into the true nature of the mind, step by step. Yes, it is true that beginning meditation requires that the mind be quieted or calmed, but this is not the end result or goal of meditation. Calmness is not the primary goal of meditation, but just a preliminary step. In other words, until the mind is calm, we can't see beyond the endless activity of our mind into its true nature. Since most that meditate here in the West never manage to calm their minds, then the successive steps remain mostly unknown to us, thus the popular concept that meditation is (somehow) just relaxation, trying to calm down.

In the East, when the mind is calmed or quieted down, the teacher proceeds to give what are called the "pointing out" Instructions, and this pointing out is considered the next major step in the process of examining the mind or meditation. There are probably endless ways that the nature of the mind can be pointed out.

And be clear that pointing out the nature of the mind is not the end result of meditation instructions, but just the next step after the mind is quieted enough to work with. When we grasp or see the true nature of the mind, that is not enlightenment, but just the beginning of real meditation practice. A common analogy in the tradition of meditation is that what the teacher points out to the student is like pointing out a wild stallion running in a field. As my teacher puts it:

A herd of wild, disheveled, and dirty stallions are racing across a plain. The teacher points to one particularly gnarly stallion and says, "There, that is your stallion. Can you see it?" If the student can see the nature of the mind, that is: how the mind works, that is not the same as enlightenment. That is simply pointing out the nature of the mind, so you can recognize and begin to work with it. We first have to become aware of the stallion before we can gradually tame it, much less ride it.

The pointing out instructions result in the student becoming aware not only of how wild and unruly the mind is, but of the various obstacles that impede or block us from knowing the true nature of the mind, and perhaps chief among these obstacles is the ego or Self, the very same self that here in the West we are so familiar and enamored with, and yet so schizophrenic about.

This great Self and Sun is shining now in the darkness of our mind. It is everything we think of and everything (seemingly) we have ever known. When we think, we think of and with our Self, this great central source of our identification. It is who we think we are, who we refer to, and who we (as far as we now know) have always been. Who else is there?

In other words, when we go to look into the true nature of the mind, this sense of Self is just inside the door waiting for us. We can't get around it, because we think we ARE what we would be trying to get around. It is, after all, our Self.

WHO YOU ARE

If who you are is who you will be,
And who you will be will be who you were,
Then:

Who you are is not who you are
Or who you will be.

So, who are you?

Sunrise

Again, in the East the Self is said to be nothing but a composite, meaning it is a collection of god knows what, accumulated since god knows when, that we think of as us. We have become habitually attached to our Self. In fact, we have almost completely identified with it, at least to the point that we feel that everyone has a self, and thus all the references to "selfishness," etc. that we have mentioned earlier on.

This sense of Self is so ingrained in us that we can't just see it for what it is. At the same time, we can't see through or past it, because it literally takes all our attention; it distracts us just about all of the time, forcing us to consider it as our main focus or filter, like one of those unwanted ads that pops up on our web browser. We can't see beyond the self to the true nature of our mind, if for no other reason than we think we "are" the Self.

The Asian approach to dealing with the ego or Self is not through a frontal attack. You don't run at it head on. Wrestling with the self just draws more attention to it. Instead, a gradual and more sidewise approach is usually offered, one that takes time and patience on our part. This is not the place to go into it here, but in general, what happens next is that the mind (and self) is examined very carefully to determine what it is or is not.

This concept of the Self is a lot like the old game of "Pick Up Sticks," where a bunch of sticks are tossed on the ground, and become a tangle, with sticks pointing every which way. Then, stick by stick, each stick is removed, being careful not to disturb or upset the remaining pile. Gradually, all the sticks are removed, until there are none left.

Examining the mind is something like this. With the help of a qualified teacher, and with a lot of looking at the mind on our part, little by little, the dense nest of our "Self," becomes increasingly transparent, until such time as we actually can begin to see through it to the nature of the mind itself. In other words, we not only don't need the Self to see the true nature of the mind, but the Self is the chief obscuration that prevents us from seeing that nature.

I probably have given you a little too much detail here, but the point is that what we refer to as our Self is never going to find anything (other than itself), much less lead us to knowing the true nature of the mind. It hogs our attention, and its endless activity is itself what clouds the mind from true insight. That, in general, is the problem.

BEYOND MY EXPECTATIONS

Looking at the mind,
It's not what I'd expect.
Expectations can't define,
And you can't expect to find.

That's the nature of the mind.

Beyond the Heart Center or Sun

This has been a bit of a long-way-around to get back to how this relates to the Sun, as used in astrology. The Sun is, of course, a quintessential part of astrology, ancient or modern, in the East and in the West. However, we should note that much of Asian astrology is lunar based, rather than solar based. In other words, in Tibet, no one would know or care about your birthday (solar day you were born). Instead, they would want to celebrate your Moon day, that is: the lunar day (solunar angle, like 4th Quarter, etc.) you were born in the solunar cycle. But that is another article.

My goal here is to point out something about the nature of the Sun and Self, and that this entire Sun and solar system itself is a construct, something in front of us, that shields or covers what is behind it. That is one of the deepest mysteries: What does the Sun cover or stand for? What stands behind the Sun?

In the foregoing, I have tried to give you enough information so that you could perhaps begin to examine and pick apart this Self or Sun or at least develop an awareness that this great shining Sun or Self is nothing in itself, simply a construct, an illusion, although a very convincing illusion indeed.

Let me try to wrap this up and bring us back to the main material in this book, our journey through the various chakras in toward the Sun itself.

In the earlier chapters, the Earth or Heart Center can be seen as the goal of this journey, the place we are all trying to get to, that is: being our self. This has been presented above and this concept stands. We pointed out that those planets interior or beyond Earth toward the Sun were not places we could get to, as much as they were spheres or chakras within us upon which we might occasionally (when circumstances permit) gaze. We gaze into Venus, Mercury, and at the Sun itself, all of this deep within us.

That being said, we want to take a look at this Heart or Earth Center, this solar Self we each inherit and find shining deep within us. That same great shining center or Self that warms us by its presence and with which we absolutely identify, and have identified our entire lives is also what hides from us all that which is still within us, the inner nature of the mind.

If we want to explore the inner mysteries, those interior to and beyond the Earth/Sun/Self, then we would have to be able to see through (or make transparent) that Sun center or Self. Otherwise, its endless shining shields or blocks our view. And, as you can imagine, this is not a small task. Just try it. And that is why great saints and souls meditate and work through the obscurations in their ego or self, and learn to know the true nature of their mind, a mind not filtered by or through the Self-Sun.

I have done my very best to point out to you this general nature. I cannot instruct you on this, because like many of you, I too am standing here staring into the Sun, and only beginning to work through it. I too am warmed and thrilled by this Sun, almost a complete captive. I have very little idea of how to work through this great obscuration. I am not sure I even want to, which would be the first step, of course. I can say this:

Consider this great inner Self and Sun. As children, we could only look up into it and wait for that day when we could grow into it. As elders, we can but look back to it, still shining in our inner sky. Nothing has changed. As busy mid-life people, we are almost entirely caught up in the whole process to see anything clearly.

It is a great shining and yet it nowhere exists. It is before us; it is behind us. It is just about everywhere, but where we are, yet it is "us." It is ours, our very self. It endlessly shines in the darkness of our mind, radiating life and light all ways — everywhere. It is always in our mind, yet it has no true existence. This is the mystery of the Sun.

THE POINT OF NO RETURN

By Michael Erlewine
Feb 14, 2006 2-4 PM,
Grand Sextile Helio

A Poem for My Daughter Michael Anne

The point of the "point of no return" is that:
When you have reached the point of no return,
From which there is no return,
The point is to turn and return.

That is the turning point.

Every life has a turning point,
Whether it's in the echo of age,
Or in the very midst of life's prime.
As we reach our point of no return,
We pause,
Then we turn.
And, in turning, we begin to reflect.

In our reflection,
And rising into view,
Perhaps for the very first time,
The Sun.

Where before it was we who were seen,
And others seeing,
Now we are the mirror in which they see themselves,
And we can see our self in them,

What we once saw shining before us, as youths,
That which we gladly embraced in our prime,

And what we now see etched in the mirror of reflection,
Is our eternal Self, the Sun,
Ever burning in the darkness of our life.

That's it.
I understand this.

What I find harder to understand,
Yet still believe is:

We didn't know it then;
We don't know it now.
We never knew it. In truth,
It never was.

IT NEVER WAS;
It never will be.
It is not now,
And still, it is.

It still is:
This most brilliant illusion,
Shining in the mirror of the mind.

Reincarnation

Incarnation and Re-incarnation

Let's begin with a discussion of 're-incarnation'. Here is a concept that can be a real puzzler. It's the prefix 're' that causes all the excitement, the idea that incarnation is something we somehow can renew or do again. Incarnation appears to be a fact of life — maybe the fact of life. And yet I have always been intrigued by a line that Shakespeare wrote in one of his sonnets that suggests incarnation is not something to be taken for granted. He writes:

"You are no more yourself than you now here live."

Thus incarnation or life itself can be seen to have its moments or flux and, like all the cycles we study in astrology, rises and falls with the tides of each day. In other words, some days we feel much more ourselves than on others. Some days we live more in what we hope to be our future (where we want to go), and others are spent (often against our wishes) mired in the past.

Before we hazard a guess about how we might 're'-incarnate, it is important to know something about how we incarnate. Instead of trying to peer beyond the walls of our lifetime to we-know-not-where in an attempt to grasp this esoteric concept "reincarnation," we can perhaps see this idea at work around us now in day-to-day life as we already know it.

Incarnation — A Work in Progress

We mentioned above that our incarnation or life may not be the constant we might imagine. In fact, incarnation is more like something that is renewed or re-instated every day of our lives — in each moment.

Like waves on a beach, our every action and thought propels and shapes us toward or away from our sense of self and future.

For starters, it can be helpful to recognize that incarnation is a work in progress, rather than an accomplished fact or state. Incarnation is continuous, ongoing. The end and the means are identical. In other words, the place we are trying to get to and the way we are traveling to get there are one and the same. The place that we are trying to get to is to live happily. Years ago, I wrote:

> Look at yourself,
> No better, and yet, not worse.
> Now get yourself together in a bunch,
> And call what carriage as ye may, your hearse.

We can all testify to the fact that we are, as Shakespeare pointed out, no more ourselves than we now here live.

Bodies of Knowledge

All of us reading this are busy creating a body of knowledge for ourselves to live in called 'astrology.' This body of knowledge, astrology, is an example of a mini-incarnation. We are creating a body or vehicle in which to live and experience astrology. It is hoped that astrology can become a way for us to know and experience life and ourselves from a new perspective.

We invest energy in studying astrology through or over a period of time. The intensity of our interest and our approach or attitude will determine how we work at our study, and whether the resulting body of knowledge we create will be more or less workable or suitable.

If this knowledge body is put together right, it can serve as a vehicle for us to live in and learn astrology. We can use the knowledge to look at and understand the world through the perspective or filter of astrology. It can be a real and viable body or vehicle. It has life.

On the other hand, if astrology as a subject does not 'click' for us (and thus cohere or come together), it can be a useless vehicle too — a big waste of time and energy. It will just fall apart and be forgotten, like so many other things we have tried. It will never be realized or vitalized to become a living experience for us. Many people's lives are littered with the shipwrecks of ideas they tried to vivify and get into, but were not able to get off the ground. I have my share, for sure. On the other hand, consider carefully those areas or "bodies" where you do live, where you do have life. You are something more than just your material physical body. You live in many kinds of bodies.

Abandoned Bodies

How many things, studies or bodies of knowledge have we started, only to find them spontaneously aborting on us, projects for which we were unable to create a viable body or vehicle for ourselves, and had to abandon the effort. We found that this or that approach to diet, food, exercise, etc. was not for us. We could not make it go or work. At some point, we gave up pouring energy into it and just let it go, allowed it to drift into our past, a nice try at best, a waste of time, money, and effort at worst. At least we learned what won't work for us.

The point here is that we are always involved in creating a wide variety of vehicles or incarnations for ourselves. In fact, there is every reason to consider that our lifetime (our self or ego for sure) may be nothing more than the sum total of all of our involvements — all of our projects. We create friendships, hobbies, attitudes, fears, etc. We get involved (like it or not) in hundreds and thousands of ways. How do you answer the question 'Who are you?' or 'What do you do?' Chances are the answer to this question could reveal many of the areas of your self where you have created living bodies of knowledge. Just ask yourself those questions, and you will have a list of your bodies of involvement.

Putting Our Self into Things

Each of these involvements, these lesser incarnations or bodies, has a lifespan. Each is created, holds together or lasts for us for some length of time, and then fails and gradually comes apart. Some we manage to keep up for a lifetime. Our life is filled with countless involvements of this sort — islands in this sea of time that hold attention or last for us to one degree or another. They are like stepping stones through the waters of life. Some areas of interest are life long. Others are such that we dip into them again and again, as we feel inspired. I don't know how many times I have tried to get a real physical exercise program to work for me. I give it a spin, but it gets old fast. It does not last or cohere.

And we people our life. We endlessly pour ourselves forth into projects and things that strike our fancy. We animate the world around us with our energy and attention. We fixate or bind that energy with each new enthusiasm we have. That bound energy lasts for a time, and then breaks up and comes back to us, as our interest in the topic fades. It holds our interest, and then fails, and we are on the roam again to find some new interest. We have just so much energy and, like money, we can learn to invest it well — in things that last.

TIME OUT

What if at every out, I set an "in."
I said:
What if at each out, I set on in,

And in on in on in on in ...
And if on in,
I'm lost within?

Time is sure to see me out.

The Fixed Stars in Our Life

In fact, the things we put ourselves into serve as beacons or markers in our life. We can see to steer by them. They give us a sense of identity and permanence in our life. They shine. Our life is filled with the objects of our interest like the night sky is filled with stars. These are the fixed stars for us, and they light up our life. If everything else were to fade out, these would be the last to go.

There are many thoughts we could have about this subject. On the desperate side, we may find ourselves pouring energy into topic after topic that barely gives back any light to us. The vehicles we create don't all hold water. Like spinning coins on a table, some come apart as soon as we cease to spin or energize them. They just won't shine for us. They don't last. Thus most of us try to find the subjects of interest that will hang together, that will last long enough for us to get some use out of them.

Bind and Last

Here is where the idea of truth can come in. Time and experience has shown us that certain ideas and subjects are more worth investing in than others. They are worthy or hold our attention. And they last or appear true. We could perhaps agree that "true" and "last" are synonyms. The word 'religion' is derived from a Latin word that means to bind back or hold.

In this sense of the word, religion is the science of binding or holding fast, just as the ligaments (Latin: ligare) hold our body muscles together — the things that endure or last. In fact, religious ideas last so long and shine so brightly that they are like great Suns in our mind. Many of the great religious ideas are said to be eternal truths, to shed eternal light and to hold eternal life. They shine and shine to light our way. I felt much better about religion when I understood that all it refers to are the things that last longest. I can get behind that.

A religious statement like "we are all one" is an example of a truth that appears to stand the test of time. Most great philosophers, saints, mystics, etc. have testified to the truth of this statement. It has held true for them. It holds true for us. It is a fixed star in the life of our mind, of the mind. As my teacher used to say to me, "It is not true because I say it; I say it because it is true." I like that.

Lasting the Test of Time

Likewise, the words of great philosophers are not true because the philosophers say them. They say them because they are true. The energy and attention that they have invested in this or that idea has been well spent. Ideas that last are not just made up; they are discovered, and they have always been there, by definition.

True ideas have stood up to the test of time and Saturn. An idea like this one shines like a great beacon in the night of our mind. Each of us can invest and attest to its verity for ourselves. In this sense, perhaps it is an eternal thought, what we could call a fixed star in our consciousness..

The idea that I would like to see forming here is that our life is built upon things and ideas that last more or less well. Picture a world only as solid as the concepts and thoughts of which it is made up. That's us. Time defies just about everything that is created; we know that.

However, some concepts defy time's (Saturn's) every attempt to destroy them. They last. Others last or hold for but a moment, and then undo themselves to release the energy that was them, that we put into them. It seems that we spend much of our energy finding out which topics and ideas will last for us. Religions are built around ideas that a group of people have found to endure, lasting ideas, truth. They shine like suns in the dark night of time. They are light. The rest is darkness.

Nothing Lasts Forever

It is easy to see this concept at work in the world. Take popular music. Some songs are made or built around ideas or thoughts that can hold our attention for many listenings. This is why certain songs are called 'Old Standards'. On the other hand, there are songs we can't bear to listen to even once, so little do they hold or last for us, while others we can listen to a dozen or even a hundred times. They are of lasting importance to us, landmarks in the great hall of our life.

A writer like Shakespeare has written so well that, centuries after his death, his work still stands unraveled. It lasts. Those of us who go to read Shakespeare, to test and try to get into him, end up listening to what he has to say. He satisfies us before we get very far into the inner workings of his prose. He fills us up. We can't see through or beyond him. We never get to the bottom of Shakespeare. His work is a ground we can stand on; it supports us. We are entranced by the brightness of his star. We can see to guide our way by it. This is how it is with great writers and thinkers.

And yet, someday, we can imagine that we may get underneath (or behind) even old Shakespeare. Nothing lasts forever. No thing lasts forever. Shakespeare, too, will, in time, unravel and release all of the energy locked within his work, energy of his own creation, and energy from the millions who have read his work and found satisfaction, who also have invested. We will not have Shakespeare to stand on or base our life on, and will have to come up with something or some other genius that becomes terra firma for us. For that which lasts is the ground we walk on. Our hearts are highways over which our life can run.

The Birth of Stars

There will be still other new stars for us to live by, other Shakespeares. Our every thought, word and deed are miniature time capsules, set to wear off sometime in the future. They will last until then. When they go off, they will gradually release the energy that has held them together. That energy will be free to be used for something else. That energy could be our very selves. Our Self is, according to the Buddhists, a composite or thing, something that is a construct, rather than a verity. That idea is too difficult to go into here, but amounts to the difference between much of Eastern and Western philosophy.

It is clear that our greatest artists, authors, saints, etc. are those who have built their work around enduring or true ideas. They have made themselves a coat or personality out of truths, things that last, and their personality shines for us still. Their work may be almost indistinguishable from the pure truth itself. It will last and last. Look around you the next time you go to the supermarket for examples of ideas that won't prove so useful — that won't last.

In summary then: who are we? In some sense, we can say that we are the end result of all our involvements, literally, the living end. We are what we care about and, more important, we are the way we care about them. We are embedded in all of the things we do, all of the different bodies (bodies of thought, knowledge, etc.) that we create. We are endlessly involved in the care and tending of all of the areas of life where we find interest and concern. We bind ourselves into every part of our life. In time, we learn to spend our effort on things that last, on true things. We all find a religion of our own making, if only to economize, to save time and energy.

The Sum Total of Our Involvements

I have pointed out elsewhere in this book the fact that our entire life can be seen as the sum total of our particular involvements. 'Involvements' here refers to those areas of our self and life where we find ourselves interested, concerned, or working. In other words, what we are into — our personal incarnations.

Although we like to think of our life and incarnation as one big lump, when we examine that lump we find that it consists of a lot of smaller parts, like the strands that make up a rope, some more real to us than others. We concern or embody ourselves here and there in the subjects (bodies of knowledge) that interest us. More important, we then live in these islands of involvement, set in the midst of the life process itself.

Shakespeare says "You are no more yourself than you now here live". At any given time, our life is lived in those areas where we are working and have an interest, in fact, wherever we find or catch ourselves, are drawn toward (or repelled from) — all our attachments. Examples of such mini-incarnations or bodies within the larger body of our lifetime should be easy to locate. What are you into?

The Body of Knowledge

In this book, we concentrate on the body of knowledge we are building called astrology. If we love astrology, we really spend a lot of our time in the body-of-knowledge called astrology. Try looking at your body as those things in which you are involved and live. My teacher had a saying that he would often quote from the "Gospel According to Thomas" to the effect that:

> 'Blessed is the man that eats the lion,
> That the lion becomes a man,
> Cursed is the lion that eats the man,
> That the man becomes a lion'.

A more popular version of this is 'sometimes you eat the bear, and sometimes the bear eats you'. The idea here is that most of us fluctuate from being able to manage life (be in control) to being unable to handle anything (be out of control). Any of the areas of interest (hobbies, prejudices, etc.) in which we find ourselves oscillate or show signs of cyclic behavior. We alternate from being able to manage and use them (be in control) to getting stuck in them, not able to get much use from them (to be out of control), etc., thus the above sayings.

The Point of No Return

For example, any subject of knowledge (like astrology) has its seasons. We have a surge of interest and understanding, during which we build or deepen the knowledge body "Astrology." The interest wanes. Perhaps we bite off more than we can chew. Perhaps we simply spend all our energy for the current round or cycle. Whatever the reason, the end result is that we tend to get left, stuck in a subject — in over our heads. We reach a point of no return, where nothing seems to add up anymore. We can go no farther, at least at this moment. And we do this all the time. I leave it to you to verify this fact and process in your own life. It is this phenomenon that we are discussing here.

When we reach the point of no return with any subject (body), we stop investing, and we turn around, return, and try to get ourselves out of it, since we can't seem to get any more life out of it. That is what the point of no return is all about, investments and returns.

The main point presented here is that any 're-incarnation' that takes place can be seen and studied on a day-by-day and issue-by-issue basis. In brief, we commit ourselves or say 'I do' or 'I will' all the time to life.

When we feel on top of life, we ask for more of it, and we do this each day. When we are under it, we wish we had never gotten into whatever it is in the first place. It is a very simple thing for you to verify this to your satisfaction. This involves developing an awareness of what is taking place all the time. Here is how that can be done:

Our Flood and Ebb Tides

Pick any subject that you regularly involve yourself in — any topic of real importance to you. It could be your study of astrology. Now observe for awhile or, if you are in a hurry, reflect on the history of the topic over the last few years. Everything does have a season, and there are times when the floodtide of our enthusiasms carries us over obstacles and into real experience and understanding of a subject. On the other hand, there are ebb tides too, that find us stranded and lost in the midst of our work. We awaken some days to find that nothing makes much sense, and even wonder why we have spent so much time studying or working with the topic. We feel at a loss. Am I right or wrong about this?

When We Say "I Do"

Here is the point: It is at the high-flying times of real control, when we feel we can manage almost anything, that we say the cosmic 'I do' and the 'give me more.' We ask for it, because life then feels really good to us. We are on top of it. At these times, we have the subject firmly within our grasp. This kind of experience, where everything seems to click and work together, has sometimes been termed an 'out of body' experience by many. When we are outside of our problems or in control, we find it very easy to say 'Yes' to life and to ask for more of the same, more of it. It is not unlike the Bible, where God looks over the Creation and says 'Yes, this is Good'. We do the same thing all the time. Check it out in your own lives. We are the ones who choose our own destiny.

The converse is also true: at the ebb tides of our life, when we are caught up in a situation with no feeling of relief or return. Here is where we cry out and complain about our lot. And yet, if we will observe, we will see that we usually have brought it on ourselves. We have asked for it. One cannot but wonder what life might be like if we did not ask for more of it at those high moments of life.

We manage to involve ourselves all the time in creating bodies or mini-incarnations. Getting into and out of these many experiences (our involvements) comprise much of our day-to-day life. Some of you might prefer to look at it as being in (or within) control, as opposed to being out of control of a subject or situation. Since these opposites alternate (follow one upon the other), most find it more convenient to look at this kind of phenomenon as cyclic, as cycles. We are now ready for a general look at the cycle-like nature of our experience or consciousness.

Our Cycles of Up and Down

It is not difficult for most of us to recognize that our life is filled with ups and downs of many kinds. They come and go and repeat themselves: they cycle. What is important to present here, and for each of you to observe and verify, is just what happens with us during these ups and downs. It can serve to explain a lot.

At this point, I have presented, and it is important that you understand, that our body and the bodies of our various involvements are something that we get into and out of on a regular basis. We have mentioned investment and returns. Some days we are more involved in one aspect of ourselves or life than others. We have moments and times of greater clarity and understanding, as well as times of confusion and general fogginess. Our consciousness or awareness on any particular topic or body of knowledge (such as astrology) changes and varies. In fact, we cycle or circulate from one extreme to another and on around again. We are into it. We feel out of it. We feel into it again, etc. Our consciousness circulates from feeling free and able to manage it all, to getting caught up in it, trapped, out of control, and so on. It is this cycling or circulation that we will now look at. We are moving into and out of the body all the time. Out-of-body experiences and in-the-body experiences are natural and can easily be seen, if we learn to look.

Extending Ourselves in Experience

It is important to point out that we continue to get involved, have extended experiences, and draw conclusions (get out of) these experiences. We make short or long trips into different subject matter or experience, and get some return (we return) from these experiences. We get something out of them. If nothing else, we ourselves get out of them. We return, and that is indeed fortunate. We have bouts with various subjects. We can look back at our involvement, and have thoughts as to whether it was worth it — whether we would like to do this or that again, and so forth.

I am indicating here that we fluctuate from being very involved in a given subject or experience to being less involved — at any given time. Often, at times of intense involvement and experience, we have very few thoughts about that experience. We are too busy being in it to think about it or to see it as a whole. Later, when the experience part dies down, we find ourselves getting past, beyond or outside that experience. We can look back on, get our mind around, and understand the experience for what it was. We can appreciate and appraise the experience.

We Ask For It

Here is a very important point: When we are able to manage or be in control of an experience, when that experience is comprehended or is very clear to us, something special happens. It is then that we may make commitments or declarations concerning the experience, that is: when we have gone through a real experience, when we have learned to handle it or have it under our belt.

When we have lived through an experience and gotten far enough past it (or around it) to feel that we can handle or manage the experience (at least it didn't kill us), it is then that we ask to do that again. We have become a 'big' enough person to handle it. We have struggled through to mastery and have (so to speak) gained control of that experience. This is often when we wish for or ask to: do it again. It is then that we reincarnate or ask for more or another incarnation, at the high times. This is not the case, when we are at the low points, however. Then, we tend to decry our fate.

Moment by Moment Incarnation

In other words, we re-incarnate on a moment-by-moment and day-today basis, almost on an issue by issue basis. And we do this when we are feeling good or high, and in control. In fact, these times have often been called in the literature "out-of-the-body experiences." We can contrast them to in-the-body-experiences, when we are fed up with, lost in, or have more of a given project or experience than we can handle.

It's up to you to find examples in your life that fit this description. How many times have you agreed to do something in a good or 'high' mood, only to perhaps regret that agreement when the time came to actually carry it out. It is a different day, and we feel differently. 'Sweet in the mouth, bitter in the stomach' is the proverb. We are forever asking for more, when we are in a good mood, and forever complaining about our state, when we get in the thick of it. Right?

Let Me Have It

The above concept provides us with an important clue as regards ideas of incarnation and re-incarnation. We incarnate or re-incarnate on a day-to-day, and on an issue by issue basis. When we are in a high or a good mood, we are willing to forget the hard or rough times and say Yes! to life. 'Yes! life is worth it'. And 'Yes! I want more of it', etc. "Sock it to me!" "Let me at it," or "Let me have it."

We commit ourselves to life on a piecemeal basis. We say "yes" to this and "yes" to that. Or, we say "no" to this or that. We do this when we get high or out-of-the-body of an experience enough. Here again, it is not enough to read these words. You must find out for yourselves if this, in fact, is the case. When you feel on top of an experience, do you ask for more of the same? Do you ask for it? If so, then you will know that you alone are responsible for the way things are with you.

I am not saying that it is wrong to ask for more. It might be an interesting experiment to go through one of these high times without asking for more. Accepting it for what it is, without re-instating it. It is written that if you do not ask for more, that you will accumulate no additional karma. That intriguing concept is beyond the scope of this article, however.

The point here is that it can be helpful to think of your incarnation as something other than just your physical body and as something more than just one lump. You are caught up in life in a myriad of ways, each more or less incarnate. Incarnation is an ongoing process.

Reincarnation: The Sun Is Shining

Everyone claims to know something about or at least wonders about personal death, the death we all look forward to sometime at the end of our future. My comment, which is an age-old refrain, is that if we did in fact really get this message, we would live a lot different life than we actually do. I am not running any "holier than thou" rap on you either. I am just like anyone else as far as keeping these thoughts in mind and enjoying life today goes.

For years I have used the following image to communicate about the difference between the personal life and the common life. And, to a large degree, these differences amount to the difference between the way the East and the West look upon death, and therefore, life. Try it out.

Honeybees and the Hive

We all know that honeybees live as a society or colony. One image to grasp is that the hive persists through an endless series of little bee bodies that are born, live, and die. The hive of bees is still there each year, but the members are ever changing. There is another fact of bee life that provides a perfect simile for what is called the monad in the esoteric tradition. Here it is:

In winter, to keep warm, the hive clings together to form a solid ball of bees. At the center of the ball, there is constant motion, as the bees that are in there dance and move with great force to generate precious heat which then radiates outward throughout the ball of bees. It keeps them from freezing. As the bees dancing at the center of the hive tire, they cease dancing, fall asleep, and are replaced by still other dancers. Sleeping, they are, over time, worked from the center to the circumference of the ball. Reaching the outside of the ball, where it is cold, they awaken and burrow in to the center to dance once again. Thus, through a convection-like motion, the hive endlessly keeps moving. This is why they don't freeze to death each winter.

The Constant Generation

The opposite of linear time is the cyclic process of life, irrespective of bodies, just as the bee hive has a life irrespective of this bee or that bee. The generation of bees, like a fountain of bees pours forth. Always eggs, always larvae, always adults, always birth, and always death. The hive of bees exists via the process of the life of the colony. Countless bee bodies line the track of the history of a hive. Year in, year out, the flame of life burns, fed by the process of life. When you go to the hive, you find the colony of bees. You don't think about the fact that these bees are not the same exact bee bodies that were there two years ago, anymore than you can step in the same river twice. The colony remains, fed by the process of constant generation and life.

What about those little bee bodies? They are gone. Death is a specter that hangs over many of our lives like a threat. We each can puzzle out the fact of our death, although we would as soon forget it as keep it in mind. We can guess at the years before us and count the years behind us. The Shakespeare Sonnets, the early ones in particular, are about the closest thing in accepted world literature to a description of the esoteric knowledge I am pointing to. Here is his 13th sonnet:

> "O, that you were yourself!
> But, love, you are no longer yours
> Than you yourself here live.
> Against this coming end you should prepare,
> And your sweet semblance to some other give.
>
> So, should that beauty which you hold in lease,
> Find no determination; then you were,
> Yourself again after your self's decease,
> When your sweet issue
> Your sweet form should bear.
> Who lets so fair a house fall to decay,
> Which husbandry in honor might uphold,
> Against the stormy gusts of winter's day,
> And barren rage of death's eternal cold?
>
> O, none but unthrifts!

Dear my love, you know you had a father — let your son say so.

The Life in Common

Throughout the early sonnets, Shakespeare wastes no time and quickly points out the succession of bodies required to maintain our common life. This is about as close as we come in the accepted literature of the West (the kind every school kid is encouraged to read) to the concept of reincarnation — a succession of bodies with one life. There is no mistaking Shakespeare's message. He hammers away on this theme all through the first twenty or so sonnets. If you have not read them, you have missed one of the few great esoteric lessons in western literature. Take a look sometime.

Yet why, then, are we so dumbfounded by the Eastern concepts of reincarnation, karma, and the like? Is it such a strange and monstrous thought that some common something survives through the endless succession of bodies in the world? There is no question that the majority of people living on this earth (Asians, in particular) accept as a matter of fact that we endure through and by means of the many bodies we have used through history — reincarnation. It is the West that is in the minority and, as the world becomes more of a global consciousness, it is embarrassing that westerners don't update their take on reincarnation.

The Terrible Crystal

The Eastern concept goes even further. Not only is there a common life shining through our many bodies, but we are each responsible for our own life, actions, and predicament. Each of us must pick up on that responsibility and live with it. The fact that the East fingers the person is like each bee in the hive being responsible for the well-being of the hive, and, if you have studied bees, you know that they are, even to the point of dragging their little bee bodies to the edge of the hive to die, so others won't have to carry them out.

Here in the West, we skip right past that common message and insist on understanding reincarnation to mean that I, Michael Erlewine, with this and that mole on my body, will continue to exist. We hear people speaking of being the re-incarnation of Nero, Dante, or some similar personality. Personalities don't reincarnate. Personalities are the result of our action in the world, what the poet Gerard Manley Hopkins called the "terrible crystal," the crush of our own personality in the grip of time, causing each of us to burst into flames and burn, to some degree, and give light — become a star.

In My Past Life

It is the spirit, whatever we could agree on that is, that reincarnates through and beyond any person, beyond our personality. How like us, here in the West. We focus right in on the fact stuff of a life, the personality, and ignore all that is common, the spirit. We miss the whole concept of the hive, and worry instead only about the dead bees. I wish I had a nickel for every time I have overheard an astrologer using the "dead bee" concept of re-incarnation. "In my past life, I was one of Caesar's mistresses". We never hear statements like "I am ageless, eternal. I live forever," or if we do, we tag that person for the loony bin. We have to go to the American Transcendentalists to read that concept right.

Instead of becoming one with the life of the hive, we are obsessed with the remains of the process, the dead bees. The common life that we are living and that lives through all of our efforts, that "life" is the one that we, as astrologers, ought to be conversant with, the life that, irrespective of persons, we all inherit and share. The passing forward through time of personalities (Nero's, etc.), if true, could only be the frosting on the cake. The common life is the cake itself. We all eat that.

Re-Incarnation: More

Let's return to the concept of 're-incarnation', and please forgive me if I repeat concepts that are in other chapters or sections. Repetition is a key way to absorb these esoteric concepts.

Instead of trying to peer beyond the walls of our lifetime into we-know-not-where, in an attempt to grasp this concept, we can see this idea at work everywhere within our life.

We incarnate everyday in every thing we do. We mentioned earlier in this material that we are busy creating a body of knowledge for ourselves called 'astrology'. This is an example of an incarnation. We are creating a body of knowledge or vehicle in which to live and learn, and from which (out of which, through which) we get something — a return, an experience, or, at the very least, ourselves.

We invest energy over time. Depending upon our interest and how we apply ourselves, the body of knowledge we create in our study of astrology will be more or less suitable or workable.

A Moment's Infatuation

Consider, for a moment, some of the many enthusiasms you have had over the course of your present life. Notice how some infatuation or another started you off in a particular direction, on a project or a course of study or thought. Think how you brought together or created some vehicle to experience that subject, how it held together and served to hold your attention for a time, and then how you lost interest in it and, in time, it fell away and took a backseat in your life.

You got into the subject, held to it for a time, and then withdrew. What you got out of the subject was yourself but, with more experience. In this way, our many interests and involvements are a learning ground. If we look with care at our life, it is possible to observe that perhaps we are no more than the sum total of our mini-incarnations or involvements, and that we withdraw from life only with the experience we have gained. If not that, then who or what are we?

The Word Must Be Made Flesh

If we are sincere in our interest in astrology, it is important that we learn all we can about this incarnation and re-incarnation process. I can tell you about it somewhat here in words, but you will have to elaborate and explore these ideas, as you can find them active in your day-to-day life. To the best of my knowledge, that is, in my experience, it was not enough to go once-over-lightly these ideas. They must be exampled and extended, until they are perceived working throughout your life — at every turn. You must do the work, or have these thoughts remain locked in your head, a mere intellectual exercise. It is up to you to make them flesh and live them out.

A next step will be to note that, in very many cases, we have more than a single fling at a favorite subject. We get into it (create a body of knowledge), spend some time learning and living in this body, and return (get some return) out of it. If we like what we see or get out of the experience, we find ourselves re-investing even more time and energy in the matter. And so the process of life goes.

Sowing and Reaping

With our favorite subjects, we are always sowing and reaping, investing and returning — getting returns. It can be easier to see this process if we consider areas of study or concern where we have made a great investment, spent some time in the study, and gotten some real return. Many people get into astrology in this way. They do some work, get something out of it, and rest awhile. After a time, they get inspired once again, and get into it even more, and then perhaps get even more out of it and so on. In and out, in and out. Each time, they are creating a stronger and more perfect vehicle or body of knowledge. Professional astrologers can spend a lot of their life living in the astrological body of knowledge that they have created and are perfecting. Do we not?

What I am working up to here, and the point that I want you to consider and explore, has to do with incarnation and 're' incarnation. We invest in a subject, get a return from our investment (get more of ourselves out of it, but with experience), and in the light of these returns, we re-invest. Sowing and reaping, giving and taking. We live through and by means of these investments and returns, these different bodies that we create for ourselves. And we don't have to be quite so abstract as to only look at bodies of knowledge or studies. A marriage is an incredible investment or a child. Just think about it. Look at how we invest in our own self!

A Child is Life

What an investment is a child, and can any real parent not agree that a child is something we have created that we too get a lot out of? A child or marriage, from this point of view, is more than just a new body or contract. It is everything we pour into it.

What parent does not, to some degree or another, live in the life of their own child? As your child succeeds and finds joy, does not the parent? And it is more than some passive observation. I know this from my own experience. Their life becomes, to some degree, my life. Our life is filled with and consists of nothing else but those areas where we are connected or have investments. This is where we identify, and this is our identity, not just "in here," but very much also: out there.

We are looking here at investments over which we may have some control (like studying astrology). We will leave aside, for the moment, areas of connection or incarnation where it is not obvious how we have any control — like our personality, physical body, etc. That would be too direct an approach for now, but please take note. At this point, we will be content to approach this concept from the side.

Most of our interests and experiences can be viewed as a series of incarnations or bodies. Further, most can be seen to be cyclic or reoccurring — again and again. These are the cycles of which our life is composed. It is these we must study, if we wish to learn astrology.

Saturn the Sequencer

Shamanic or esoteric astrology is something we hear little about these days. My interest in astrology has always had an esoteric base. The inner workings of me, my psyche (psychology) and the rites of passage (my inner journey), have been much of the fuel for my particular astrology.

Mamy astrologers are mostly time keepers, and modern astrology is too wrapped up with the concept of time. The great and small cycles of the planets provide the guide for most of what passes for time in our world. It is often commented how many astrologers are also musicians. Music, too, is all about time. In Tibetan Buddhism, the study of astrology is part of what is termed the Kalachakra Tantra. Kalachakra means the wheel or cycle of time. This section is about Saturn and time.

Cycles Are Returns

Even beginning astrology students know that Saturn (or Satan) is the lord or prince of time. Saturn rules time and the material world. And understanding of Saturn and its sequence of time is essential to any serious study of astrology.

The return of Saturn to its natal position around the age of 30 (29.4 years helio) is an important astrological event and is what is called a climacteric year. "Never trust anyone over thirty" is, by now, a well-known slogan. The completion of ANY planetary cycle, especially for the first time around within a lifetime, marks a very significant point of change in our life and consciousness.

The return of Mercury in the chart of an infant at three months marks the onset of what has been termed "adult awareness." Around this time the child's motor responses switch from reflex to voluntary, and he or she begins to see in color! The return of Venus at some 7 1/2 months is when the baby first can discriminate between itself and its mother. A duality occurs that allows appreciation.

At one year, the Earth return, most children get up and begin to walk.

The "terrible twos" (18 months) marks the Mars return, when baby discovers emotions and struggles for independence — looking outward for the first time!

And at 12 years, Jupiter returns, marking the onset of adolescence and the beginning of a real adult sense of time. After the Jupiter return, the individual begins to pick up on and to monitor the most definite of cycles, that of Saturn, time itself.

In physical terms, the most dramatic return has to be the return of Saturn to its place around 29.4 years of age. In a very real sense, it marks the end of time for an individual. And here we begin to dip into what is called shamanic astrology, an area not well understood even by most professional astrologers. I have always been fascinated by it, and I had a good teacher.

Saturn or Chronos

Saturn (Chronos), the great marker of time, drags out its wheel or cycle for a full thirty years. During all of this time, Saturn is tracing out, degree by degree, new territory (for any given individual) against the backdrop of the zodiac. Saturn is going around for the first time, with no repeats thus far. We have all seen the beer commercial that tells us that "You only go around once!" Most astrologers wouldn't agree with that slogan, but we do know that first cycle or circle of zodiac experience for each planet is an important one.

The first cycle of Saturn (first 30 years) fills the life with a sense of the future, always leading toward somewhere. The great time measurer, Saturn, keeps time for us like a metronome. In fact, we measure our life against Saturn's constant ticking, and that beat appears to lead us toward the future. This regular sequencing of events plays our life out like a movie score — a great and constant heart beating within us, giving birth to the moment.

Saturn is concerned with the external and the sequence of external events that provide our particular set of circumstances. As each of us grows up, we come to depend upon its very regular movement. We are cradled inside this first Saturn cycle, like a baby in the womb. It never occurs to us that this very constant beating, like the surf washing up against the shore, could ever change, much less lose meaning for us. But change it does.

Life beyond Saturn or Time

Very few of us are prepared for what happens on the esoteric plane at the Saturn return, when Saturn does complete the circle of the zodiac and begins to repeat itself — to go around a second time. However, as most of us are wrapped up in time and its circumstances, Saturn's return (whether we are aware of it or not) marks a dramatic change in our life — how we conceive of or experience time itself.

The image I would like to convey to you is that of a child leaving its mother's womb. With the Saturn return, we pass beyond the grasp of Saturn or the cycle-of-time, and begin to walk out into eternity. Like a space ship leaving port, we sail straight out into the blue. The image of the astronaut floating out there in space on the end of a thin tether is a good one. As each of us reaches our first Saturn return, we are born beyond gravity or the grave, and begin a new weightless or enlightened existence.

Sound strange? Perhaps, but keep in mind that we are studying esoteric astrology here, an astrology that monitors our inner life and soul's journey, and thus its connection to shamanism.

The above metaphors offer a fair description of the actuality. Here is an esoteric truth, yet a truth so exact and real that it boggles the mind. At our Saturn return, each of us passes beyond the grip of Saturn (the physical) and floats beyond the grave (gravity) into middle age.

As Saturn turns to repeating itself and begins to go over ground (degrees of the zodiac) that we have already covered in this life, our absolute fascination with it fades. Saturn has, up to that point, offered us a bewildering display of time, year after year, and then, with the Saturn return, that display begins to repeat itself, and we gradually start to catch on to that fact — deja vu. We have seen this before. The enchantment is lost, and we begin to lose our fascination. We start to wake up to the fact that there is (somehow) no longer a sense of "newness." The deer-in-the-headlights stare we have had all our lives is broken or breaking.

Our Soul Memory Stirs

In the middle of life, after thirty years, our soul begins to stir, and we wake up from our sleep of life to a life beyond time. There are many names for this experience in the occult literature. Perhaps the most common is the term "silence." We are said to "enter the Silence." Perhaps entering the silence is nothing more than stepping beyond the noise or music of time. Can you hear the silence? Emptiness? However you may wish to spell it, we do go beyond time, and not at life's long end, but right in the prime or middle or life, at around 30 years of age. In esoteric astrology, this is considered a major initiation or rite of passage.

Another of the great esoteric or shamanic truths is that death is only an illusion. Or, if we must think in terms of death, then the death that all speak of (and perhaps fear) comes not at the end of life, but smack dab in the middle of life, at that first Saturn return.

The Prime of Life

The so-called prime of life of the physical body also marks the passage from within life (within the grip of time) to beyond time and into a new life — a threshold, a rite-of-passage, where we are passing beyond or passing on. This is where the phrase "born again" comes from. Being born again is not something just for Christians. It happens to all of us, whether we know it or not, and when we realize that fact, we are said to be "born again."

This great event, and the rites of this momentous passage from within time to without or beyond time, is the Saturn return around the age of thirty years. And this passage follows on the esoteric or psychological level the exact same sequence of events found in the physical birth. In other words, there is the birth canal, the moving down it, the birth of the head, the birth of the body, and then moving free of the mother, etc., even the birth of the placenta!

Each of us peeks out and steps beyond time at about thirty years of age. However, very few of us are prepared for this event, can actively witness to it, or have the least idea of what is happening to us. We lack the preparation and training needed to prepare us to experience this great initiation with consciousness or awareness. Most of us are numbed or knocked out by the sheer magnitude of what happens. It is practically never spoken of publicly. It can take years for us to register or become aware of this momentous event, even though it is over and already in our past. Some never remember or put it all together, and are just not able to become aware of what is so obvious.

Hide in Plain Sight

Let me slow down a bit and repeat the main idea being presented here: All planet cycles measure our life and are important objects of study. As astrologers we know that. Yet time, and the kind of event consciousness that the everyday world measures, belongs to which planet? It belongs, astrologically speaking, to the sphere of the planet Saturn. Saturn (Greek: Chronos) measures and rules time, circumstances, and the sequencing of everyday events.

Keep in mind that much of esoteric astrology is concerned with what is hidden in plain sight, what goes without saying, what is never spoken of. Time or Saturn is only one planet. Therefore, the cycle of Saturn, and its return at around the age of thirty years marks an important esoteric event or initiation. This event is so profound and pervasive — SO VERY OBVIOUS — that there is little or no conscious recognition of it by society. Literally, it goes without saying. Instead, there are endless innuendoes and oblique references to this great passage from within to without, from having time to having none. There is a constant subconscious murmur taking place, a hum or buzz of reference to this initiation, this event that takes place in the lives of each of us.

Never Trust Anyone over Thirty

What I am saying is: time (Saturn) stops at thirty. The trickle of new events that have always led us toward the future ceases or falls away when Saturn begins to repeat itself. A great hush falls over our life, as we sail beyond the circle or cycle of time into what can only be called eternity — that place beyond time. Like the astronaut pushed free of the mother ship, each of us spins off into space, turning and floating, adrift — trying to figure out what has happened.

When time begins to repeat itself, it stops, for all practical purposes. No more does it call and beckon to us with the promise of an endless linear progression. We each begin to experience and grasp the circularity of it all, whether consciously or unconsciously. We begin to develop what is called "wisdom." That is what I mean by "time stops." Your watch does not stop ticking, but the timeline you have followed so raptly up to that point gradually becomes meaningless. Going where? Can you tell me where please?

Under Saturn's seal or cycle (under age 30), we are led toward the future as to some place that we might achieve or actually get to. Time is conceived of up to that point as linear, a straight line stretching off into the future. At the Saturn return, that very straight line begins to be seen, however subtly at first, as a great curve, a circle that returns on itself. We gradually start to lose sight of life as just a straight line. Time starts to curve back on itself. We are going nowhere in particular unless it is to our grave.

At thirty (and after), we begin to realize that our mode of travel, our way of life, is a goal in itself — the way to go. In other words, the place we are traveling to becomes also our mode of travel, the way we get there. In a poem I wrote years ago, I said "Call what carriage as ye may, your hearse." Chuck Berry said it too: "no particular place to go."

Leaving the Womb of Time

The movement I am describing here is from within the womb of time or Saturn to outside (without) or beyond time or Saturn. Once outside or beyond our Saturn return, we begin to view those still within time's grasp (those under 30 years of age) as like babies still asleep in the womb, while we are born free of time for the first time in our lives. We are just out there! Younger people are in there. We have time; it no longer has us.

A palindrome is a word, verse, or sentence that reads the same forwards as backwards. "Able was I ere I saw Elba" is a famous one that refers to Napoleon. The fascination with palindromes becomes an obsession at the level of the esoteric. There is a point when each of us begins to read life backward as well as forward — no difference! The symbol of this is the Sun and the statement: the Sun is shining!

Better yet, we begin to read life as a circle or cycle. The Saturn return stands out like a great beacon or turning point in our lives. The age of 30 is what is called a climacteric year in the esoteric tradition. There is a great stream of souls leading up to this event, this Saturn return, and another stretching off into middle-age.

From the un-manifest emerges an endless stream of bodies forming, building to the prime of life. From the prime of life, stretching off and fading to old age is another stream. Think of these streams as rays and the prime of life as the center of the Sun. This is the image of the esoteric Sun.

The Noise of Time

The younger souls (those under 30) can but imagine what someone is talking about who has taken the Saturn return initiation. Their life is filled by the incessant hum and drum of the Saturn cycle laying down each beat and measure of time. Saturn fills the mind up with activity, with noise. It is a bewildering display or show. A few sensitive souls, with a thirst for the esoteric, can peer beyond the womb of time for snapshots of what is to come — glimpses of eternity. The older souls can tell the younger of what is coming, but most young listeners cannot hear these thoughts all that well. They have no experience or faculty to measure these words.

And, we might ask, what is the point of hearing or prefacing such a natural event? Why not let nature take her course? There are many possible answers to this question. My own feeling is that once upon a time we were trained or prepared for esoteric events such as the Saturn return. We were prepared to experience it in a more conscious way, to appreciate and know what it is that is happening to us at the time it happens, rather than to piece together some ghost story from hindsight many years afterward.

What I am speaking of, in terms of preparation, is nothing more than developing an "awareness" of life that all esoteric studies encourage. Awareness of what, in fact, IS and is happening — happening right now: to measure and appreciate life as it happens and preparation for these events can be important.

Setting the Sails

Just as the doctor may have to adjust the infant in the womb so that it enters the birth passage in a natural way, so too esoteric knowledge given (that is: pointed out) at the right time can help to set the sails for our inner birth. Like a sailing ship, we come from within the womb of time and sail beyond time into our particular version of eternity. It can matter to us how our sails are set and how our sails take the inevitable winds of change.

This is why I write on this subject. I had the good fortune to receive instructions on this subject prior to my Saturn return from a Rosicrucian initiator. And although I had great difficulty understanding what was being presented to me at the time, some glimpse into the reality of this passage did filter through to me. Like a baby in the womb, I did try to prepare myself for what was coming and I did experience at least a portion of it with awareness or consciousness. And yes, it was more than worthwhile to do so.

But I should say this: I am sure I was not a very apt student, but during those years I spent with my teacher, before he died, I hardly ever said a word in his presence. It was unspoken between us that he would go over material, again and again, and I would try to just absorb it.

I heard these concepts over and over and over. In fact, he would say to me things like: "Michael, I am tuning you like one would tune an instrument. Years from now, you will respond to what is being placed in your care." And I did.

To give you one clear example of how potent were his words, one thing he said to me was: "Michael, imagine yourself standing at the center of the Sun," then he would kind of growl, and say "That is hot stuff!"

I had no idea what this meant or why he was saying it to me, but years later I naturally discovered what has become a life-long interest in heliocentric astrology that has fueled most of my work. And it is hot stuff. That is how it worked with this teacher.

After the Fact, There is but the Poetry

It does not matter if you are under 30 and within Saturn's grasp (and return) or over thirty and beyond that grasp, if you can grasp what is being pointed out here, it will make reading any other esoteric literature much more sensible. This will be much harder to grasp for those of you under 30, but not impossible.

In closing this section, I would like to quote from a journal I wrote years ago about this type of experience. I know it is florid, but for days or parts of days in our lives, we do sometimes have poetry:

"No matter what you think about me, about my person, I know in time you will learn to recognize me as yourself and you will love me as I have learned to love myself, as I have learned to love you, like it or not."

Journal: Person the Product of Time

Context: Awakening after the Saturn return.

"My person has not changed. How could it truly? For "person" is the product of time, and my person, like a freight train, rushes on at the future. It always has. Only I, stepping off my person, am with you now. I am myself. I turned off or away from time's endless matter at thirty. I dropped my body or sense of gravity. It proceeds on without me, or rather, with my perpetual care and love. But I am not only my person. I am as well one with the creator of my body, of anybody. My faith informs me. Each day's passage frees and reveals my past, presents my past and clears it open."

"Where was but an endless accumulation, layer on layer, is now removed with every passing day. And as the layers lift, it is clear to me that there is nothing there worth worrying. All the past lives I have are presently living, are become clear. Nothing to go back to. No place to hide. No cover. I am born free, held awake by all that lives. Where before I could not keep my eyes open, so now I cannot shut or close them. No closure."

"From my subconscious pours my past. Cloudiness clearing, it is my present. My placenta is being born, turning out all of which nourished me. I can clearly see all that clouds this stream of consciousness is but a searching, is itself but a frowning, a looking to see, a pause, a hesitation that, caught and unfurled in the eddies of time, becomes clear, and laughing, I leave it go clear, and turn from a darkening or dimming of my mind to light. And it came to pass, and I let it pass."

Journal: Personal Ties

"The morning's brightness lights the day. And when that day is gone, the quietness of evening here approaching settles to sleep that restless world. Hard can I hear the frantic rush, as I turn away from the edge out into floating rest am I. It is not my conscious direction doing this but, as a head down-turned all life now turns up a blossom to the night, the night of time urges me open, at last a flower too, open to life. Already the dawn."

"Still, around me, urging caution, a retinue of persons set my spirit, like a jewel is set, in time. But where before my worry, now my rest. The tide rolls on beyond me. Ever changing, it rocks me now asleep. And in my sleep awake am I, so clear a bell is ringing."

"The smart of persons lash and crack to drive me at time's edge. My personal ties are slipped as floating out I'm gently tugged. Too long have fought to force my thought and not, at ease, arising like some cloud to pass. My work undone, yet done, I rise. Drifting though strains, I sieve and pass myself, open out to nothing thoughts to touch back not once more. A clear sleep is soft; its ever-blooming sound is silence. Now to find my way among the slips of time, and slip I will, now lost to striving, and lounge in this room of emptiness. To lay back in time, behind its edge and ever look eternally. No way to pass this on. This is: passing on.

Slamming against the walls of time, I shove off into eternity, spread open a flower, so wide."

Saturn the Timekeeper

We all should be familiar with the concept of Saturn as the great timekeeper and ruler of the physical. I have pointed out that the Saturn cycle and its return at around 30 years of age ("Never trust anyone over thirty!") marks a climacteric or critical year in the lives of each of us. Before we continue, it is important to recap the material that you should be familiar with.

The return of each of the planets to its natal place has always been important to astrologers. In particular, that first return for each planet during a life has special significance. Our whole consciousness and living can be seen as a series of investments and returns. If we are at the point of no return with anything, that something is lost to us. It is only by the steady returns of life (like the waves beating against the shore) that we know we exist.

The Moon returns each month, and the planets begin bringing us returns as early as three months of age (Mercury). As each planet returns (completes its circle or cycle), it has described for us its basic orbit and sphere of influence. It then circles on and begins to go around again, and its cycle becomes a constant in our lives — a part of our inner life. Our consciousness and experience moves beyond that orbit, beyond the time of that planet, and we begin to pick up on the next outer planet which has not yet completed a cycle. After we have completed a Mercury cycle, we begin to pick up on the track that Venus is laying down in the heavens, then Earth, and so on, all the way out to Saturn. This is what is called our "formative years."

The Circle of Repetition

The idea to consider here is: before a planet repeats itself (returns) in our lifetime, we don't know its limits through our personal experience, because it has not completed a cycle during our lifetime. The information we receive from or through the planet as it counts through the zodiac, degree by degree, is new to us. It absorbs our attention. There is seemingly no end to it. It might as well be a straight line, as far as we know. It is somehow altogether new, as far as that planet is concerned.

However, when the planet has completed one circle, the information or tone changes for us. We now have the whole of that planet's message or cycle within us, within our personal life experience. Its ability to entrance us falls away or is now included within and as part of our experience, and we begin to pick up on information about the next outer planet. I was first exposed to this idea in the book by Grant Lewi called Astrology for the Millions. And, although I am quite well read in the literature of astrology, this book is still one of the single most important work on astrology that I have ever come across that relates to time. It is, in my opinion, the definitive work on transits. Everything published since amounts to a footnote to Lewi's book.

The Womb of Time

For example, Jupiter makes its first return at about 12 years of age and signals adolescence. At that age we begin to monitor and pick up on the beat and measure of the great keeper of time, Saturn. It seems that almost all of us get caught up in time. Before our first Saturn return, we are held within the sphere or cycle of Saturn like a child forming within the womb. These are our formative years, years during which we are growing up and completing our physical form, that is: Saturn, the physical form.

As Saturn completes a great circle or cycle and begins to fade to repetition, its hold on us somehow lapses and we start to see beyond time and catch glimpses of a time-less state — of eternity. It dawns, for most, very slowly. We find ourselves standing outside time as we have known it. The transition from within time (Saturn) to without time (the passage), and the rites of this passage is our theme here. In this sectione we will go a little more into this esoteric idea of time.

Go Spell

The word "time." My teacher would always tell me to "go spell" (gospel). The word "time", he said, spells "Tie me," and if you turn it around and read it backwards, it says "emit". There you have the whole concept in a word. Within the cycle of Saturn, we submit to the force of time and we "form" or tie ourselves up and grow our body (incarnate). After the Saturn return, when we are over the age of 30, we begin to untie or emit. We start to break up or come apart, to shine!

This same teacher made it clear that we are launched, like a space vehicle, at our Saturn return. Our formative years are then over. The time to perfect the launch vehicle (the physical form) is before the launch, before the age of thirty years, while we are still on the ground, so to speak. Once launched, we find out just how well made or tightly wrapped we are — how long we last. We then begin to move beyond the protective sphere of time (Saturn) and submit ourselves to the test of time, Saturn or Satan. How long can we endure?

The Monad or Space Ship: The Silence

At the Saturn return, our physical body (now full formed) heads out beyond the womb-like Saturn cycle. Ready or not, here we come! We are launched beyond time's (Saturn's) first protective grip and begin to stand the test of time, to see just what we are made of — just how and how long we will last sailing out there. Time releases or lets us go and off we float, freed for the first time from all sense of gravity and the grave. However, the awareness of this event that takes place at around 30 years of age to all of us may take years to develop.

At this point, at our Saturn return, we are cut loose and, like some great ship, we begin to float off into space. It is as if some vast generator has been switched off. Our consciousness moves beyond time and Saturn into a new state of mind. We begin to enter what has been called "The Silence."

This great event is given almost little or no fanfare in our modern consciousness and society. We have lots of asides and jokes about growing older, but few direct references to this great transformation, this rite of passage. Most take these changes in a very private and solitary way. We each get a little crazy from time to time, and that is for sure. During these lapses in our normality, our loved ones hang on to our various tethers, as we float out toward the wild blue yonder. After a while, most of us come down to (or find) Earth again, but perhaps with an altered view of things. We reorient and that is called, appropriately enough, the "Turning Point."

The Quality of Time

Those of you who have ever played with time know that the quality of time is far more important than the quantity of it. Just a little bit of real or quality time experience can light up a lot of life. And the inner eternal sense that can be found in our intense moments provides a real clue as to what time is all about. I am reminded of part of a poem I wrote years ago...

"The hour's heartbreak conceals the whole of what we have not hated."

To a great degree, time is a social convention lived by the majority — a consensus. We don't always remain within that convention, but in odd moments, days, and hours of our lives, we may wander into more unusual (altered) states of mind and time.

Eternity does not somehow exist at the end of history or linear time. Eternity exists now, deep within (or without) time. Time does not extend to some end. Individuals extend time and we endure for that length. We last until then. We go between time, stretch time, make time. We extend ourselves. In moments of great vision, we leap between the seconds (beyond time) to the day of creation itself. We each have and develop our own sense of time, and sometimes what we see can be quite unconventional. This is particularly true for the shamanic among us.

The Rush of Time

Over the course of life, our sense of time changes. In the rush of linear time, it can become impossible for us to slow the flow of events. Time then seems like a freight train hurtling through the present, carrying us toward we know not where, we know not why. There is no rest when things get tight. We are having a "bad" time, and hang on for dear life.

We also know moments and days when the rush and clatter subsides and is not the main focus. The freight train slows down, and we can smell the flowers once again. The gentle roll and swell of events now flow by like a great lazy river. On those days, there is no place we have to get to as important as the way we are feeling at the moment, the way we are going. This is a "good" time.

Many of you reading this column will have had minutes, hours, days, and perhaps years of your lives when you were thrust beyond that general consensus into a time zone where you knew that you were on your own, having a good or a bad time. Those of you with a tendency for the shamanic view, will spend a considerable amount of time beyond what we could agree is conventional time. The task is to reintegrate our experience, so that it can benefit both ourselves and society.

If you made it back from those moments and glimpses beyond the normal, and were able to put what you saw to good use, then you have had what are called "moments of vision". This is pure shamanism. If you got trapped out there, or were (for some reason) unable to integrate what you experienced out there with your everyday life, then you are said to be experiencing some kind of mental problem. All of us have had both experiences, to one degree or another.

Time Curves

As pointed out, time does not just extend on forever in a linear progression, although that is one definition of time. Time (like space) curves, wrapping us in its cycles. There is also eternity to consider. Eternity, as all wise men have been telling us forever, is "now here" (some spell it "nowhere" or "erehwon") with us. Eternity is the salvation of time. In fact, we go between the seconds of the "now" to have these eternal moments, not down the road to some far end.

We can reach within the crush of sequenced time to touch eternity and slow time down to nothing. Time is tempered by eternity. Time slows down in the really full moments. It just stretches, that's all, and we go between those clock-ticking seconds into a dimension that is, somehow, timeless — beyond time. I don't know why it works this way, but I have experienced it, many times.

As any musician knows who works with time, laying down each beat and measure, the moment opens just like a flower to expose its timeless quality. I mean: eternity can be found only within time. Time stops or slows and we bloom in the moment, having all or enough. The seconds stretch, and although the metronome ticks away, there is more and more quality, more eternity between each tick, until we have all the time in the world. We have time and not vice versa. We have conquered time. An astrological aside: I should mention that the conquering of time is the domain of the planet Jupiter, our guide through time. This is covered in the main body of this book.

Beyond

As an astrologer, I have tried to understand what astrology is. For one thing, I am certain that it, in the popular sense, is all about time and the sequencing of time, at least on the outside. Yet, the heart of astrology is concerned with the eternity that is somehow beyond or deep within time. We all find eternity, just in time. (That's my particular sense of humor talking now.)

The relationship of eternity and time (the eternalization of time) is, well, my kind of astrology, and shamanic in nature. Every religion I study tells me that somehow we must redeem time, renew it, and find or make our little piece of heaven within what, in fact, "is", like that old phrase, "On Earth as it is in Heaven". All of the books about making the mundane everyday world sacred, bringing the sacraments of life into our everyday reality, are what I am talking about here.

Over the last few years, I have had trouble with my classical astrological training. I have let a lot of what I had been carrying go, because I had reached a point of "no return" with it. And, if astrology is about nothing else, it is about returns. Things that produce no returns for us are things lost to ourselves. We live only by and through the returns that keep pouring in each moment. That is an acceptable definition of consciousness for me. We "are" only by returning or continuing on around.

Time and Eternity

I am fascinated by the relation of time and what we can agree to call eternity — whatever may be said to be beyond or embedded within time that is timeless. I am entranced by the concept of overcoming time in favor of eternity.

It does not come as a surprise for me to learn that there are groups who have concerned themselves with the eternal moment, the eternality of time. Most of the world's religions do little else but attempt to guide us toward this part of ourselves. Among others, the Native American and the Tibetan Buddhists have kept a vigil over the eternal flame of the "now." It is the sole power of eternity to transform linear or sequenced time. We must touch upon it, if we are to open up time and let it blossom. How much better for us to view time from the vantage point of eternity, than to view or glimpse eternity from what can at times be the prison of linear time.

And, this is just what the Saturn return is all about, a passage or passing on. This passage (and the rites of that passage) is one of my major astrological interests. Since this is not the focus of the great many astrologers, I guess that makes me a practitioner or student of esoteric astrology — a shamanic astrologer. Some of you, no doubt, are too.

Saturn the Sequencer: More

Looking Forward to Looking Back

Here we will look at the esoteric concept of Saturn and its time sense and sequences. As youngsters we look up to adults. We dream of when we will be old enough, grown enough, able to take full possession of our earth inheritance, our own life, and be our own boss. Within the womb of the Saturn cycle (that is when we are under 30), we gaze toward our Saturn return (one of life's great event horizons) as to a bridge into another dimension, which it is. After thirty we (very gradually, perhaps) begin to look back. Looking forward along the line of time; looking back down the line toward our youth. That is linear thinking. Time is most often seen as a sequence of developments, one leading to the next. Leading where?

On a day to day basis, this makes a lot of sense. Time does tend to lead us, to point forward to the next event in any developmental sequence. It is easy for us to slip into the habit of seeing our life as linear, as a straight line. That line leads to our personal death; make no mistake. This very basic fact urges us to look for some other way of understanding our life than as a one-way trip to the grave.

The Straighter the Line, the Finer the Curve

The reality is that we have within us a burning ball of fire, spirit — the esoteric Sun. Looking up from childhood at it, we know it not yet. Looking back from old age, we know it not now, except in memory. In the prime of life, we are too busy to notice it or see it as clearly as we did earlier, and will later on, because we are in the midst of it. The Buddhists explain to us, and they are correct that, for these reasons, the Sun or Self is but an illusion. How easy that is to say and how hard to realize!

It is part of esoteric training that, as we learn to understand life, our linear sense of time begins to curve, until it has wrapped around itself. When we see that the Sun in the sky is a burning ball of fire, we see just right. The esoteric or spiritual Sun is the same.

In the center of the lives of each of us, that is, in the center of our life (our common life) burns the primordial Sun, William Blake's "Tiger, Tiger burning bright, in the forest of the night..."

This esoteric Sun stands at the center of our life and at the center of our lifetime. In all truth, it lights up our life, just as the physical Sun gives us light and warmth. We are blinded by its brilliance when we are young, warmed by it when we age, and lost in it when we are in the midst of life.

Of course, the esoteric Sun is the sum of all the planets that encircle it. Here we focus on the cycle of Saturn, since this planet rules time, the event consciousness, and the sequence that we have come to know as the external world.

The Event Horizon

Like a stream of consciousness, we grow up and toward the event horizon of our Saturn return at around the age of 30. Imagine a brilliant throne toward which this procession leads, a long line of visitors moving, day by day, closer to the throne to make a presentation, perhaps their fifteen minutes of fame. Only here it is ourselves (or so we like to think) we present to the world.

A second line leading away from the throne into old age also exists. In fact, the esoteric tradition tells us to throw away the image of a line and just see a ball of fire, the Sun, and an infinite number of lines or rays stemming from it in all ways. That is the correct image of the Sun.

The young are inside, the old outside. Where they meet is the fire up front, a fringe of fire burning bright in the heavens — the so-called Prime of Life, the Self or Sun.

Like the rays of light that stem from the real Sun out into space, the fire is at the surface, at the event horizon. Beyond that horizon, the fire is not as hot. Within the core of the Sun, it is very hot. We have the premonitions of the young, the memories of the old. And we have the experience itself, the transition, the very passage from within to without, from within life to without life. This is the exchange of energy to light. Then, we might ask, what is life? Life might be defined as a process — a passage.

Here is a poem I wrote years ago, when I was learning this:

> Whether,
> That which is within will out.
>
> And when out, with all within,
> Will out without Within.
>
> And then within,
> With all without,
> Will out as in.
>
> And In,
> When out,
> Without an in,
>
> Is out when out,
> And in when In.

The Sun is Shining

"The Sun is Shining" was the title of my first book. The above concept is what that title was all about. The Sun of the prime of life is always shining. It burns and burns and burns in the firmament of our inner lives. It is all that we see as we look up from our amorphous adolescence. Its splendor is all that we can see from the vantage point of old age. The Sun is shining today as it always has shone. It blinds us from seeing it.

Straight is the gate, and narrow the way. No doubt. A translation of light, not unlike a magician's sleight-of-hand maneuver — nothing inside, nothing outside. What then, is there? There is the translation, the going itself, the passage, and there are the rites of the passage. These rites of passage are what we study here.

My message is that there is existence itself, that ball of fire that shines through and in our life. We are coming to be; we are being; we have been. An endless stream of souls pour through the threshold of Saturn and out to eternity beyond. Where are they all going to?

Nowhere. It is the going itself, the living, the shining, that is the goal, and this is called the Earth Chakra. We are going to, toward: living. We are going: to live. We tend to live. The movement from within to without is the shining of the Sun. That's all. I once wrote these lines:

> I am in it all the end,
> And that's all,
> And the ever its coming to be.
>
> And in me is out,
> The shadow of doubt,
> And the in that is out,
> Well, that's me!

Karma & Re-incarnation

The fact that the West conceives of the idea of re-incarnation and karma as somehow a degraded concept is laughable. It matters not to Westerners that the very great majority of the world's people find reincarnation an accurate description of life. We find these Eastern ideas weird, to say the least. What is weird is not the Eastern approach, but our own ignorance of the entire subject. The inane remarks coming out of the average astrologer about reincarnation, etc. do not reflect on the ideas themselves, but rather on our superficial knowledge of them. "Do you believe in re-incarnation?" is equivalent to the classic "Do you believe in astrology?" Very few modern astrologers would credit that astrology is a matter of belief. The same is true of re-incarnation. Either you have looked into it and have some knowledge or experience of the subject, or you have not. It is useful to you as a tool or it is not.

It is pure arrogance on the part of the West to consign these very detailed doctrines to the realm of pure speculation, an idea that we may toy with when in certain moods, as if any idea in this world is that far from reality that we could take or leave it — humorous. The Eastern concepts describe the mechanism of the process of this endless life, this burning Sun.

What do we obtain by studying these subjects? Perspective, humility, and thus an even better perspective. A study of this material tends to break the habit of hoping and betting on the line of the future — linearity. It forces us to today, to now, to living. It can aid us in abandoning the linear idea of progress, of getting "somewhere" in particular, where we are better off than we are right now and here. These ideas can be a godsend for the here and the now. It forces us to look now for our future right here, where we are now.

The Shining Sun

Let us look at this idea of the esoteric sun shining. Please stop, for a moment, that linear thinking about getting older, growing younger, etc. Stop thinking about growing along a line to your physical death. Think instead about growing into something, taking possession of yourself, like filling your own shoes, growing into your potential, being fulfilled. And then passing through, passing beyond, passing on. At first not enough (young), and then perhaps too much (older). Where is that middle ground? Is it anywhere?

We know that all the stars shining out there are burning stellar fuel, converting energy from one form into another, and producing a lot of light in the process. This process drives the whole galaxy. If this is so pervasive, and it is, could it be very distant from our own life process?

It is the conversion process I am referring to here, the transition, the passage itself from one form of energy to another, from one form to another. Within Saturn, we have one form of energy. We are in our formative stage. Our bodies are growing to the tune of the Saturn cycle. If Saturn and the sequence of time is all that has meaning for us, then we can plan on being reduced or extinguished as life passes. Is there life beyond the bodily sequence? Is there life beyond death?

Beyond Saturn, and its return, we have another form of energy. The periphery of the sphere, the fire itself, is the point of conversion, the translation to light, the very passage.

Outgrowing Our Body

Our body may reach full growth and stop growing (it does), but our consciousness does no such thing. Our mind outgrows our body; make no mistake. Or better yet, we begin to be more aware of our mind when the body stops moving or growing, and by "stopping moving," I am not referring to the death date of our physical body, but when it stops forming or growing, around the age of 30 years, at our Saturn return. That is the point we really die.

This ball of light, the Sun, itself a sphere, moves through space. In fact the earth is traveling (as we speak) at 67,000 mph around the Sun, and the Sun is traveling at 500,000 mph around the galaxy, so we are not exactly standing still, ever.

The track of this ball through space is what we call history — linear time. But the real story (his-story or her-story) is the endless exchange, the fringe of fire, the fire up front. This eternal energy conversion process is the "eternity," the process that drives time itself. Any knowledge of history or linear time (West) must be balanced by an awareness of the eternal aspects of the cyclical process of life (East). East meets West. It is this awareness that we find in the East, what they call "Awareness Awareness."

We each pass through the flames, from inside looking out, to outside, looking in. We are the youngster looking up toward age, and the elder looking back. What I am getting at here is the movement, from inside to out, a controlled fusion or conversion, a light giving. This whole process is what is called the Monad in the esoteric tradition.

Beyond Time

We are even now being born out of time, beyond time. We are formed in time, under Saturn's rule, and then born or borne beyond it. We can go beyond time at any time, that is: in time, perhaps, just in time.

Instead of a line of history, think of a sphere, a ball of light shining in the darkness. Or, go outside and look at the Sun. What is that ball of fire? The center of life is where the shining takes place, where the light is made, the light of the prime of life, the light of health balanced with the wisdom, the knowledge of life. The Sun is shining!

The awareness does not dawn for most until we are cut off from the ever-growing Saturn cycle. When

Saturn goes around once and turns to repeating itself, we come awake (or bolt awake) in the time after, like waking from a deep dream. Slow or fast, we start to put it all together. We shoot out into space, born beyond the circumference of Saturn — beyond time as we have come to know it. And then we wake up.

Beyond the Saturn return, we slow down real fast. We go from pushing forward through life to our future, to hanging on for dear life to today. The future that we sought one day to achieve becomes the present. We are then in the future that we pushed toward. Worse yet, as some fear, we may already be looking back. Did we miss something?

Do Look Back

Until our Saturn return, we have never looked back, because we have been looking forward. There has been nothing all that important to look back to. And then we cross some subtle threshold, and are pushed out beyond time's grip. We "reflect" for the first time, rather than are reflected. We feel something moving inside us, rather than feel ourselves moving inside. The baby is born. This is what is called discovering our inner life, discovering the Self.

No, this does not take place in a flash for most of us. It takes place (in awareness) over a lifetime. Are we inside looking out or outside looking in or somewhere in between? We go through a conversion process. We are converted from one way of seeing life to another. In all truth, we ARE born again. Being born again is not just a Christian experience; it is a universal experience.

Be the Book

We can have our library of astrological treasure books. There is a time for that, and a place for these books in our lives. We hunt and dig through them for clues or pointers that point us on toward real understanding. The great astrologers point us on toward understanding ourselves. God knows I have spent enough years poring through books, abstracting them, trying to fathom them — anything. Yet, there comes a time for each of us when we, ourselves, must become the book. Maybe that is what the term "living Bible" is all about. We must ourselves become a living resource, our own reference source. My teacher in esoteric astrology used to say to me, "Michael, someday you must become the book!"

Another way to say this is that, at some point, it may be easier to leave off with marking the important passages in books and just go within ourselves for this same information. Not easy, perhaps, but easier. All of the knowledge we seek is within us right now. Accessing it is as easy (or difficult) as breaking the habit of looking outside ourselves for it and recognizing the outside as inside, etc. This kind of statement rolls off the tongue, but baffles the understanding. We each must make it real.

What You See Is What You Are

One of the most important lessons I have learned is that anything that I can see, appreciate, admire, etc. is already a part of me. I am already that. Otherwise, I wouldn't even see that. Or, as they say, you can't see the phenomenon, if you lack the faculty. If you can see the phenomenon, you already have the faculty. This principle already points within. The really portable astrologer is one who can read way back or within him or herself. It is a technique that can be learned, like any other technique.

Here in the West, it seems we have focused on the "facts" of history to the exclusion of the process of that endless life. What does man see when he goes into outer space or eternity? Well the Sun/earth, of course. That is a key point.

The Sun is a ball of fire that fills our lives with warmth and energy. The esoteric Sun is burning in the firmament of our mind, right now, day and night — always. As young people, we look up to that Sun; as old people, we look back at the Sun. The whole thing is not a line, but a sphere, and the process or differential is one of conversion, inside to out. When we are in, we look out; when we are out, we look in. The symbol for this process is the shining Sun. It is that simple or that complex.

Saturn: The Body of Our Enlightenment

Young people, those under thirty who have not had their Saturn return, are often intrigued with stories of out-of-the-body experiences, with ideas of spiritual awareness and enlightenment in general. Many young people imagine that if they could just get outside their body far enough, if they could get a glimpse of what is beyond the physical, that with a little enlightenment, they could better see to manipulate and control the actual body of their day-to-day experience, and perhaps avoid some of the obstacles they see in their path. From what they have heard and read, they think that enlightenment and greater control might help them escape from the limitations or obstructions of the body or situation they are now in. This is very common.

Older people know only too well that without some actual life experience living in bodies, without some life savvy, that control or manipulation of them is impossible. It would be like trying to drive a car from a book, but never having been in one, much less had a driver's training course. Young people often seem willing to ignore and/or leave their bodies prematurely, to trade up, in order to get some degree of desired awareness, to get a peek outside of their current circumstances. They believe that if they can just get a little farther out, they will somehow get a bigger picture, which will help them get the hang of life, and come into the promised land of better self-control. In general, this is just not true.

An Object is the Product of its Use

Older people know: An object is the product of its use, and this includes our life. Rushing out from the body only produces a disembodied state, as helpless to effect change with, as the previous body or embodied state was. We have a genuine "Catch 22." In fact, in one view, enlightenment is no more than getting far enough out of the body to realize the value of being within the body in the first place: the real use of the body. This is a key point, so give it a moment.

If younger people drop everything and make an exodus from the temple of the body, without first fully determining themselves in the body, they will only find themselves bodiless, and with no spiritual muscle or life experience built up thru years of a young body's work.

The Body is the Ultimate Talisman

Yes, they will know something of the out-of-the-body mystery and secrets, this esoteric knowledge, but they will be able to do very little with that knowledge. Formal knowledge is not wisdom. They will have gone outside, only to have the door to the body closed firmly behind them. What is needed is a co-operation between older and younger souls, so that the younger soul (with the stronger body) can hear what the spirit in the older soul's openness is saying and telling them about, and build that information into their young body, so as to better act out that truth — cooperation.

What is being pointed out here is that perhaps the most basic error in much of the spiritual work of this time has to do with our relationship to our physical body. For starters, many people today do not understand the full meaning of the physical. In their wish not to be too materialistic, they do not understand that the physical body is of ultimate value in our spiritual realization, and that without it we cannot fully realize ourselves.

Rush To Leave the Body

The body that you call your physical body is not all of what I mean here, when I use the term. What I do mean is more like: your workload or karma or, in astrological terms: your Saturn (the obstacles in your life), the densest point or nadir of your physical life. This dense point or workload (Saturn) is the occult meaning of the term "physical body."

When we are young, under the age of thirty, we have great workloads to accomplish with the strength of our strong young bodies: great karma to work out, while we have the strength to do it. After all, we are busy forming our body. Many of the spiritual students working today have an incorrect idea of what the physical body is and can be used for. The majority are trying to find ways to escape, dump, and get out of their bodies as fast as they can, to grow up, to be adult, to "get there." Where?

They are trying to grow up too fast. They have read that attachment is bad, and they want to detach from the physical as soon as possible. They "think" that to be spiritual is somehow to not-be-physical, and that non-attachment means no feeling of the physical, in all of its many varieties.

These quasi-spiritual types ignore any and all real opportunity for spiritual growth, and live in an artificial atmosphere, mostly of their own making. Their spiritual workload sits waiting to be done, and in many cases it will be right where it is today when they are eighty years old. They believe, because they traffic in refined spiritual thoughts and refuse to allow any of the more physical experiences ever to happen to them, that they are pursuing a truly spiritual existence. This is a big mistake, and a 'fool and his body are soon parted'.

Getting Some Body Out Of Our Body

Our living body, like any cycle, has a prime of life: a center of greatest such-ness. How could we imagine that this too, this prime of life, would not exist for some definite purpose, when everything else does? In many respects, our physical life is a procession up to our prime of life, and a recession leading away from this event toward old age. This living body of ours is made for work, and needs to work to build not only the physical muscles, but also the spiritual muscles of discipline through the experience in the body. I am not talking about an exercise plan, either. Using our growing experiential strength, we can work thru our karma and create spiritual muscles and character — like an ark that we can use, long after our physical muscles fail. This is to be done before our Saturn return, while our blood runs warm and is not yet cold.

The Esoteric Concept of Bodies

"You are no more yourself than you now here live." This quote from Shakespeare is to the point. Furthermore, we 'live' not only in our physical body, but also in all of the various bodies of interest we have created. A photographer lives in his photos and cameras, a teacher in the teaching process, etc. We actually spend a lot of time in these special areas of ourselves. As astrologers, we live in the body-of-knowledge we call astrology that we have created, and so forth.

Our sense of self and who we are fluctuates or oscillates. We have ups and downs. Most of us go through a regular rhythmic process or cycle that alternates from feeling very good and in control, to feeling not-so-good (not-so-in-control), to feeling good again, and so on. We tend to look for that happy medium (ourselves) where we feel 'just right', not too emotional, and not too distant from life. 'When you're hot you're hot, when you're not you're not'. How true.

High Times

During times when we feel good or are 'right on', we tend to move ahead in all areas of our life. We are in an expansive or forward-moving phase. We are eager to fulfill existing responsibilities, and we feel we have the energy and insight to take on even more.

In these good times, we extend ourselves into new areas of life or make a deeper commitment in areas of current involvement. We do this based on the high energy that we feel at the time. It can be very hard to remember during those times that there may be another side to our story — that we may not always feel so 'gung ho', and that the high energy push that we are riding may in time flag.

We could spend reams of writing on just why and how we manage to fall from the good times and lose our extra energy or great attitude. The simple truth is that just as there is a flood tide to life energy, so is there an ebb tide. Sooner or later, most of us wake up one day in a situation that is driving us rather than vice versa. We have over-extended ourselves, based on the very great sense of energy that we felt, and with the assumption that this energy or attitude would remain a constant. We bit off more than we could chew.

Low Times

The tide changes and we find ourselves stuck within a situation that we created, but without the guiding light, energy or attitude that first put us there. Furthermore, we do this over and over again. This kind of cycle happens in little and in large ways. It happens large on the level of our basic self-confidence, and it happens small in any of the many subjects where we find ourselves involved.

There is a tendency to bite off more than we can chew during our flood times. And we may get stuck in a situation during the ebb tides, and have to wait for the next high tide to pick up where we left off. In fact, the process is not dissimilar to the action of waves washing a log up on the beach. Each new wave of energy pushes us a little farther in the course of our life. In between waves, things tend to remain just where the last wave left them. When the energy and light are there, we explore and pursue what interests us. When it is gone, we wait for the tide to come back in. At times we may even cry out for help. Learning to work with this pulse of life is an important part of astrological study.

When Words Live

As astrologers we should be able to verify this cycling process as it relates to our study of astrology. There are times when we can understand what is written in the astrology textbooks, and other times when nothing seems to register. We have times when it all clicks and we sense the way things hang together or work. We can see connections on many levels. There are other times when we wonder what we ever saw in the very same books and thoughts. The life energy or light is, for the moment, gone. In summary, our interest (and self) appears to pulse or fluctuate. This happens over and over. It cycles. For now, it is not important for us to attempt to link up this or that cycle with the movements of the planets, aspects, and what-not. Here we will work toward a better understanding of this cyclic process itself — the pulse of our life.

Our incarnation can be seen to consist of all of those areas of our life where we are involved, attached, and connected. Each of these smaller life areas has a pulse or rhythm of its own, just as we have seen that our interest in astrology waxes and wanes. In addition, we have a larger sense of self that could be seen as the sum total of all our involvement. This large sense of our self or well-being also has its ups and downs.

As Above, So Below

The point here is to provide the setting for a very simple (but important) observation and that is: incarnation is indeed an ongoing process. It consists of all the smaller series of involvements in which we find ourselves, and each of these has its own pulse. If we are to speak of 're' incarnation, we must look to see how that works in the cycle-like process of life itself. Re-incarnation means to somehow live on or again. It may be difficult to grasp the process of re-incarnation at the lifetime level. However, it should be clear how this works by examining the much smaller cycles of our day-to-day life. Here we may find a clue as to how this re-incarnation process works.

Such clues are not hard to locate either. Every passion or subject of real-life interest, whether it be a study of astrology or a love of philosophy, has its seasons, its cycles. There are times of inspiration, when we are fired up and when great progress and understanding is possible. At these times, we have a real feel for the subject. Everything falls together and makes sense. We feel great. We are on top of the world, in control, and able to manage all of the unwieldy and difficult passages. And here is the point:

When We Say "Yes!"

It is during these 'good times' that we 're'-incarnate, if it can be said we reincarnate at all. It is at the high times that we look over our life (our creation) and judge it good and worthwhile. We say 'Yes' to life. It is then, at these high times, that we ask for more, that we desire to feel this way forever. At the high times we find it hard to remember the other side of the process — i.e. the low times. Were we better able to do this, we might think twice before asking for more of the same.

It is standard procedure in many spiritual disciplines to take the high and the low times without preference, to abide in whatever state we find ourselves, desiring nothing other than what is present. We could speculate that this kind of attitude might be a key to balancing out some of the cycles in our life, at least in those areas where we tend to plunge from very high to very low and back again. Sometimes it might be better for us to not ask for anything more.

Issue by Issue

Our purpose here is to demonstrate that we invoke or ask for continued incarnation in the odd moments, hours, and days of our lives, where we sense a real oneness, continuity and unity. And we do it piecemeal, issue by issue, rather than saving it up for the end of our life. We are the sum total of our desires for life. Today we might be at the top of the cycle as regards our study of astrology. We see the reason for it in our lives, give it our blessing, and opt for a continued subscription. We subscribe to life on an issue-by-issue basis. Tomorrow we may approve or re-subscribe to something else. We ask for it, and what we ask for adds up to our continued involvement.

You might be tempted to jump to the conclusion that it is being suggested here that one ought not re-subscribe to life, not re-incarnate. Not so. The goal here is only to develop awareness of an ongoing process, so that we might better understand what it is that is happening to us, and have a choice in the matter. Let's subscribe to the issues we choose.

Recapitulation

In closing, let's recap the flow of our discussion. Understanding the process of re-incarnation involves examining each of the areas of interest in our life that we find ourselves alive-to and living. We re-commit ourselves to each of these areas on a not-infrequent basis. We do this when we feel very good and in complete control (at one) with the subject. We also do this, in general, with our whole life. On those very, very good days, when we are at one with life and all is just right, those are the days when we desire to do this forever, to live forever.

There is this endless process of incarnation, of desire. As a child is born, he or she picks up the mantle of the desires of his or her generation and continues on with it. It is an endless life and an endless 'One' who is living that life in all of the bodies that now exist, have ever existed, and might ever exist. The wise tells us that death is but an illusion. We might add that it is, at the least from our 'un-wise' perspective, a 'Grand Illusion'. If we find it convenient to see the endless birth of each new generation as a 're'-suming or 're'-incarnation, fine. There is evidence that it might be even more convenient to conceive of life as an endless incarnation or fountain of life, incarnation, rather than reincarnation.

The Last Judgment

I would like to introduce you to another very important esoteric concept, that of the "Last Judgment." I hope that the following will serve to get you started working with this material, until I can present it in still greater detail sometime in the future.

At any moment, an event can occur that causes us to re-evaluate our entire day of incidents and decide then and there that we have had a good or a bad day. The glance, the phrase, and the smile are sometimes the points on which can turn a successful day. A fortunate event or thought that comes later in the day can change how we view that whole day that went before. A change in perspective is capable of reordering the importance of events, how we see the entire sequence of events.

We have been told by wise men and women that the only future open to us is the present, "The future is now!" "The future is embedded in the now," etc., this sort of thing. Most modern astrologers understand this concept. Yet, the converse principle is not recognized. We might also say "The past is in the now," because the present can also control the past. This is the idea being presented here. If you think about this, it makes sense, that the "now" would control both the future and the past.

He Who Laughs Last

This is the concept of the last judgment. It is something like the "he who laughs last, laughs best" sort of thing. Your past, my past, and our past can be "redeemed" or reordered by an experience we may have not yet had, and this is a very important thought.

The esoteric truth I am pointing at is much more profound than I can communicate here. I will try to sketch it out just a bit of it. History is only in the reflection of the present. It can never be more than how we manage to see it. We remake history in our own image each generation and probably each day.

We complete our thoughts with the help of those we link to or are aware of from the past.

Making Choices

This concept holds true without changing any of the facts of the situation, although facts are not as always solid as we like to think, but that would be another article. What changes is the way it goes down and the view we have of that. We each give our life by following our own internal genius and muse. We put our life on the line each day by choosing this rather than that path or direction. The main result of our intuition and the choices we have made in life is the position we have placed ourselves in or have been placed in. If we are positioned in the way of what we might call the general "Will" or trend of things, it becomes our will, and we get to go along with or do the greater will.

If we live what is called in religious books the "life that never dies," we will attract to us those opportunities for growth, the new ideas, the insights that we need to continue with that life. If the course of history is looking for ways to grow, and we make ourselves one with those ways, like standing in front of a freight train, history will have to come to us and happen through us, through our person. We can hitch a ride. And there are nothing but opportunities for this kind of growth. Placing oneself between a need and the fulfillment of that need is one of the principle rules of good business.

Credit With Interest

We can practice all this by giving credit where credit is due. Funny word, "credit." Is it like credit at the bank? Will someone else use this credit, with full interest?

We offer ourselves to those who go before us, picking up where they left off. In some sense, we are controlled by their wisdom, and their need for completion, to have their work completed or carried forward. These famous men and women from the past are the touchstones and impetus for much of our own growth. We complete what they started, and we, in turn, are completed by those who come after us, and they, by those who come after them.

If we labor in a particular niche or field, we first unearth the value of those who came before us; we expose their light for the world to better see, as lights to guide us. We get in line. Our job, which may seem a lot like waiting, is to live, and to be ourselves. The great works of art in history, the lineages, are almost collective efforts based on a string of men and women who are inspired to complete each work they do, illuminated by the light of those they have taken inspiration from. Each work of art, a beacon in the night of time, like a fixed star, must be loved anew by each generation or it is soon forgotten. And this appreciation or love can't be faked. It either is there and done, or it is not, and forgotten.

That kind of appreciation and love is not a passive thing. It is an active giving, an extension of ourselves, a giving of life itself. We pour our own life blood into the things that we love, for they are literally the beacons that light up our life. They serve to guide us, and without them we cannot see. In this way, works of art, science, and what-have-you are like the fixed stars in the firmament of our lives.

W. H. Auden, on the death of Yeats: "He Became His Admirers"

A great poet is kept alive by those who read him or her. The very words on the page move and change with each generation, molding themselves to fit the needs of the times. One year, the early poems of a poet are valued, a few years later some other period of his or her work. Or, that same poet, a few years after that, may shrink out of sight into obscurity. It all changes, depending on what is needed now, what works for the present.

It is the channel, and the open link that marks the genius. All manner of form can fill that channel. We might take life from Shakespeare's sonnets during one generation, and from a couple of his plays during the next. History is based, to a real degree, on what we need in the present, now.

Perhaps something is not important. Some works are worn out of time in short order, and soon lost, while others stand the test of time to light our way. We return to them, generation after generation. Still others come in and out of prominence, like a variable star, as the need arises.

Whatever you love, whether it is astrology or any other subject, receives your lifeblood. We pour ourselves into what is most important to us. In this way, the past reshapes itself to reflect the current moment, and grows to meet the needs of that moment. Our life energy streams through these portals. Thus, what appears as the most modest of gifts, perhaps a single clear thought or good intention, can grow into a pivotal work of art, become a channel, if the need exists.

A Crack in Time

What you or I do today, while it may seem insignificant to us now, will become the foundation for our future life. It is what we build on. A single effort may appear, in the light of time, as a pivotal gesture — the straw that broke (or saved) the camel's back.

Perhaps this is getting too esoteric for most of us. The message here is: don't underestimate your own contribution, if it is indeed your own. In time, it may appear to be much more than what you now take it for, like the single pebble that plugged the hole in the dam, and prevented untold catastrophe from taking place. You never know.

A sincere action that we make could be the way or crack into the future through which all of mankind must pass. A simple path, hardly a trail, today often becomes a highway tomorrow. Your heartfelt actions can become a highway over which an entire generation can run.

Your own willingness to love what is excellent, to serve that which is noble and true in your life, may itself be the key to the highway of the future. Great thoughts, poems, and art may not stem so much from an inherent gift or talent, as from a sincere willingness to be of use. That willingness may be an openness or gap in an otherwise unyielding present that can lead to the future, through which great things can pass.

Our current generation's need or focus can raise one author from the dustbin and send another to it. It has to do with what we see we need. We look backward and forward, but we see the same thing: ourselves. Anything from the past is like a lens through which "we" peer. That lens can and should be polished and kept clean.

Personal Choices

We each build our personality by the choices we make, and time will tell if we have made the right choices or not. We all would like to have an attractive or interesting personality, and the endless stream of popular magazines is testimony to the fact that imitating what is considered cool is the way many personalities are put together these days. We copy, big time.

But real personal power, the actual power of the person, has little to do with imitation or copying what works for others, and has everything to do with the choices we make in life. And this happens to be pretty easy to explain, so I will give it a shot. And this is what makes the concept of the "Last Judgment" so important.

At any given time, like today for example, we are surrounded by choices, and are free to choose so many different paths and directions. We can't travel all the roads that life offers us, at least not at the same time, so we must choose one and leave others un-traveled. In many cases, we won't know if we have made a good choice until much farther on down the road, until much later in our lives.

Unconventional

Choosing what everyone is choosing, as shown in the popular magazines of the day, copying what others do, does not guarantee that these personal choices will result in a personality that reflects how we really feel inside ourselves, or what is good for us, what we really need. Using what is now current or popular is (by definition) peaking or already peaked and will probably not be very useful down the road of time.

Not choosing what is popular at the time, holding out for something better or more true for us, may also, by definition, be unpopular and very risky. We go against the grain, against what is conventional. How will we know if we have made the right choices?

We will know later on down the line, for better or for worse. Let's take an example, someone living in the 1960s, where there was so much flux, and so many alternatives to choose from.

Future-Oriented Choices

Back then, we might have chosen to home educate our children instead of sending them to public schools. We might have had home births, rather than hospital births. We might have chosen to eat more whole and organic foods, as opposed to eating more processed foods. We might have preferred self-educating ourselves, rather than pursuing a more formal course of study. We might have elected to experiment with alternative states of mind, rather than the excepted religion of our times, and so on. You get the idea. These are choices we might have made back in the day.

At that time, way back then, these choices were not all that clear. I know, because I was there. These choices did not stand out, because everything was all mixed together in the present moment, and there was more like a haze of confusion than a list of clear choices to make. We had to go by our gut feeling in making choices. Unconventional choices were just that: not conventional. They went against the grain or trends of the time. Some (many in fact) even carried penalties, imposed by society, like choosing to not finish high school, or choosing to educate yourself rather than get a degree. It took guts to make those hard choices and there were few rewards other than personal satisfaction.

Now, let's jump ahead some 30 years and look at the personalities that result from these different choices.

Most Significant Subset

Today, a person (personality) who chose (way back then) to self-educate themselves, to home educate their children, to have home birth, to learn about whole foods, and alternative religions, would at least (today) be very distinct and probably more interesting to society than a person who chose to follow a more conventional route. Why?

Because, as time changes, certain qualities are found to be more useful or interesting to society, and these are sought out and promoted, and those persons who have these qualities have a personality of more interest (of more use) to society at large, than one without these qualities. Both types have personalities and as personalities go, neither is more or less a personality. Why is one more interesting?

The process of time and change naturally selects the qualities most needed for the present time, and if a particular person happens to be composed of the most significant subset of these qualities, that personality will be interesting, perhaps even scintillating. Everyone wants to learn more about what it takes to be that way, because today it is considered useful. Ecology and clean air is a good example.

I grew up in an era when almost everyone smoked, in planes, and trains, buses, and cars. There was no apology for blowing smoke where you breathed. You just had to suck it up. Those who did not smoke, like those who never touched a drop of alcohol were frowned upon — teetotalers. Ugh. They had no fun. But today, all that has changed, thanks to one person at a time giving up those habits and daring to defy convention.

Another example: If in the 1960s, for some reason, you had decided to learn the Chinese language, your skills would be in great demand today. English speaking Americans who know Chinese can get a job anywhere. Who could predict that China would become so powerful, although, if you think about it, this should have been a no-brainer.

A Stellar Personality

The point here is that one way of looking at our personality is as the result of a series of choices we have made in the past. Someone who, for whatever reasons, has managed to make five or ten really good choices in their past, will appear as a most valuable and fascinating "person" today. Others may kick themselves for not having made the same choices, and try to imitate those choices now, but this is usually just a little too late to bring about the same effect for themselves. The die has been cast.

In other words, there are real practical rewards for developing our instinct for making good choices. What I am pointing out here is that a stellar personality, one filled with many points of light, was made long ago (just like stars in the sky were), not just by natural talent, but through a process of making careful correct choices.

We may not all be Leonardo Da Vinci material, but we each can learn to use our own mind and intuition to make choices that will bring forth a destiny worth living. Choices that we make today, which may seem very unpopular now and even separate us from acceptance and popularity can, in time, result in a personality that is key or crucial for the society of the future, even precious. This is the idea of the last judgment, personified.

That Fascinating Person

When you meet a really fascinating person, take note of what about him (or her) is so fascinating, and you may end up with a short list of the significant choices he made, choices that others did not make. He invested his time and energy in ways that have proved useful to society today, although at the time, that choice may not have raised any eyebrows, or even seemed like a waste of time. This is called having the courage of our conviction.

Today we are the most significant subset of all the choices we have made, and if most of those choices are now relevant, then our person appears almost unique. You get the idea. That is how personalities of note are made. If you believe that the truth will win out in the end, then this helps in making and standing by good choices.

Saturn and Cycles

Saturn, sometimes called the "reaper," brings forth all things in time. Where do they come from? We can learn to find or discover the source of life within us, that from which all good things pour. In the process, we must become the road or the way itself, that through which news and life pours. The cycles of life, large and small, continue to turn, grinding out their respective portions of life. The large cycles keep the succession of days in line with the nights to bring us years, and so on. Within this succession of days and nights, within time, we live. There are cycles within cycles within cycles. The ebb and flow of spirit in our lives brings us dry and full times.

We often seem to wait for something to happen, for signs in our life that will give us direction. We seek to get to the promised land of significant living, moment by moment. Yet, the very anguish of waiting, the lonely vigil may be what we do best. We stand and mark time, waiting for the gap or glimpse, for the "sign," and then shoot through that narrow passageway, the cleft in the barren days, making a move toward a better life, whatever that may be.

The Tracks of Time

The roar of life's meaning all around us often finds us down on our knees, feeling our way along the tracks of time. It is indeed a question of worlds within worlds within worlds. In the realm of Mars or meaning, everything points onward or inward toward the very heart of meaning, toward what it all means, what it is all about. We gather clues in the books and through the teachers that we know, clues to what we might call the meaning of our life — what we are all about, why we are here, etc.

As counseling astrologers, we often serve as guides on this inner journey. To do this, we must first find our own way within the spheres within spheres within spheres. We have to know our way around, to be able to read the signs along the way for someone else. Reading the signs of the zodiac and planets is no different than reading the signs around us in day-to-day life, signs that pop up to point out our way.

The Astro-Shaman

To me, the return of the astrologer to an accepted social standing is synonymous with the return of the shaman. Our integrity is our life, the living of it. To be true to ourselves, that is the test, to follow our heart as a guide, no matter where it may lead, to be able to lay down one direction and pick up on another without missing a beat, if the signs are right.

Jupiter is the guru that guides each of us beyond Saturn or time. Saturn wears everything out in time. Physical death is inevitable. We find freedom from the facts of time, what has been called "the terrible crystal," through Jupiter, the guide — the guide within. We don't usually seek that guide within until we have been turned out by the Saturn cycle, until that cycle goes to repeating itself at thirty years, at which time we are subjected to the destructive test of time after that Saturn return. Then we look out into the mists of the future, and begin to put two and two together. After the Saturn return, we feel the bite of Saturn, the promise of a lifetime of test. At that time, physical death starts to become real to us.

Our interest in the external, what is out there, wanes a bit. We find freedom from this outer test within ourselves, by going within. We begin to pull in our horns. And the first planet within the orbit of Saturn is, of course, Jupiter. Jupiter becomes our guide through Saturn to what is still further within.

Within or Without?

Are we still within the first turn of Saturn or are we already outside its womblike protection? If we are exposed to time's test (over thirty), then how aware

are we of that fact? Have we begun to cope with it, to overcome time, to succeed?

If we are young enough, within Saturn's cycle, then Saturn is the planet to become aware of. For anyone in the Saturn chakra, Jupiter becomes the key to life, to how to go inside ourselves, and deeper within, to Mars, then Earth... and so on.

The astrologer must be able to negotiate time, must deal with Saturn. History will justify our good intentions and our efforts. We don't even have to worry about it. It will take care of itself. It is enough to live life as we have to, carefully, mindfully, moment by moment. By our efforts, we can become the path or way onward, not only for ourselves, but for others, for those who follow.

For Saturn is not airtight. The vents or cracks in the mundane or material world, like some great vortex, will collect around themselves whatever significators are needed to mark their presence. The rush of spirit through these cracks in time will collect the necessary bric-a-brac, assume the form, and provide the signs for others to find the way to and perhaps through us, if, indeed, our life becomes part of the way through to the future, if our heart becomes the highway over which life itself will run. We become the very road itself.

IN OR OUT

In is not within the out,
And out without the in.
No,
In is without the out,
And out within the in.

The Last Judgment

This is, then, the story of our personal history, and the concept behind the Last Judgment. The idea of spiritual practice, such as meditation, is nothing more than being aware, observing our mind and waiting for those openings or gaps in time that do come. Spiritual insights come in blossoms and streams. Time spent quietly looking at the mind itself is what is called "practice," waiting for the moments of opening, and seizing those moments to look even more deeply into the nature of the mind itself.

The straighter the line, the finer the curve

Planets As Chakras In A Natal Chart

It may be useful to some of you to go over, however briefly, how these techniques might be integrated into an astrological practice.

The main planets of interest to the counseling astrologer, from a shamanic (life journey) point of view, are Saturn, Jupiter, Mars, and the Earth/Sun. It is not that the Moon, Venus, Mercury, and Uranus, Neptune, and Pluto are not important. Of course, they are, but, in general, the main chakras that can be counseled are those of Saturn, Jupiter, Mars, and Earth/Sun. I will explain why.

The inward spiritual journey from Saturn, to Jupiter, to Mars, to Earth, represents the typical path of awakening that each of us goes through sometime after our Saturn return at the age of 30 years, and these four planets are the most accessible in the counseling situation.

We say Earth/Sun here, because many of us look at both the standard geocentric natal chart (Sun) and the heliocentric natal chart (Earth). I have looked at both charts for all the readings that I have done for some 35 years, and I always look at the heliocentric chart first, for that is what I call the "Dharma Chart," the key. The Sun and the Earth (which are always opposite one another in the chart) represent the same principle, usually identified as the Self, our heart essence, how we will end up (our future), when all our changes are done.

What Interests the Client?

Once we have spoken with the client, heard what his (or her) questions are, and asked a few questions ourselves, we should have at that point a good idea of what chakra or chakras he or she is most active in, and thus be prepared to present to him the information they will most benefit from concerning where they are now at or of the next chakra inside the one they currently are in. For the most part, the clients need help in either adjusting and working with the chakra they currently are in, or help breaking through to the next inner chakra. Or both.

In fact, all of this could be done without even looking at their natal chart, provided that you, the astrologer, have a solid grasp of the various chakras, know the signs that point to activity in each one, and are familiar with the possible remedies or directions-to-go involved. This information in itself may be enough for a complete reading, and you may never need to even look at the planet's positions and aspects, etc. on the client's natal chart. However, using the chart is very much recommended, and provides us with much of the chapter and verse your client may need to hear and benefit from.

Looking at the Chart

Many of you will, no doubt, have your own personal way (and training) in looking at the chart, so you don't need my recommendations. However, for those of you who may be just learning all of this, let me at least lay down a few general guidelines.

Using the natal chart, you will want to look at the position of Saturn, Jupiter, Mars, and Earth/Sun in the chart to see how strong and well-positioned each of these planets is. In other words, do we have a strong Jupiter or a weak Jupiter? How you measure strength and weakness is up to you, but traditional ways would include by zodiac sign, house, and full-phase aspects.

For example: is the particular planet part of a larger pattern of aspects or is it alone in some area of the chart, essentially unaspected? If it is strongly aspected (locked in), what kinds of aspects are we talking about here? Is it conjunct another planet? What aspect phase is the aspect in? Is it waxing or waning? Are there lots of challenging aspects or are the aspects more energy-giving, like trines and sextiles? You will want to do this for Saturn, Jupiter, Mars, and Earth/Sun. Of course, looking at the rest of the planets and bodies is also important, but here we will concentrate on these four planets

Strong and Weak Planets

The point of accessing the strength of these planets is to determine if the planet is strong and able to carry out its normal function, or weak and possibly in need of some form of assistance or compensation. On the other hand, a planet can be too strong, and we may have to compensate for that as well. Let me give an example:

If a client is living primarily in the Saturn chakra, and struggling to survive and make ends meet, we know that they need to invoke Jupiter (the career), which is the key to Saturn, the means to reverse or control the power of Saturn in that chart. However, if Jupiter in their chart is debilitated (very weak), we are alerted to the fact that this may not be an easy task, and the client may have to go to extraordinary measures to compensate for Jupiter's inherent weakness. Somehow, the client will have to balance that.

In fact, we need to look at all four of the planets (Saturn, Jupiter, Mars, and Earth), carefully, to see how "healthy" each of them are, much like a doctor might check out our arms and legs for strength.

Saturn represents the physical challenge and circumstances the client faces. Jupiter represents the way through Saturn, how he or she will succeed, the particular path they must take. Mars represents the kind of energy or activity-space they can look for to propel the Jupiter to make or tread that path, and Earth tells us where we will end up, just who we are, when all is said and done. Earth, oddly enough, is a place we each are trying to get to, and not part of our birthright, by our just being born. We are trying to take possession of our life.

Planets: A Process and a State

These four planets (Saturn, Jupiter, Mars, Earth/Sun) represent the living process of our life, and are interdependent, and inextricably connected one to another. In fact, while it can be helpful to view each planet as some sort of state or realm (chakra), we should never forget that it is also important to view the planets as interconnected and part of a continual process. All of the planets interlinked with each other describe the journey each of us is taking through life. We are a living being.

For example, when we speak of Jupiter as the planet of career, then we are speaking of Jupiter as a static state or chakra, as if it were a place we could travel to and remain in. This is fine, and we do tend to remain in a particular chakra for long periods of time, until we get the hang of it.

However, when we speak of Jupiter as our path or guide, the way we go through life, then we are speaking of Jupiter more as a process. Jupiter is the process of success or succession, how we get through whatever (Saturn) faces us with.

Interdependent

In other words, each planet can be viewed as a process and a state, much like the heart is an organ (state), and a pumping station (process). In real life (which is where each of us now is), the various planets are hopelessly intertwined (one to another) into a living organism, forming ourselves and the life we are involved in.

The form we are in (Saturn), the way we go through that form (our path or career — Jupiter), the kind of energy or atmosphere we are capable of generating and maintaining (Mars), and the place we are trying or will get to at last (Earth/Sun), are both interdependent and interconnected, one living process, which is our life.

Astrology and the planets are but a description of that process. We are using astrology to examine and talk about our life. The life journey is the point, here, not the astrology. If the astrology is good, it is transparent, and gives us a window into the life process and journey. It is doing its job.

Astrological Techniques

As mentioned, astrology as a method or technique should not be confused with why we use astrology, which is to look at our life. We study astrology or seek out an astrologer not for the sake of the astrology, but for the information it can provide about us about our lives. This is the old razor and shave analogy. We don't care that much about the razor; it is the shave we are after. The same is true with astrology. It is the life information we are after, and astrology is one way to access this information.

There are countless astrological techniques and approaches to astrology, probably as many as there are astrologers in the world. And there are even more astrological clients, each of whom hear or receive astrology in a slightly different way.

Astrology as an Oracle

What is important is that we each find an astrology (or astrologer) that speaks to us, and that offers a window into our self, into whatever information we currently need. This is why astrology is, after all is said and done, essentially an oracle through which the heavens speak to us. It is this deep information we are after, not what astrological technique is used to provide it.

This is not to say that there are not proven and solid astrological techniques that astrologers use to arrive at this life information. There are. But also keep in mind that when the astrological muse speaks, it could be through who-knows-what astrological technique, and also sparked by the background music, the warm breeze through the window, and the candle or the incense. We also have to be in a frame of mind to be receptive, to hear what the cosmos is saying.

Astrology Is About Our Lives

The point here is that receiving a good astrological reading, having the heavens speak to us, may well be through the very most tried and true astrological techniques, the very best astrologer, and so on, or it may be through what might appear as the corniest and most flimsy of astrology techniques, along with the particular brand of incense playing. When the spirit within us speaks, we listen.

It is the communication to us of useful information about our lives that is the purpose of doing astrology, and it is difficult to say just how, where, and when this information will be communicated. When we do astrology, we try to set the stage and create a mood where this kind of inner communication can take place.

That being said, make no mistake, it is not always easy to get on our contacts and bring through meaningful astrological information, and to make the heavens speak. That is why astrologers, like myself, work to find the very best astrological techniques, ones that tend to work every time for us. I have an axiom I use in my own astrological work: astrology must work for me, not I for it. In my early years, too many of the techniques I tried to use took more from me than they gave me in return. I was working for it, not vice versa.

If this sounds just the opposite of what I said above, well, in a way it is. On the one hand, astrology is an oracle that can speak. On the other hand, making it speak clearly can require just the right astrological technique. Both of these statements are true.

Can Astrology Predict Events?

I am asked this a lot and it is a good question, but one that does not have a simple answer. There are astrologers who claim astrology can predict just about anything, and there are clients of astrology who claim it has done just that for them, things like: exactly how many children they will have, their sexes, the stock market, and so on. With this type of testimony, there seldom is room for discussion, much less debate.

Here I am distinguishing prediction, of the kind suggested above, from simple astrological profiling, such as saying that I am a homebody, because my sun-sign is Cancer, or because I have the Sun in the 4th house, that kind of thing. What each one of us who practices astrology might better ask ourselves is: what can I predict for myself or for a client, using astrology? This will be the limiting factor for us, regardless of what other astrologers can or cannot do. When I ask myself that question, it is clear to me that I cannot predict things like the stock market.

Financial Astrologers

I once held a conference on financial astrology, in particular, about predicting the stock market and other financial markets. Some 21 speakers or experts attended, most who had a financial newsletter of some sort that they sold to clients on a subscription basis. As far as I could tell, and without meaning to offend these fine folks, it appeared that virtually none of them had been able to use their astrological market savvy to make themselves any money. Most were broke or close to it; many had to have help even paying for their way to the conference.

It would seem to me, if I could predict the market using financial cycles, much less advise others how to spend their money, the first thing I could and would do, is to make myself enough money so that I could live comfortably and have plenty of time to do my astrological research. This did not seem to be the case with this group of investment counselors.

I was amazed at this fact, for I had been only too willing to believe the hype these astrologers presented to their clients. Previous to that, I thought it was just me who could not make money through financial investments using astrology. Neither can I tell you how many children you will have and/or their sexes. That is just the way it is, for me. If some of you astrologers reading this can do any or all of the above, how about teaching the rest of us how to do it, so we can successfully invest in the stock market and live comfortably.

What Can Astrology Predict?

If astrology is not able to predict events like the stock marker's rise and fall, just what can it predict and how?

A better approach to astrological prediction, at least for me, has to do with understanding the nature of cycles, and the phases that any cycle must pass through. While we perhaps can't predict a solitary event, we can look for certain phases in a cycle to represent events or a particular part of an event landscape.

For example, if we accept that the Full Moon is traditionally a good time for social gatherings of one kind or another, than we can predict that social gatherings may occur (or be successful) around that time. Or better yet: using electional astrology, we can pick the Full Moon time as perhaps an optimum time to throw a party.

Electional Prediction

In other words, prediction here is achieved more by an electional process, than it is by some form of out-and-out prediction, and this form of electional prediction is perhaps the most used by astrologers practicing today. I know that there are all kinds of stories and claims to the contrary, but I am unable to find astrologers who can show or teach me to predict in the sense of saying "such and such will happen on this or that day, period." Perhaps it can be done, but it seems more to be through some psychic ability, than it does a straight-forward astrological technique.

Since astrology is pretty much all about returns, and all returns are about cycles, and all cycles have phases, then by being aware of these phases, we can elect (or predict) appropriate times (particular phases). This is about as close to prediction as I have been able to come. But I must say that this kind of electional or phase-oriented prediction is very useful, both to me personally, and to the clients I have worked with.

For example, take something as simple as the Saturn return, an event all of us go through. We could write an entire book about the phases before, during, and after that particular return, a book filled with very useful information.

Perhaps electional prediction is, in a way, kind of backing our way into what the public expects from an astrologer by way of prediction, but this electional method at least works, and on a reliable basis.

The 'Last' Of Life

We learn to make the things we do last. Great art is made so well that it lasts and fascinates us for a very long time, often far longer than the civilizations that produced it. We still love the Bible and the Odyssey, thousands of years after the cities of the men who lived and wrote these books have turned to dust.

Shakespeare has defied the combined ears of centuries to fathom and to exhaust the ability of his words to last. Only absolutely true actions hold together long enough for us to see anything in them.

It is like gathering our light into little pockets, little balls of crystal (crystal balls) into which we gaze (and last) into the future. Things done or made well collect light and are the solidified product of the light of our experience.

They are like Suns shining, bringing light. These sources of light, these "things" that we do, are one of the esoteric meanings of the fixed stars. In each of our inner selves, we make and discover, one by one, things and facts that never fail us, but ever last, giving us light. Finally, our whole inner world is ablaze — filled with the light of these true things we have made or found. We, literally, guide our way through life by these stars, we astrologers.

Collecting Light

As we grow spiritually, we learn to make more and more things last in our life, and we, in turn, develop more and more light. The things we do well collect light and give us sight. Once we have made or found one star shining, we can see to make more by its light, and the more light we have, the more we can make, bringing still more light, until we have built an entire body of light. In this way, we light up our life.

When we succeed in making some part of our life really well, that section of life no longer demands attention, and we can turn our awareness to other things. Spiritual work is the process of taking permanent or perpetual care of more and more of our loose ends, tying these down so well that they don't require further attention. We then have time to more fully appreciate and be aware of what our life is about.

Teachers are master craftsmen of the spirit, who demonstrate to us how to get ourselves together into a form that will truly last a long time. A teacher is a perfect crystal that can collect all available light, bind it, and let it shine like a pole star in the direction of our life.

When we meet someone with more time, more freedom of the moment than ourselves, we know that they have somehow built a stronger vehicle than we have managed, and we are free to ask them to show us how to do the same with our life. Teachers, having more time on their hands, are free to shed light all ways. They are fountains of light.

Realized Realization

Our spiritual strength can be measured by what we can afford to realize in our daily life. It is easy to afford private spiritual vision that we cannot share with the world, and that no one but ourselves understands. This might mean we are empty inside.

It is work to afford real spiritual treasures such as obtaining a perfectly realized friendship or having a real sunrise or real peace. Ask yourself when was the last time that you saw a real sunrise. That should tell you what I mean here.

Realizing the spirit in the closest areas of our life takes courage and a great amount of work. How about real parents, like we always imagined that they could be, or a real job? Only when we are very rich inside do we have the strength to bring this through and act it out on the physical plane. Just what can we afford? These are not even luxuries, but necessary steps in our spiritual unfoldment. We must realize them all. Could we afford not to have real parents or real brothers and sisters and still claim to have any unfoldment at all?

Spiritual Work

True spiritual unfoldment starts from the center — where you are now — and radiates in all directions outward, like a pebble dropped in a still pond. The rings, starting from the center, spread equally out in every direction. We don't have to say a word, think a thought, or even breathe.

Spiritual work will realize every part of our existence. Spiritual work is the process of making the spirit matter or mean something in every contact we make, and the greatest signs of this work accomplished are not visions and flashy experiences. If that's all we have, then we have very little. The greatest signs are found in the most common things, and always with constants like: breathing, our food, a real home or a real husband or wife, or having a real teacher in the flesh.

I once asked a mentor of mine, who was a poet, why he had not written any poems lately, and he responded: "Michael, my best poems are walking around," meaning the time he spent with people like me. Enough said.

Inner Teacher

Externalizing the inner teacher and acting out this inner drama in two or however many bodies is a sign of faith and strength. Living alone in a world where only we are truly alive is not living. Inner strength is the power to realize all and every form we contact, and to draw it to its fullness — not try to hold it back.

These realizations will not come about, if we do not want and ask for them. We must ask very deeply to prove our life by full realization of its every aspect. A real guide or teacher may take years of work to bring into the physical plane — the same (even more) for a wife or husband. These things that make up and take up 99% of our life, are the most important signs of life we have. If our realization ends within our own thick skull and does not extend by its radiance from every opening in the body, an aura of light to everything that is, then we have realized very little.

Just Passing Through

Saturn is something we each pass through or more correctly, Saturn is our way of passing, or perhaps most correctly: Saturn is our way of passing through us every thing in our lives.

Saturn is something (like a landscape we at first appear to be passing through), that over time becomes for us our particular way of passing (how we manage or do it) and, finally, we realize that this is how we pass or take (handle) everything in our lives. In the end, we realize that we are just passing through; it is "we" who are passing though.

The forces of generation in this vast process are one of continuous labor and outpour. When any body enters the world, this formative world, they undergo massage and formation in accordance with what IS already there. In other words, they are shaped by what "is," by what we must go through. Our formative years are ones of slow formation, increasing growth, a process of incrementing, and of gradual increase.

The Degrees of Experience

In our formative years, we are growing each day; something new is added. Each new degree of experience reflects Saturn's transit through the circle of the 360-degrees of experience that define our space. Until the age of thirty, there is always this forward leaning or urging, an ambition or future-oriented quality, this continual leading us on during our formative years. Another way to say this is that we look forward to growing up, to becoming an adult, to coming into "our own." The seeming-endless bewildering display of Saturn, through time, catches each of us in its headlights.

We had long ago (at 12 years of age) first experienced Jupiter's transit, and the gradual completion of Saturn's transit is a much longer process (1.5 times), consuming the greater portion of our young life. Longer cycles, like that of Uranus at 84 years, is beyond comprehension to a young person, at least until Saturn completes his first round and begins to slip into the groove of repetition.

Endless Description

As we grow up, we gradually include within our personal lifetime experience these longer and larger cycles, and also continue to sustain the repetition of the smaller ones. Each larger cycle describes the same sphere, the same circle or cycle of the 360 degrees of the zodiac, yet each longer cycle reveals these degrees in a slower and more methodical manner, exposing or holding our attention fixed to a given degree for increasing lengths of time. Sooner or later, we are bound to learn each degree, for they are etched into our memory.

What we went over rather lightly in a two-year Mars cycle, that entire circle of the zodiac, we spend about six times as long when Jupiter passes over the same area. Certainly this will be more revealing, perhaps six times as revealing as it gives us, like it or not, six times the exposure. Of course, Saturn is very detailed. So, as we personally age, we are having the whole of our life exposed or described to us in ever-increasing detail and elaboration, the 360-degrees of our experience. Time leaves its mark.

The Straighter the Line, the Finer the Curve

In a very real sense, we are or become the rhythms of the cycles we have experienced. Any body entering this world of generation, this material world, is formed or shaped according to the laws and cycles of that world. We are gradually exposed to the formative cycles of time indicated by the various planets, pulling us out of the womb (the unmanifest) into existence, holding up or maintaining us for a while (our prime), and passing us (our body) again from this world, thus changing our form — arising and passing away.

As we know well, the human form has an average time of formation, endurance, and passing. We measure this in years, and we experience very regular and predictable changes in physical structure: growth to our prime, the sustaining of that growth for a time, and the falling away and decay of what has grown — our trajectory.

As much as we might like to imagine how different we are inside or spiritually, if you investigate, I believe you will find that our spiritual and emotional bodies bear a direct correspondence to the lifetime of our physical body and are not in some random relationship. As I like to say, our physical body is our ultimate talisman and significator. It pays to study the planetary cycles that form us through time.

The Hierarchy of Age

In spiritual matters, it is common in our times to deny the relationship of age and spiritual knowledge. Instead (so many claim), there is (somehow) a random-like relationship between the average spiritual growth and rebirth, and the physical map of the age of the body. I have been told this again and again.

People balk at entertaining or accepting the idea that there is perhaps a hierarchy of aging that is, in general, as indicative of precise spiritual events as it is of the physical events (like your second set of teeth). People will accept the physical roadmap of age and growth, but still persist in the belief that their spiritual roadmap might be randomly related or randomly oriented to their physical age, and that spiritual experience can just happen any old time. I have not found this, for the most part, to be true.

Gradual Exposition

Age is the spread through time of the process of life, the gradual process of building to a fullness of our physical body and a tearing it back down. If we are serious, if we are sincere students of astrology, we will investigate this general series of events, the smaller cycles in our life that compose the average lifetime.

As we grow up into and pass through this world, more and more is revealed to us through the gradual exposure, the exposition of the forces of time, and we all measure time by the precise movements of the planetary bodies and by the changes we experience. Through this revelation and repeated exposure, the cycles of the planets wear or imprint themselves into our memory. They serve to point out each degree of our experience. They are how we measure our memory. We become used to the more quickly-repeated cycles, and only gradually learn of the slower cycles.

Falling to Repetition

As each more gradual cycle completes its return and continues over zodiac degrees we have experienced before, we become that cycle, that is: we incorporate it and include it within our life experience. We have it under our belt. It is somehow inside us. We are bigger now than that.

As each planet falls to repetition, we somehow "get it" and are no longer as interested in what that particular planet has to tell us, as it begins to repeat itself. It no longer holds our attention as it once did. We have done that, experienced that. It is already a part of our experience.

That particular planet's cycle becomes old hat, as it falls to repeating itself, and we pick up on the new revelations of the next larger cycle, the next greater cycle, and are intrigued and fascinated by the continual revelation of THAT body's movement or transit through the degrees of experience that we call life — the circle of our existence, our circumscribed life. All the planets tell the same story of the 360-degrees of our life, but each successive planet has its own flavor, and tells that story more slowly and emphatically.

It is almost as if, and I am being humorous here, that because we didn't get it the first time around, we get the story told to us again, only more slowly, and with a different angle or flavor. As we complete and "know" the complete cycle of any given planet, it falls to repeating itself or sustaining its pattern, and our awareness or interest is somehow freed and reaches beyond that planet's sustained repetition, and begins to pick up on the next larger cycle, the planet next beyond. Each successive planet-cycle reveals basic areas of our existence and, caught up in all this activity, we are gradually led to the confines or outer limits of this physical world, which is defined by Saturn.

The planets Mercury, Venus, Earth, Mars and Jupiter are all within the sphere of Saturn, and it is Saturn that lends to each of their cycles that physical or material feel, sense of linearity, as if we are going somewhere. The ever-changing display of Saturn as viewed through the filter of each of these inner planets, like the northern lights, presents a bewildering and mesmerizing quality to our life. We are caught up in it. When Saturn stops or returns at thirty years of age, we fall out of trance and that is a major experience for each of us.

The Limits of Time

The limits of time are defined by the cycle of the planet Saturn, beyond which we begin to pick up on the vibrations of the cycle of the planet Uranus, which is quite different, in that relatively few people personally ever live to repeat it (84 yrs.), and even then they only repeat a small portion of it. Much of how we learn about these outer planets is information passed on to us from above the grave, through word of mouth, from mouth to ear, through the various religious and spiritual lineages. The same is true of any other planets beyond Saturn, such as Neptune and Pluto.

As young people, we are relatively comfortable within the womb-like physical confines as indicated by the 30 year cycle of Saturn. Almost everybody lives to experience at least two cycles of this planet, and while doing this, they are working on experiencing most of a Uranus cycle, and increasingly smaller portions of the more distant planets. The Uranus cycle reveals constantly the degrees of the physical cycle as indicated by Saturn's transit. It gives each degree incredibly more exposure, each single degree of possible experience.

An interesting exercise is to look at those areas of the zodiac covered by Pluto, Neptune, and Uranus, for they are, for each of us, the most thoroughly defined parts of the zodiac in our lives. Even though we have not been initiated into the cycles of the outer planets, that is: even though we have not lived long enough to experience that entire cycle, those particular degrees that we have experienced under Uranus, Neptune, and Pluto during our life may be special to us. I have wondered about this, but that is beyond the scope of this book.

The Beat of the Planets

We are always experiencing ALL the planets all of the time, each marking a particular degree of the zodiac, but it is only when each planet completes its return do we appear to pick up and register the beat of the next planet beyond, although it has been there all the time. I learned about this idea from Grant Lewi in his book Astrology for the Millions, and I believe it just came to him. I have not seen it mentioned in depth anywhere else.

Modern science bases its standard on the Saturn cycle, on the limits as defined by the physical. We are only learning now as a group consciousness to feel beyond that Saturn cycle, get a sense of those still larger cycles (Neptune and Pluto), and to interpret in our shorter lives something of the knowledge of these longer and larger cycles. This is part of what is called initiation, where knowledge is communicated by an initiate (one who has the experience of the whole, of larger cycles) to someone who has not yet taken that degree of experience. These initiates are our mentors and guides to these other worlds.

Where we have spiritual inquiry in our lives, we are (pretty much by definition) inquiring into the cycles of those planets beyond our personal experience, each successive planet, and finally the outer planets, called: transcendental, metaphysical, spiritual planets, etc. And these planets and what they signify are still relatively new to our conscious experience. But as time wears on, we will grow very comfortable with their presence and better learn to appreciate them, not just personally, but as a world culture. Their message is filtering down to us now.

Time's Noise

Until the return of Saturn is experienced, (and by the return I mean the circumscription of our physical world, the end or limits realized), it is very difficult to experience or feel what planets exist beyond that physical Saturn. We can read about it here, talk about it, but actual realization before this time is still difficult.

We are each too much caught up in the activity or buzz of time, which is Saturn, to measure and pick up on the more subtle outer-planet vibrations. They are drowned out. Their signal is lost in the noise.

This activity of time, which is Saturn, this continual revelation of the physical, takes up our focus (like white noise) and makes it more difficult to be awake to or have awareness of what is beyond time. There is too much static. It is a rare youngster indeed that accurately can appreciate or be in tune with these outer planets before their Saturn return takes place. These concepts fall on deaf ears for those under thirty years of age, unless they are "sensitive."

The Roar of Nature Living

The roar of nature living that we have come to know as silence, as we mature, remains a roar until Saturn completes its description to us of our confines, our limits. We feel virtually "unlimited" until Saturn returns. Why? Because Saturn IS the limiter. Saturn is the law, and the law protects the juvenile, those who have not yet matured, those still in their formative years, within the womb of Saturn.

And as for this experience of no limitation: while within that Saturn return, it is so difficult to listen to our elders warn or indicate or tell about life beyond Saturn's wall, about these outer or "other" worlds. The ongoing revelation or noise of our day-to-day Saturn experiences leads us on in our continual discovery of life, and younger people cannot long listen to anyone who speaks of this world they think they know so well as having an "other" side or static quality to it. It is not yet within their experience, just as the grasshopper could not heed the warning of the busy ant as summer waned. Don't I sound like a fire and brimstone preacher here?

Of Purgatory and Hell

All of the books and tales of religious experiences, all of the warnings of purgatory, of hell and fire, damnation, all are written by souls who (having passed beyond Saturn's wall, beyond the physical, these souls who have somehow died and gone over there) attempt to aid and warn those who are now living younger, who are still within their Saturn return. They try to describe an experience that has not been experienced by the younger person, and so talking "about" it is all that is possible. When that younger person actually experiences what the older soul is describing, then and only then does this material rise up in the mind and become of real use. In a very real sense, this kind of the other-side-of-death (or life) can be read, like a script, into the mind of the inquiring younger person, where it will remain in a dormant stage, until awakened by the appropriate signs, as the younger soul begins to come of age. At that time, when the signs are right, the script is remembered, revived, is suddenly understood internally, and serves as the guide it was intended to be.

Most of you reading this may be familiar with the concept in the "Tibetan Book of the Dead," where spiritual advice is read into the ears of those recently departed. This same principle is what I am pointing out here. We are all relatively dead, dead to one phase in our life, and not yet born to the next. Hearing "scriptures," descriptions of what is coming, does not just go in one ear and out the other. Some of it is retained and stored in our mind, waiting for the life experience needed to stimulate the memory synapses, whereupon it springs to mind and: we get it now! That is what esoteric traditions are all about.

The less abrasive and more sophisticated of the fire-and-brimstone preachers simply present themselves, tell how it is with them, not what one should or should not do to realize this spiritual life which is coming. They realize the impossibility of communicating what must be, by definition, a personal realization. Others, less subtle perhaps, don't mind the preacher attitude, believing that, regardless of personal judgment of themselves by their readers, some of what they are saying will register and be of use when that reader comes himself or herself to the brink of eternity and begins to pass over into a new and, for many, terrifying experience.

As for myself, my teacher was not a fundamentalist, not even a standard Christian. Christ to him was a great spiritual leader, among many. Buddha was even more important to him. His approach to me (as to this material) was one of repetition, going over and over the material, very carefully placing it in my mind each time as if for the first time. In some way, what he did reminds me of a very precise ritual, like the Japanese Tea Ceremony — very carefully executed. It happened again and again and again.

I knew what was being presented to me was very important and, unlike talkative me, I sat very, very still and let it sink in. I hardly ever spoke or asked any questions. At the end of six or eight hours of intense listening, I was totally exhausted. Somehow, I knew that this precious script was being read into my consciousness, swallowed up whole in the midst of that day, only to float to the surface and be read internally by me many years later.

Here, I am trying to write some of these same ideas down for those of you who have the inclination (attitude) and stomach for it.

Have You Heard About the Lord?

Who are these esoteric teachers? Many of them, having been themselves once lost, terrified and alone, who are able to call to us from the other side, wish (at any cost to their persons) to reach out a helping hand to those younger than they, that they might have guidance and be better able to take these changes and experience them in a more useful manner.

I used to be so annoyed by fundamentalist evangelical Christians who always assume that anyone other than themselves has not been saved. Gradually, I have learned that a more pro-active approach is best. When evangelicals knock on my door, I now invite them in on the condition that I get equal time, that is: I listen to them for ten minutes; they listen to me for ten minutes. They don't like, for the most part, to be on the receiving end of things, and soon are out of there. I have learned that if I listen carefully to what they say, that beneath all the pride and arrogance is this same knowledge we are discussing here. There is only one story to tell.

"Have you heard about the Lord?" We can hear that asked on your every street corner. These street-side preachers are not expecting you to understand what they indicate, but to pave the way, to plant the seed in you, that you may most benefit from the coming experience (and it is coming) and pass to inherit a heavenly world, and not in your terror, be plunged into a hell through which you will endlessly search.

How we take the changes of this life greatly influences what kind of life we have.

As for myself, I am not really a fundamentalist, not a preacher, and not interested particularly in orthodox Christianity, but I am working here to describe a process that some of you may understand, that is: if I can manage to point it out well enough. I feel it is worth the effort on my part to present this material, so please forgive me if all this sounds repetitive. From my point of view, if you do not yet understand it, this material is at a root level, and you can't hear it enough. Repetition does help.

Shamanism and the Bardo States

An obvious question is what is the relationship of these various Astro-shamanistic techniques to the Tibetan Buddhist concept of the bardos, the intermediated states between death and the next rebirth? This is something I have thought a lot about, but I must make it clear to you that I am not an expert in the area of the bardos. However, I have studied it.

As background, I have been interested in the bardos and the "Tibetan Book of the Dead" since the late 1950s, and have read whatever I could lay my hands on about this subject. For the last 32 or so years, I have been practicing various Tibetan mind-training practices, and working with the same dharma teacher, a Tibetan Buddhist lama, for over 26 years. These practices included a couple of sets of what are called the preliminaries, and various additional practices and sets of mantras dedicated to Amitabha Buddha, the Buddha of the Padma Family, which traditionally has to do with death, dying, and rebirth in the Buddha Realm called, in Tibetan, "Dewachen."

I have also been instructed and empowered to practice what is called Phowa, one of the traditional Six Yogas of Naropa. Phowa is a very detailed technique for ejecting the consciousness from the body at the time of death, and this can also be used to help others eject their consciousness, in the period immediately following death. While I have also learned to read the Tibetan script, my knowledge of written Tibetan is still very inadequate.

An in-depth article on the bardos would be the size of a short book. What I can do here is to go over, very generally, some of the main points about the bardo states as they relate to astro-shamanism, with the hope that this will give you enough of an overview to decide if you want to pursue this topic elsewhere on your own.

The Bardos

The Tibetan word "Bar-Do" means "gap," literally the space between two bodies or houses, the intermediate time between two places to live or lives. Perhaps the most famous text on the bardo is the "Tibetan Book of the Dead." The Wylie transliteration of this title is "bar do thos grol ," which transliterates in phonetics to "BAR-DO TÖ-DRÖL," and translates to "liberation by hearing on the after death plane."

Although the popular misconception is that the bardo realms take place after death, in fact the Tibetans make it clear that are a number of different bardos, and we are in one of the bardo realms at all times. Let's briefly mention the six major bardos:

The first bardo, the "SHI-NAY BAR-DO," or "Bardo Between Birth and Death," is just that, a bardo that extends from the moment we are conceived until the moment of our death, our last dying breath. We are in that bardo now.

The second bardo is the "MI-LAM BAR-DO," or "Dream Bardo," and this refers to the dream state we all have when we sleep. This is usually considered part of the first bardo.

The third bardo, the "SAM-TEN BAR-DO," or "Meditation Stability Bardo," is also considered part of the first bardo, and refers to meditative states that can be experienced by the accomplished dharma practitioner.

The fourth bardo is the "CHIK-KHAI BAR-DO," or the bardo of the moment of death, and is said to begin along with the signs of approaching death, and extends until a very short time after the last breath is taken.

The fifth is the "CHÖ-NYI BAR-DO," or "Bardo of the Experiencing of Reality," begins a short time after death, and usually lasts for a period of several days, a time during which most fall into a deep sleep or unconsciousness, and then gradually begin to awaken..

And the sixth and last bardo is the "SI-PA BAR-DO," or "Bardo of Becoming," which lasts from the moment of reawakening after the death swoon until the next birth is taken, which is an indeterminate period of time, usually put at 49 days, but it can be much longer.

This last bardo, the "Bardo of Becoming" is what most people mean when they use the word "bardo." Now let's look at some of the basic ideas of the bardo realms.

What Is Ignorance?

Before we begin, a KEY concept is that of our own ignorance of enlightenment. According to the Buddhist teachings, we are now and have always been (since the beginning of time) in a state of profound ignorance. We have all heard that term before, and many religions say the same thing, that ignorance is the cause of this or that. This, therefore, is an important term to understand.

Ignorance, here, means (literally) to-be-ignoring the-truth, ignoring what is real. Ignorance is not simply some state of unconsciousness or stupidity, but an active ignoring of the true nature of the mind and of the real, at least the inability to look at the truth. It takes effort to do this, and this ignoring is a deeply ingrained habit, extending back endless years and lifetimes. We do it habitually. We have always done it. We will always continue to do it, unless we learn otherwise. It is responsible for most of our pain and suffering. As I understand it, we choose it.

Mind Training and Meditation

If you understand this fact, then you can grasp what all the excitement about meditation and mind practice techniques is all about. Meditation is not, as many people like to think, various relaxation techniques or therapies, but, rather, active techniques to examine the mind and the nature of the mind. How are ignorance and meditation connected to the bardos?

Many of us will remember the game of Pick-Up-Sticks we played as kids. There were all of these colored wooden sticks, about the size of darning needles. We would scatter the sticks in the pile, and the game was to pick the pile apart, stick by stick, without disturbing the rest of the pile, until all the sticks were gone. We could also use the old analogy of the layers in an onion.

Mind training techniques are somewhat similar, in that the mind, and particularly our concept of the Self, is examined and picked apart until there is nothing left — nada. When you take all the layers of an onion apart, there is nothing in the center. So it is, the Buddhists teach, with our personal sense of the Self. The Self (our self) is said to be a composite, and can be picked apart, until nothing remains of it. And this is the "why" of the meditation techniques.

My point here is that these meditation techniques are about the only way to pick through our ingrained habit of ignorance, and to reach the point where we begin to cease to ignore what we have been ignoring all this time, and start to pay more attention. Using meditation techniques, we gradually reach the end of our own ignorance, we stop ignoring, and begin to have awareness and awaken. Remember that the Sanskrit word "Buddha," means to awaken — to become aware. Buddahood is simply the end of ignorance and the advent of full awakening. So, what's my point, and what does all of this have to do with the bardo states?

Meditation and the Bardo States

Tibetan Buddhists are VERY concerned with the state of our mind at the moment and time of death, and much of Buddhist meditation practice is little more than working to prepare the mind for that moment when we each will die. Why?

Because it is at that moment, when we are suddenly freed of all of our personal habits and body, that we come face to face with the unvarnished reality of our mind, just what we have been ignoring all of this time — the true nature of the mind. The Tibetans say that after we die, we are suddenly nine times as aware as we were in life, many times more aware of just everything in our mind AND in the world around us. We are also very, very sensitive, like the skin of a newborn baby. It is as if a veil has been lifted.

And in that much more aware state, it is much easier for us to get past our habitual patterns of ignorance (of ignoring) and to see the true nature of our mind, which at that point begins to appear to us. We have that opportunity. The Tibetans use the analogy that this "true nature" appears to us in the form of various brilliant colored lights — stunning. Depending upon our habit of ignorance, these lights can appear to us as very, very bright, blinding us with their brilliance and making us flee to the shadow life, or these can be seen and recognized as what they actually are, the true nature of our mind — something that has always been there with us.

The Mind's True Nature

Right after death is a chance to see the actual nature of our mind, but the shock of the difference between what we habitually are used to seeing and our mind's true nature may be more than we can stand, and we may be frightened and forced to turn away.

Using a metaphor: it is said that the brilliance of this sudden illumination is so very great, so stark, that we can easily not recognize it as the truth that it is, and habitually turn away from it, seeking out some place that is darker and more familiar to us — our familiar ignorance once again. We agree to forget what we find so hard to remember.

In that brief moment, we can, instead of recognizing that light as our true nature, turn downward and choose another lifetime of continued ignorance, and thus: the many forms of suffering. I am very much generalizing here, so please don't forget this is just a metaphor. The point here is that instead of awakening from our ignorance after all this time, we fall right back into it. We choose it.

If we can stand the shock of looking at the truth, the utter brilliance of it, then instead of falling back into ignorance and another birth and lifetime, we can hold that realization and become enlightened enough to not reincarnate as a lower birth, but remain in a realized state. Each of us has this opportunity, this chance of realization, soon after the moment of death. This fact and opportunity is very important to Tibetan Buddhists, therefore understand:

Preparing the Mind

The greatest majority of all of Buddhist meditation practices are done to better prepare the mind of each of us for that singular moment of death, and the coming face-to-face with the true nature of our own mind. And here is a crucial point: we don't have to wait until we die to begin recognizing the true nature of our mind. We can do it right here in this lifetime, now. We can train for this after-death experience. And that is what many forms of meditation are all about, or lead to — recognizing the true nature of the mind.

In fact, the closer we can come to recognizing that true nature of our mind in this, our waking life, the greater chance we have of recognizing that same nature in the after-death state, and achieving a more enlightened state, one in which we see clearly ourselves and can begin to benefit others as well.

With true recognition, we won't turn away into a darker place (a womb, for example), but will walk directly through and into the light, and realize our mind's true nature from that point forward. As for what happens then, this would require a whole book and I am not aware enough to write it.

And we should point out that this kind of after-death experience does not seem restricted just to the Tibetan Buddhists. The Buddhist are very quick to say that these after-death experiences, just as they are described in the Tibetan Book of the Dead, will appear to all of us, regardless of religious upbringing —Christians, Jews, Muslims, Hindus, and so on.

NOTHING IS SOMETHING

Thank you, Rinpoche
For pointing something out:
That there is nothing to be pointed out,
That nothing can be pointed out,
Including "Nothing."
"Nothing" also cannot be pointed out.

To me: That is really something

What Is Pure Land Buddhism?

In many Asian countries, there is what amounts to a cult of devotees who are practicing the meditation techniques that we have been mentioning here, and who want to achieve liberation at the moment they enter the bardo, and by that to thereby skip the bardo states (described above), and go straight on to being a realized being at one level or another. This is the principal concern of what is called the Pure Land School of Buddhism, and we need to at least introduce this concept of the pure lands or Buddha fields. It will help explain this whole movement.

In brief, a Buddha field or "pure land" is a realm spontaneously produced by the merit of a Buddha, a place where enlightened beings can go and congregate. There are a great many Buddha fields, and it is considered very advantageous for each of us to ultimately get there, a place where we can most benefit ourselves and also the rest of sentient beings.

That being said, there is one Buddha field that is said to be the easiest to gain entry into. Why it is easy is a long story, but, in brief, one particular Buddha aspired deeply that this Buddha field be accessible to almost anyone who aspired to reach it.

Amitabha's Buddha Field

Even ordinary people who aspire to this realm can obtain it. This particular Buddha field is called in Sanksrit, "Sukavati," and in Tibetan, "Dewachen." It is, for the reasons mentioned, the most popular Buddha field, because any of us can aspire to go there and actually have a chance of achieving that goal, even if we are not fully realized or enlightened right now. Otherwise, it can take many lifetimes, perhaps even entire kalpas (very long time), to become enlightened and reach one of the Buddha fields.

By going to a Buddha field, we cease to take births, and instead are enlightened and can be of great help to all beings. This form of Buddhism that wants to reach Dewachen (Sukavati) is called "Pure Land Buddhism," and it is (in one form or another) immensely popular in China, Korea, Japan, Vietnam, and of course Tibet.

By understanding the idea of Dewachen, perhaps you can begin to see why the great concern with the bardo states, in particular the Bardo of Becoming, the one we encounter right after dying, is so important to Buddhists. It is at this point of death that, if we are mentally and spiritually prepared, we can recognize the true nature of our mind, and pass directly into the Buddha field of Dewachen, bypassing the various bardos, and cease to incarnate.

As my teacher has often pointed out, we are (those of us living today) all of the souls who never up to now, through all millennia, have managed to stop ignoring the way things actually are long enough to become enlightened. We are, as he says, the stragglers, the hard cases.

The Bardo Realms Are the Default

So, that is a brief account of the big rush to get to Dewachen, the nearest and most easily accessible Buddha field. And, since the main entrance to Dewachen, is at the beginning of the bardos, this explains some of the concern and study with the bardos. But what happens to those of us who can't get on board that train to Dewachen, and that is probably most of us?

Well, Dewachen aside, that is what all of the rest of the tradition of the bardo states is all about. If you do not make it to Dewachen, that is: if you turn away from the bright lights, from the way things are, then you enter the Bardo of Becoming, and eventually take another life, and not necessarily as a human being, but that is another story which we don't have time for here. As I mentioned, this is not the place, and I am not the expert you need, to properly describe in great detail the various bardo realms. That would be a book on Tibetan Buddhism, however, let's go over a few of the main points where the bardo teachings and astro-shamanism are similar.

Summary: Astro-Shamanism and the Bardos

In many respects, the bardo traditions and the Shamanic traditions are in parallel. The person who completes their Saturn return, also finds themselves detaching from the physical (Saturn), and floating off beyond time, wandering in and through a progression of chakras. They too most often do not know they are dead, and cannot understand why they cannot communicate with those around them, those who are among the living now, where they once lived.

The idea that we die and yet don't know we are dead is common to both approaches, as well as the gradual realization that death has occurred, and all that goes with it, such as: being unable to connect or reach the "living," not being able to get back into your old habits or body, hypersensitivity, some kind of remote viewing or out-of-the-body experiences, and so forth.

In other words, if you read the "Tibetan Book of the Dead" or writings on the bardos, you will find a lot of similarities to the journey through the chakras described in this book, the dying to one level or chakra and the process of being born or incarnating on another. These two traditions don't fully dovetail, but it is clear that they are talking, if not about the same kind of experience, then in a similar manner.

Astro-Shamanism and Meditation

When I am asked what are the most important resources for the astrologer interested in shamanic techniques, some are surprised and disappointed to hear that learning the proper kind of meditation is at the top of the list. It is almost as if it is somehow unfair or not part of astrology to make such a recommendation, almost as if it were somehow politically incorrect. We need to examine this.

Whereas in the East, in countries like Tibet, China, Japan, Nepal, Korea, and so on, there are hundreds of types of meditation and words for it, here in the West, we pretty much have just the one word, "Meditation," to cover anything to do with the mind and its training. To make matters more confusing, the most popular concept of meditation in America (perhaps because of the success of TM — Transcendental Mediation) is that it is some form of relaxation or stress-release therapy, a way for us to cool out. Meditation is often also associated in people's minds with cults, trance-like states, hippies, and alternative religions, in general.

And it is anyone's guess what those relative few who do "meditate" on a regular basis range actually do, everything from practicing the actual Eastern methods of mind training to mood therapy, psychedelic music, incense, and lava lamps. It is a fact that there is no general agreement as to what meditation is all about in this country, so it is no wonder that the vast majority of individuals steer clear of meditation entirely, and this is unfortunate. Let me explain why.

Our Western Tradition

We have a long and distinguished philosophical tradition here in the West, but it has one major flaw, which is that, in general, that tradition seldom focuses on the mind itself. In other words, we don't use the mind to look at the mind, but rather we use the mind to look at the various contents of the mind, subject matter, like existentialism, mathematics, linguistic analysis, and so forth. For example, please look at who is reading this page this moment? Direct your mind to look at itself, to look at the looker. Difficult, is it not?

Well, this is part of what the Eastern methods of meditation and mind training are all about. By and large, we don't do this form of mental practice here in the West. For centuries, we have been lost in a simple dualism that conceives of a looker and a "looked at." We have bought into that dualism, although philosophy and science are gradually coming to accept the concept that the looker affects what is looked at, and that "how" we look makes a difference.

What little we know about looking at the mind itself, we have assimilated from the Eastern philosophical traditions, under the very broad term, "meditation," and, even then, it has a very foreign feel to it for most people. Mind training of the type I am describing is not a natural part of our culture, but rather something that has come to us from cultures outside our own, in particular from Asian countries. Why do we need it at all?

What's In It for Us?

For starters, we need this type of meditation to overcome the dualistic way of thinking we just spoke of, and to prove to each one of us that the looker and what is looked at are interdependent, and not independent, of one another. Our most sophisticated scientists, psychologists, and philosophers now understand this, but it has not yet filtered down to the rest of us as a fact of life.

In studying astro-shamanism, we need these meditation or mind practice techniques to help us get beyond the time-oriented (read: Saturn) materialistic techniques we have inherited from this dualistic way of thinking, and into the timeless or more-eternal areas of our own mind. In this area, our religions have failed us. Western religions, by and large, offer the concept of faith to us, but precious little by way of a methodology of the mind, that is: step-by-step practical techniques to work with the mind to look at itself. And we need those techniques, for all the reasons given above. Asian religion and philosophy, which are themselves more unified than here in the West, abound with techniques and methods of mind training. We need them at this point in history.

The Ego or Self

The actual mind-training techniques themselves are too involved to go into here, and there are many books and teachers available where you can learn them. I will give some references later on, but let's briefly look at how these techniques might be helpful.

We are all familiar with the Western concept of the "ego," sometimes called the "Self," and selfishness. It is very much a part of modern psychology as well as spirituality. This ego is, as many Tibetan poets have put it, like the single cloud in the otherwise cloudless sky of our mind. This ego makes seeing into the nature of our mind very difficult, and is more of an obscuration to mental clarity than a window into our mind.

When we study the various chakras and their natures, and the same goes for the bardo states, we need as much clarity as we can manage, that is: wandering in the bardo states or the alternate realities of the various chakras requires all the awareness and acumen we can muster. Anything that is an obscuration to clear seeing must be removed.

Sooner or later, our ego or Self obscures our inner vision into the mind. Certain kinds of meditation techniques are designed to skillfully work with the ego, to break down some of its over-controlling tendency to hog or block all our internal airtime. In other words, through mind training, we can deconstruct and take apart some of the ego's defenses, allowing us at least a window through which to better glimpse the true nature of our own mind.

Is The EGO Bad?

You can decide that yourself. It is not about whether the ego or Self is good or bad, but whether it prevents us from getting to where we want to go. Let me give you an example, that should make this clear;

I like to kid myself and say that I must belong to the Forest Gump family, in that I have had many near brushes with fame. While I never became famous, some of my acquaintances did (Bob Dylan, Iggy Pop, Gilda Radner, etc.) did, and even more of them became almost famous. It is the almost famous ones that I want to speak of here, and I won't name names to protect them. After all, even after what I am about to say, they are very sensitive.

These "almost famous" types, in general, have at least one thing in common, and that is that they like to hear themselves talk. In fact, it is almost impossible to have a dialog with them, as in: a conversation. For some reason, they have got it into their head that they are only to give to others, and never receive. So, they talk and talk, but never listen. It would be like if we only breathed out, and never took any air back in. Their transmitter is still working find, but they have turned off their receiver.

Anyway, the long and the short of it is that I have had plenty of time to observe their egos in motion, since I have nothing better to do but just listen, and I am usually too polite to confront them. What would be the point?

But it is clear that their sense of Self or ego completely blinds them from what I consider one of the most important aspects of life, dialogue, give and take, giving and taking. I can only bow toward those great Eastern adepts who state that the Self of ego is like the one cloud in an otherwise cloudless sky. Surely, each of you reading this must know what I am talking about. You too must have friends whose egos prevent them from knowing much more than their own reflection. My almost-famous friends certainly have no idea who I am or what I am doing, because I have not had a chance to tell them. Do you know what I am talking about here?

IMAGINE WHAT I DON'T KNOW

Imagining what I don't know,
And I don't know,
I imagine what I don't know.
I know what I imagine is what I don't know,
And what I know is not what I imagined.
That much I know.

I can only imagine what I don't know.

The Two Techniques

As mentioned earlier, there are probably hundreds of meditation techniques out there, but the kind of techniques we need for our Astro-shamanic work are actually quite simple, and remarkably enough, most of the major Asian religions and philosophies use the same techniques. This fact helps a lot, because it means we can be pretty confident of getting the kind of mind training we need from a variety of readily available sources. There are two basic techniques that almost every meditation student is taught, and the Sanskrit (oldest) terms for these are "Shamata" and "Vipassana," and they are usually taught in that order. These can greatly accelerate our work, as well.

Shamata, the place to begin, is simply a technique for calming our otherwise unruly mind. It translates to something like "abiding in the calm" or "calming the mind." Without quieting the mind, no other kind of meditation technique can be learned, because our mind is too busy. I am not going to try and present the Shamata technique here, because it is best for you to get it from someone, in person, so that whatever questions you might have can be answered. Shamata is a method to look at the mind, and by looking at it, to gradually recognize its busy or hectic character, thus allowing the mind to calm down and come to rest. In Shamata, we learn to let the mind rest. It may sound easy, but for most of us, it is not easy to just let the mind rest.

Once we have learned to let the mind rest, we can begin the practice of Vipassana or insight meditation, which involves actually looking for and directly at the nature of the mind. It is through Vipassana that we begin to pick through the ego or Self, piece by piece, and to develop an increased awareness of the true nature of the mind. By learning to look at who is looking at the mind, the looker, we can set to rest more and more of what we have always been focusing on, which is the content of the mind (the subject matter), and begin to see beyond that subject matter to the ground or true nature of the mind itself. This will not be presented here, as it should be explained by a teacher of this kind of meditation. In general, though, the point is to stop just looking at the content of our thoughts (what the thought is about), and, instead, learn to look at the true nature of all thoughts, regardless of their content.

Experience It for Yourself

Surprisingly enough, very few Westerners have ever stopped looking at the content of their thoughts, and learned to look at the nature of their thoughts. By combining these two techniques, Shamata and Vipassana, we have a powerful tool to help us get beyond the obscuration of the ego, and to experience the true nature of our mind, and this experience of our mind's true nature is what we need to explore esoteric or inner astrology. We each must experience this for ourselves. It is not enough to read about it and to intellectually understand what I am referring to here. All thought leads to experience. We each must have that experience.

I apologize if any of this sounds overly mysterious or abstract. By their very nature, these topics are not meant for casual understanding, but as stated above, must be experienced to be made real. In my own experience, I reached a point where my Western training in philosophy and psychology kind of peaked and flat-lined. Nothing more was forthcoming for me. I was then fortunate to discover a teacher skilled in meditation, who (very slowly on my part, I must add) helped me to learn to use the mind not just to look at ideas, but to look at itself. This was not, for me, easy. It was r eally tough to change a life-long habit of using the mind to look at things and ideas, to looking at itself. My mind had no idea how to look at itself.

Pointing Out Instructions

There are innumerable stories of teachers showing students how to look at their own minds. This is called, in the literature, the "pointing out" instructions, where the teacher attempts to point out to the student the true nature of the mind. One common analogy is that of the teacher pointing out the Moon in the night sky, and the student focusing on the pointing finger, instead of the Moon. It can be very difficult to point out the true nature of the mind, and even when that nature is glimpsed, this is not enlightenment, but rather this is the point where students begin to get the hang of it, to have a glimmer of what this is all about, and how they might do it themselves.

Don't let me romanticize all of this training. It is VERY difficult, unless of course, you just get it. And, we all like to think we get it, but that usually amounts to an intellectual understanding, which is what I am imparting here. That is relatively easy to get. The actual experience of understanding how to look at the true nature of your mind is, for most of us, not easy, but difficult.

Taking the Training

I hope I have given you here enough of an idea so that you can decide for yourself if you want make the effort to get this training. As for where to get it and from whom, all I can say is that it is best to be conservative. Browse the internet for places near you, triangulate sources, and stick with the best known authorities and teachers. What you want is taught by most Zen schools of Buddhism, by all schools of Tibetan Buddhism, and most all Buddhists, for that matter. Similar techniques are also available in

Vedanta, but I am not familiar enough with that approach to give you recommendations. I learned these techniques from the Karma Kagyu Lineage of Tibetan Buddhism, and Kagyu.org is one place you can look for a list of locations. They have centers all over. In no way am I saying that this is the only place to get this training. It is not. However, it is one place I am certain teaches these ancient techniques of mind training properly.

And I should add, this kind of training, and being introduced to these meditation techniques, is NOT something you should pay for. Real teachers do not charge you for showing you how to meditate, which is not to say there are not courses for which you might pay. In my experience, you find a place you respect, call them up, and request meditation instruction. The teacher sets a time and a place, you show up, and they instruct you and often a bunch of other people at the same time. It does not even take long. It is important to get meditation instruction from someone who has been empowered to give it, and who extends to you the blessings of the long line (lineage) of meditation teaching that they belong to.

My Personal Story

Remember, you want first to learn Shamata, and that is all you need to get started. Much later, you can learn Vipassana. In closing this article, let me tell you a personal story.

I did not start meditation until relatively late in my life. I was suspicious of all forms of meditation, largely because of all the crazy people I had seen practicing and advocating it. Also, I had no idea what meditation was, other than my own (false) preconceived notions. I kept putting off checking it out for any old reasons I could think of.

Then I met a Tibetan lama and teacher with whom I connected. I arranged to have an interview with him. In fact, I drove 800 miles on the coldest night of the year to get there. And I had my whole family with me. We had to scrape the frost from a tiny spot in our windshield just to see out, as we climbed up the dark mountain road for the meeting. You get the idea. It was special.

At last we got there and I met the teacher, a Tibetan rinpoche. I explained to him how very many years I had studied astrology and spiritual subjects. I was hoping to place out of meditation 101, and get to some of those advanced subjects I had been reading about, which I felt I was worthy of, and so on. The rinpoche listened very patiently, and then told me that, although he could see I had studied hard and had never hurt anyone by my practice of astrology, that when it came to meditation, I was a beginner, and it was best for me to start at the very beginning. Of course, he said, all of this was up to me.

To say the least, I was very disappointed not to have placed out of at least a grade or two, and kind of humiliated that, at my age, I had to start at the very beginning. In fact, after that interview, I had a moment of hesitation, where part of me wanted to just cut and run, and just forget about learning meditation. However, I liked the teacher so much that I decided to take his advice and just start at the beginning, like everyone else. Forget about what it looked like to others.

All I can say is that I am so VERY thankful I did not let my pride rule me, and that I submitted to starting at the very beginning with meditation. It has been the single most important tool in my spiritual education, and has proved to be the key for my astrological research and education, as well. As the rinpoche explained to me, the mind is a wish-fulfilling gem, the single greatest asset that we each have. It cannot be enhanced, but it can be trained. I am so grateful I took that training.

THE REST OF THE MIND

You cannot rest the mind,
But you can let the mind rest.
Just let go,
And don't mind the rest.

I have spent years trying to find a way around this information, trying to make it more exoteric or external, make it fit in. Now, I am at the point where I want to share my thoughts and interest with others. I want to know who else is interested in this branch of astrology? Well, are there any of you out there who respond to what I am writing of here? If so, let's hear from you. How about today? I have been writing articles like this for many years now. I can't expect this writing to get a universal response, but there must be some of you there who are on this particular wavelength.

I am reminded of that fine poem by the American poet John Burroughs called "Waiting." In it are the lines "My own shall come to me... what is mine shall know my face". If there are a group of us, I am ready to get to know you better, and to share this kind of information. I would like to talk face to face. How about it? Anybody home? My email is Michael@Erlewine.com.

Waiting

by John Burroughs (born April 3, 1837 - died March 29, 1921)

Serene, I fold my hands and wait,
Nor care for wind nor tide nor sea;
I rave no more 'gainst time or fate,
For lo! my own shall come to me.

I stay my haste,
I make delays.
For what avails this eager pace?
I stand amid eternal ways
And what is mine shall know my face.

Asleep, awake, by night or day,
The friends I seek are seeking me.
No wind can drive my bark astray
Nor change the tide of destiny.

What matter if I stand alone?
I wait with joy the coming years;
My heart shall reap where it has sown,
And garner up its fruit of tears.

The waters know their own, and draw
The brook that springs in yonder height;
So flows the good with equal law
Unto the soul of pure delight.
The stars come nightly to the sky;
 The tidal wave unto the sea;
Nor time, nor space, nor deep, nor high,
Can keep my own away from me.

The Teacher

I would like to say a few words about mentors or teachers. First, let me say this: in my experience, having a good mentor or teacher is perhaps THE most important single benefit a student can have. That is why the Tibetans call their best teachers, "Rinpoches," which means: precious ones. They are.

A mentor can not only save you years of misguided work, but (and more important) for many types of esoteric knowledge, they are the only way to receive this information in a timely way, as in: in your lifetime. I credit my teachers, and I have had some great ones, as making all the difference in my own inner education.

That being said, finding a teacher is not always that easy. In my case, before I could find a teacher, I had to reach a point where I wanted one. That was my greatest hurdle, for I was naturally untrusting, having been burnt any number of times trying out teachers who were not helpful, at least to me.

For the longest time, I viewed every other outside person as suspect, and perhaps someone to actually compete with. That kind of attitude on my part was literally antithetical to finding a teacher. It will never happen.

Before I was able afford a teacher, I had to work that attitude out of me, and this took time. There is an old saying that when the student is ready, the teacher will appear. From my own experience, this seems true. I could not find a mentor or teacher anywhere, no matter how hard I looked, until I had emptied out all of the suspicions and mistrust I had locked inside myself about taking anything from anybody. You get the idea.

So, there seems to be a lot of confusion about how to select a teacher, and about how to tell if you have a teacher that will work for you. Unfortunately, I can only be of limited help in this department, because each of us must pick our own teachers, and there are no fixed set of rules as to how this must be done. Here is what I have learned about teachers, and I have had the very good fortune to have very good teachers.

Let's first dispense with the idea that some teachers are supposed to give us hard lessons and a hard time, because we need it. Of course, we can learn the hard way. I am assuming we all know that, and that we know enough to steer away from those who will teach us by manipulating or taking advantage of us. Money should NEVER be involved in working with a teacher, unless it is a class in yoga or whatever — that kind of teacher. We all know the old saying, "Fool me once, shame on you! Fool me twice, shame on me." Those experiences are not what I would call teachers.

The Rule of Personality

I am talking here about spiritual mentors or teachers, what the Tibetans call the "Tsawi Lama," the root teacher. When I was younger, I would try to get close to and learn from anyone who had confidence and seemed to have knowledge of life. Many teachers of this kind ruled by their personality, by their magnetism, and by their forcefulness. They subjugated others. Unfortunately for me, I did not know any better, and tried my best to fit into their demands. Lucky for me, I could never get comfortable, and ended up having to move on and search elsewhere. Real teachers, what are called root teachers, do not teach by commanding you or using force. Again, some of you may require it, but I can only tell you of my own experience.

Being Recognized

When I met my first real life teacher, I suddenly understood what a teacher looked and felt like, and I was never fooled or taken in again by those who pretended to be teachers, even if they meant well. Here is what the actual experience is like:

What I was aware of was that this outside person whom I had just met cared more for me than I knew how to care for myself. It was not about how important or powerful HE was, but how much he cared for me, and about who I was. And, he recognized me for who I was, and accepted all of me, warts and all. There were no conditions. It was unconditional. In a word: he KNEW me and I could see that. He recognized me, as a mother would recognize a lost child and he welcomed me. I was home, spiritually speaking, for the first time. Teachers are, above all, a refuge in the maelstrom of life.

In the business of life, my teachers found me, identified with me, and welcomed me with open arms. That is what teachers are like, as far as I know. They had no agenda. Money was never involved. A teacher-student relationship is way more personal than money.

Giving In

In other words, a teacher is not an imposing persona, but just the reverse, a lack of resistance, an opening, and an acceptance. A teacher is very giving, but here I use that word in the sense of 'giving way', and making room. A teacher makes room for you in his or her life, and when you push forward, they give in, and you fall into their mandala or sacred space. A teacher is a refuge and a safe place.

Encountering this lack of resistance, we fall in, and the hard edges that we have used to protect ourselves up to now have nothing to push against, and we are free to change in whatever direction we are already tending, with the passive shaping and help of the teacher. A teacher is a way on into the heart of our life, rather than another barrier to that life.

I like to think of a teacher as being like the astrophysical Black Hole, an invisible space that we fall into, drawn by our own forward momentum or gravity, where we are changed forever, emerging on the other side in a more enlightened state. A teacher is like that, and changes us like that.

Meeting the Karmapa

In closing, let me share a simple story of how I met one very great teacher. My wife and I were attending the annual 10-day teaching with my dharma teacher, Ven. Khenpo Karthar, Rinpoche at his monastery in Woodstock, New York.

During our stay there, we had requested and received permission (as we did each year) for a personal interview with Rinpoche. These interviews had become almost routine. I always asked Rinpoche if there was anything special he wanted me to do, and he always responded, "No, nothing special, just keep practicing." This year was to be different.

At that interview, I outlined certain fairly severe business problems that we had been going through over the last year or two. Working with a translator, I laid out my questions and Rinpoche began to answer.

But after less than a minute, he just stopped, looked at us, and declared that he was not going to answer further himself and that, instead, we should take these questions to His Holiness, the 17th Karmapa and ask him directly. Karmapa would be able to answer our questions. Now you will need to know that, like the Dalai Lama, the Karmapa is the head of one of the main sects of Tibotan Buddhism. In fact, the Karmapa was the first Tibetan lama to reincarnate.

At any rate, my wife and I looked at each other in amazement, because His Holiness could only be found at Tsurphu Monastery, deep in the reaches of Tibet. I mumbled something to Rinpoche about, woll, that would b e great, perhaps next year, next spring or something, but Rinpoche said: "No, this summer, as soon as you can arrange it." By this time, Khenpo Rinpoche had a great smile on his face as if he were very, very happy for us.

We were speechless. He then went on to speak about impermanence, how life is short, and that none of us know the time or manner of our death. In my mental fog of the moment, I was slowly understanding that Rinpoche was directing us to go to Tibet soon, as in: that very summer, and it was July now.

Talk about turning your world upside down, our life became a flurry of activity, getting shots, passports, etc., for I wanted to take my whole family with me. The story of our trip to Tibet I have written elsewhere, in "Our Pilgrimage to Tibet," paperback on Amazon.com. Here I just want to share with you what it was like meeting His Holiness, the Karmapa, because that experience has to be the paradigm of what a teacher is. The Karmapa is now in his 17th incarnation. We were traveling on a pilgrimage to meet him.

The Meeting

After quite a journey, we managed to find our way to Tsurphu Monastery, where the Karmapa lived, and were told that he would see us. We waited.

I had not only never met this Karmapa, I had never met anyone close in stature to the Karmapa in a private situation. I knew how respected he was by all the lamas I knew, and how powerful he was from all of the stories about his previous incarnation, some that my own teacher had told me — just incredible tales. During the days and hours leading up to the meeting, I rolled all kinds of things around in my head. Would I be terrified? Subdued? You know how the mind works. We think all kinds of crazy things, and I was ahead of the curve.

We were at last summoned to His Holiness, and I slowly climbed the multiple sets (three) of ladder-like stairs, huffing and puffing in the high altitude. As we entered the interview room, there was a puja (ritual) going on, with his holiness leading the practice, accompanied by a small number of monks. We were encouraged to sit up front and settled in. Gradually I realized we were in the middle of the Mahaka puja, perhaps the most important daily practice for the Karma Kagyu Lineage. Later we found out that we were experiencing a special form of Mahakala, one for insiders, complete with the Tsok, the ritual feast offering. Karmapa was sharing this with us. There was just my family and two women who had come on the trip with us.

It was very intense, with His Holiness leading the chanting with an intent and often fierce look. Mahakala is a wrathful practice, as some of you may already know. And this one was complete with drums, cymbals, and the various Tibetan horns. I had experienced the Mahakala puja often before, but never one quite like this. I don't really know how to describe what happened next.

As mentioned, I had heard many stories about His Holiness, both this one and the previous incarnations, stories of amazing actions, all pointing to his extraordinary character. Somehow these stories help to inspire faith and confidence in the Karmapa, that he is who he is, that sort of thing. Yet these stories were nothing compared to the sheer largeness of his presence. And this kind of thing defies words. How do you explain that when you are in the presence of His Holiness, you have a different idea of yourself, who you are, why you are here, etc. I learned things about myself when I was in the presence of His Holiness that I never knew before, important things. The word is 'realization'. I realized things about myself that I had never realized before.

The Karmapa was not some towering presence that sent me cowering into a corner. In fact, the funny thing is that from the moment I stepped into his presence, I never thought about any of that kind of stuff again. All thoughts vanished, just like that.

Instead, I found myself not looking out at the Karmapa, but looking deep within myself, deeper than I had ever thought about going. And in his presence, in that room high in the Tibetan mountains, what I saw and realized was not about His Holiness, but about my own self and nature.

For one, I right-away saw through my own outer toughness and severity. There in that room with Karmapa, that same strength, toughness, or we might even say fierceness came to mind and began to be examined inwardly, but in a new light. This was no idea that I was playing with. Instead, I was examining myself or, to be more exact, I was "realizing" part of my self, in this case, the 'me' who had been "in charge" all these years.

And as this realization took place, I saw how my fierceness or toughness was but a shell covering up an extremely sensitive inside. I was tough, because I was so — so sensitive and, at heart, even kind. I was flooded with a state of compassion or rather: the realization that I was (and always had been), at my deepest part, compassionate, concerned, and caring, and that this was my natural state. This was not something to strive for, but already in fact the case — the state of my being, something to be uncovered, for sure, and opened up. I did not have to strive to be compassionate, for that was already my natural state. All I had to do was to relax, pick through mental obscurations, and let it shine through.

And, again, let me point out that this was not a concept or idea, but a realization that totally involved me. I realized that the essence of my dharma practice, of my fierce presence, was none other than compassion. It was as if, like a glove, I had turned myself inside out. Tears just flowed, as I was overcome with this, now so obvious, realization. I was, in essence, very simple — just a soft-hearted, easy mark for this world. I was easy and all of my so-called toughness, my seriousness, was nothing more than an attempt to cover over and shield myself from responding too much to all the suffering I saw around me. In that moment, I feel I understood myself and my practice, all in midst of that Mahakala puja with Karmapa. I was at peace.

My Poems

Poems,
A home for my thoughts,
Dear thoughts,
The very best of me,
All that's precious and kind,
Now sealed in words,
Like insects and amber:

Prayer flags endlessly waving,
In the gentle chalice of the mind.

About Michael Erlewine

Internationally known astrologer and author Noel Tyl (author of 34 books on astrology) has this to say about Michael Erlewine:

> "Michael Erlewine is the giant influence whose creativity is forever imprinted on all astrologers' work since the beginning of the Computer era! He is the man who single-handedly applied computer technology to astrological measurement, research, and interpretation, and has been the formative and leading light of astrology's modern growth. Erlewine humanized it all, adding perception and incisive practical analyses to modern, computerized astrology. Now, for a second generation of astrologers and their public, Erlewine's genius continues with StarTypes … and it's simply amazing!"

A Brief Bio of Michael Erlewine

Michael Erlewine has studied and practiced astrology for over 40 years, as an author, teacher, lecturer, personal consultant, programmer, and conference producer.

Erlewine was the first astrologer to program astrology on microcomputers and make those programs available to his fellow astrologers. This was in 1977. He founded Matrix Astrology in 1978, and his company, along with Microsoft, are the two oldest software companies still on the Internet.

Michael, soon joined by his astrologer-brother Stephen Erlewine, went on to revolutionize astrology by producing, for the new microcomputers, the first written astrological reports, first research system, first high resolution chart wheels, geographic and star maps, and on and on.
Along the way Matrix produced programs that spoke astrology (audio), personal astrological videos, infomercials, and many other pioneering feats.

Michael Erlewine has received major awards from UAC (United Astrological Conferences), AFA (American Federation of Astrologers), and the PIA (Professional Astrologers Incorporated), and scores of online awards.

Michael and Stephen Erlewine have published a yearly astrological calendar since 1969. Michael Erlewine has produced and put on more than 36 conferences in the areas of astrology and Buddhism.

Erlewine has personally designed over 13,000 tarot-like astrology cards, making authentic astrology available to people with little or no experience in the topic. These Astro*Image™ cards are available through a variety of small astrological programs and in eBooks. Some examples can be found at www.StarTypes.com, where there is also a link to his astrological software.

Personal Astrology Readings
Michael Erlewine has been doing personal astrology readings for almost forty years and enjoys sharing his knowledge with others.

However, his busy schedule makes it difficult to honor all requests. However, feel free to email him (Michael@Erlewine.net) if you wish a personal chart reading. He will let you know if his current schedule will allow him to work with you.

The sections that follow will give you more details about Michael Erlewine and his very active center.

The Heart Center House

1972, Michael and Margaret Erlewine established the Heart Center, a center for community studies. Today, the Heart Center continues to be a center for astrological and spiritual work. Over the years, hundreds of invited guests have stayed at the Heart Center, some for just a night, others for many years. Astrologers, authors, musicians, Sanskrit scholars, swamis — you name it, the Heart Center has been a home for a wide group of individuals, all united by their interest in spiritual or cultural ideas.

Heart Center Library

Erlewine also founded and directs The Heart Center Astrological Library, the largest astrological library in the United States, and probably the world, that is open to researchers. Meticulously catalogued, the current library project is the scanning of the

Table of Contents for all major books and periodicals on astrology.

The library does not have regular hours, so contact ahead of time if you wish to visit. Michael@erlewine.net.

The All-Music Guide / All-Movie Guide
Michael Erlewine's devotion to studying and playing the music of Black Americans, in particular blues, led to his traveling to small blues clubs of Chicago and hearing live, blues greats like Little Walter, Magic Sam, Big Walter Horton, and many others. He went on to interview many dozens of performers. Much of this interviewing took place at the Ann Arbor Blues Festivals, in 1969 and 1970, the first electric blues festivals of any size ever held in North America, and then later at the Ann Arbor Blues & Jazz Festivals.

With their extensive knowledge of the blues music, Erlewine and his brother Daniel were asked to play host to the score or so of professional blues musicians and their bands. They were in charge of serving them food and (of course) drink. Michael went on to interview most of the performers in these early festivals, with an audio recorder, and later on with video.

The interviewing led to more study and ultimately resulted in Michael founding and developing AMG, the All-Music Guide, today the largest single database of music reviews and documentation on the planet.

Erlewine started from a one-room office, and the reviewers and music aficionados of the time laughed at his attempt to cover all music. But he persisted, and the all-Music Guide appeared as a Gopher Site, beforo the World Wide Web even existed — a database of popular music for all music lovers.

Over the years AMG grew, and the All-Movie Guide and All Game Guide were born, and also flourished. Later, Erlewine would create ClassicPosters. com, devoted to the history and documentation of rock n' roll posters, some 35,000 of them.

These guides changed the way music was reviewed and rated. Previous to AMG, review guides like the "Rolling Stones Record Guide" were run by a few sophisticated reviewers, and the emphasis was on the expertise of the reviewer, and their point of view. Erlewine insisted on treating all artists equally, and not comparing artist to artist. What is important, Michael points out, is to find the best music any artist has produced, not to determine whether the artist is better or worse than Jimmie Hendrix or Bob Dylan.

Erlewine sold AMG in 1996, at which time he had 150 fulltime employees, and 500 free-lance writers. He had edited and published any number of books and CD-ROMs on music and film. During the time he owned and ran AMG, there were no advertisements on the site and nothing for sale. As Erlewine writes, "All of us deserve to have access to our own popular culture. That is what AMG and ClassicPosters.com are all about." Today, AMG reviews can be found everywhere across the Internet. Erlewine's music collection is housed in an AMG warehouse, numbering almost 500,000 CDs.

Heart Center Meditation Room

Michael Erlewine has been active in Buddhism since the 1950s. Here are his own words:
"Back in the late 1950s, and early 1960, Buddhism was one of many ideas we stayed up late, smoked cigarettes, drank lots of coffee, and talked about, along with existentialism, poetry, and the like.

"It was not until I met the Tibetan lama, Chogyam Trungpa Rinpoche, in 1974 that I understood Buddhism as not just Philosophy, but also as path, a way to get through life. Having been raised Catholic, serving as an altar boy, learning church Latin, and all that, I had not been given any kind of a path, other than the path of faith. I hung onto that faith as long as I could, but it told me very little about how to live and work in this world.

"I had been trying to learn the basics of Tibetan Buddhism before I met Trungpa Rinpoche, but the spark that welded all of that together was missing. Trungpa provided that spark. I got to be his chauffeur for a weekend, and to design a poster for his public talk.

"More important: only about an hour after we met, Trungpa took me into a small room for a couple of hours and taught me to meditate. I didn't even understand what I was learning. All that I know was that I was learning about myself.

"After that meeting, I begin to understand a lot more of what I had read, but it was almost ten years later that I met my main dharma teacher, Khenpo Karthar Rinpoche, the abbot of Karma Triyana Dharmachakra Monstery, in the mountains above Woodstock, NY. Meeting Rinpoche was life-changing.

Heart Center Symbol

"It was not long after that we started the Heart Center Meditation Center here in Big Rapids, which is still going today. My wife and I became more and more involved with the monastery in New York, and we ended up serving on several boards, and even as fundraisers for the monastery. We helped to raise the funds to build a 3-year retreat in upstate New York, one for men and one for women.

"We also established KTD Dharma Goods, a mail-order dharma goods business that helped practitioners find the meditation materials they might need. We published many sadhanas, the traditional Buddhist practice texts, plus other teachings, in print and on audio tape.

"Years have gone by, and I am still working with Khenpo Rinpoche and the sangha at the Woodstock monastery. Some years ago, Rinpoche surprised my wife and me by telling us we should go to Tibet and meet His Holiness the 17th Karmapa, and that we should go right away, that summer, and I hate to leave the house!

"That trip, and a second trip that followed some years later, turned out to be pilgrimages that were also life changing. Our center in Big Rapids has a separate building as a shrine room (see picture above) and even a small Stupa.

"I can never repay the kindness that Khenpo Rinpoche and the other rinpoches that I have taken teachings from have shown me."

Music Career

Michael Erlewine's career in music started early on, when he dropped out of high school and hitchhiked to Venice West, in Santa Monica, California, in an attempt to catch a ride on the tail end of the Beatnik era. This was 1960, and he was a little late for that, but right on time for the folk music revival that was just beginning to bloom at that time. Like many other people his age, Erlewine traveled from college center to center across the nation: Ann Arbor,

Berkeley, Cambridge, and Greenwich Village. There was a well-beaten track on which traveled the young folk musicians of the future.

Erlewine, who also played folk guitar, hitchhiked for a stint with a young Bob Dylan, and then more extensively with guitar virtuoso and instrumentalist Perry Lederman. Erlewine helped to put on Dylan's first concert in Ann Arbor. He hung out with people like Ramblin' Jack Elliot, Joan Baez, The New Lost City Ramblers, and the County Gentlemen.

In 1965, the same year that the Grateful Dead were forming, Michael Erlewine, his brother Daniel, and a few others formed the first new-style band in the Midwest, the Prime Movers Blues Band. Iggy Pop was their drummer, and his stint in the band was when he got the name Iggy. This was the beginning of the hippie era. Michael was the band's lead singer, and played amplified Chicago-style blues harmonica. He still plays.

Erlewine was also the manager of the band, and personally designed and silkscreened the band's posters, one of which is shown below.
The Prime Movers became a seminal band throughout the Midwest, and even traveled as far as the West Coast, where the band spent 1967, the "summer of Love," playing at all of the famous clubs, for example, opening for Eric Clapton and Cream, at the Filmore Auditorium. You can hear the band on "You Tube" by searching for "Prime Movers Blues Band."

As the 60s wound down, and bands began to break up, Erlewine was still studying the music of American Blacks, in particular blues. Because of their knowledge of blues and the players, Michael and his brother Dan were invited to help host the first major electric blues festival in the United States, the 1969 Ann Arbor Blues Festival. They got to wine and dine the performers, and generally look after them.

Michael interviewed (audio and video) most of the players at the first two Ann Arbor Blues Festivals, they included: Big Joe Turner, Luther Allison, Carey Bell, Bobby Bland, Clifton Chenier, James Cotton, Pee Wee Crayton, Arthur Crudup, Jimmy Dawkins, Doctor Ross, Sleepy John Estes, Lowell Fulson, Buddy Guy, John Lee Hooker, Howlin' Wolf, J.B. Hutto, Albert King, B.B King, Freddie King, Sam Lay, Lightnin' Hopkins, Manse Lipscomb, Robert Lockwood, Magic Sam, Fred McDowell, Muddy Waters, Charlie Musslewhite, Louis Myers, Junior Parker, Brewer Phillips, Otis Rush, Johnnie Shines, George Smith, Son House, Victoria Spivey, Hubert Sumlin, Sunnyland Slim, Roosevelt Sykes, Eddie Taylor, Hound Dog Taylor, Big Mama Thornton, Eddie Vinson, Sippie Wallace, Junior Wells, Big Joe Williams, Robert Pete Williams, Johnny Young, and Mighty Joe Young.

Michael Erlewine's Early Books:
The Sun Is Shining: Heliocentric Ephemeris 1975 Astrophysical Directions 1976 Manual of Computer Programming for Astrologers 1979 Seven Star Maps for Astrologers 1976

E-Books by Michael Erlewine:

The following books are available in paperback on Amazon.com or as e-books at:

www.AstrologySoftware/books/index.asp

Burn Rate: Retrogrades in Astrology
1000 pages, 153 color illustrations
Interface: Planetary Nodes
288 pages, 233 color illustrations
Local space: Relocation Astrology
207 pages, 140 color illustrations
Mother Moon: Astrology of 'The Lights'
447 pages, 304 color illustrations
Interpret Astrology: The 360 3-Way Combinations
415 pages, 360 color illustrations
Interpret Astrology: The House Combinations
332 pages, 276 color illustrations
Interpret Astrology: The Planetary Combinations
850 pages, 765 color illustrations
The Astrology of Space
512 pages, 162 color illustrations
StarTypes: Life-Path Partners
753 pages, 230 color illustrations
Tibetan Earth Lords: Tibetan Astrology and Geomancy
223 pages, 156 color illustrations
Astrology's Mirror: Full-Phase Aspects
191 pages, 145 color illustrations
How to Learn Astrology
1100 pages, 950 color illustrations

Our Pilgrimage to Tibet
260 pages, 112 color photos

The Art of Feng Shui
563 pages, 500 color illustrations

Tibetan Astrology
827 pages, 579 color illustrations

Email:
Michael Erlewine can be reached at Michael@Erlewine.net

Printed in Great Britain
by Amazon.co.uk, Ltd.,
Marston Gate.